KEY

TO

NORTHWEST

EUROPEAN

ORIGINS

KEY TO

NORTHWEST EUROPEAN

ORIGINS

Raymond F. McNair

authorHOUSE®

AuthorHouse™
1663 Liberty Drive
Bloomington, IN 47403
www.authorhouse.com
Phone: 1-800-839-8640

Published by AuthorHouse   03/17/2012

ISBN: 978-1-4685-4599-9 (sc)
ISBN: 978-1-4685-4600-2 (e)

Library of Congress Control Number: 2012901184

ABOUT THE AUTHOR

Raymond Franklin McNair was born in Arkansas, United States of America.

In the mid-1940s he and his brothers listened attentively to the 'World Tomorrow' broadcasts which led him to attend Ambassador College, a fine arts college based in Pasadena, California, United States of America. He graduated in 1953 and was ordained an evangelist later that year.

His writings include:

- *Ascent to Greatness—the Incredible Story of America's Rise to World Super Power* (726 pages)
- *King David's Everlasting Dynasty!* (32 pages)
- *A Bitter Family Quarrel . . . Solving the Arab-Israeli Impasse!* (45 pages)
- *America and Britain in Prophecy* (65 pages)

During his illustrious career, Raymond McNair launched and pastored many of God's Churches, authored articles on a large range of Biblical and related topics. Mr. McNair held the title of Deputy Chancellor of two colleges, one in Bricket Wood, United Kingdom, and Pasadena, California, United States of America.

Raymond McNair died peacefully in his home at the age of 78 (October 11, 2008), with his wife, Eve, by his side.

This book represents the intellectual masterpiece of his life's work: a thesis presented to the Graduate School Committee, Ambassador College, in partial fulfilment of the requirements for the Degree of Master of Arts in Theology, in May 1963, upon which he received his degree.

He is remembered as one of the greatest exponents of the "lost ten tribes of Israel" teachings, which is enjoying a resurgence, in part, due to his efforts.

INTRODUCTION

The ORIGIN of the peoples of NORTH-WESTERN EUROPE has occasioned much controversy! As a result, a considerable amount of confusion has been generated over the question of the racial affinities of the various branches of those peoples who inhabit primarily the coastlands, islands and peninsulas of North-western Europe.

The Bible clearly reveals the origins of the ANGLO-SAXON-KELTIC peoples who inhabit North-western Europe—and those territories colonized by them! The Scriptures are abundantly clear and convincing on this point.

The primary purpose of this thesis, however, is to furnish HISTORICAL, and ARCHAEOLOGICAL PROOF—tracing the racial origins of these Anglo-Saxon-Keltic peoples of North-west Europe who, in modern times, have become the dominant nations of the earth!

The eleventh edition of the Encyclopaedia Britannica, commonly called the "Scholar's Edition," has been used when possible in preference to later editions.

The appropriate map should always be consulted as the various peoples and areas are studied, thereby enabling the reader to better comprehend the points under consideration.

Chronology is a very controversial subject. In this thesis, however, Biblical dates used are those which Archbishop Ussher worked out—since they are deemed to be fairly accurate in most instances. Besides, exact Biblical dates are not essential in this work. (See Appendix II).

It is sincerely hoped that any repetition in this work will always serve to: (1) emphasize, (2) clarify and (3) convince the reader of the validity of the assertions, by giving verbatim many different reliable references to substantiate each point beyond question!

The length of the quotations has been pared back (only the essential part being given) in order to keep the amount of quoted material to a minimum.

Emphasis in all quotations is that of the author, unless otherwise stated!

London, England.   Raymond F. McNair
May, 1963.

TABLE OF CONTENTS

III. PHYSICAL CHARACTERISTICS OF EARLY ISRAELITES 53

IV. THE IMPORTANCE OF THE DYNASTIC NAME OF OMRI (GHOMRI) 68

MAPS

FIGURE

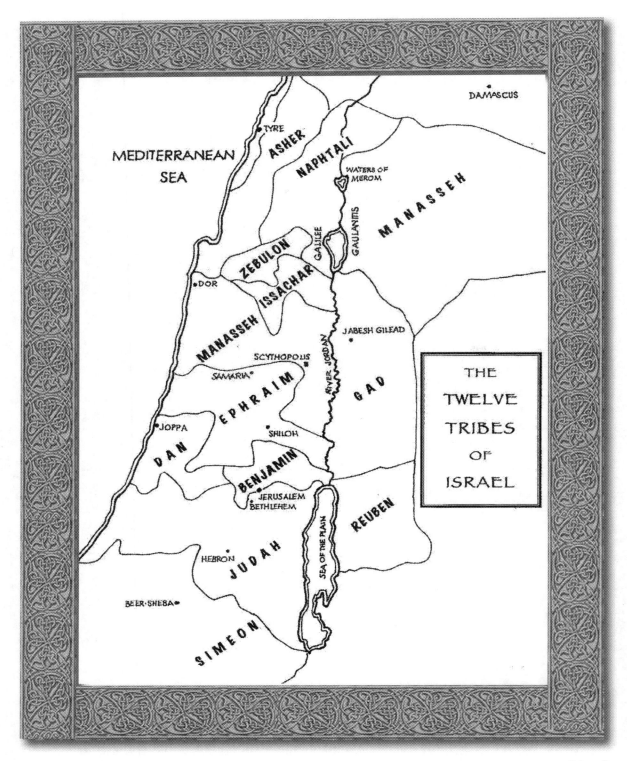

THE
TWELVE
TRIBES
OF
ISRAEL

DAMASCUS

MEDITERRANEAN
SEA

TYRE

ASHER

NAPHTALI

WATERS OF
MEROM

MANASSEH

GALILEE

GAULANITIS

ZEBULON

ISSACHAR

DOR

MANASSEH

JABESH GILEAD

SCYTHOPOLIS

SAMARIA

EPHRAIM

RIVER JORDAN

GAD

JOPPA

SHILOH

DAN

BENJAMIN

JERUSALEM
BETHLEHEM

REUBEN

SEA OF THE PLAIN

HEBRON

JUDAH

BEER-SHEBA

SIMEON

Map I

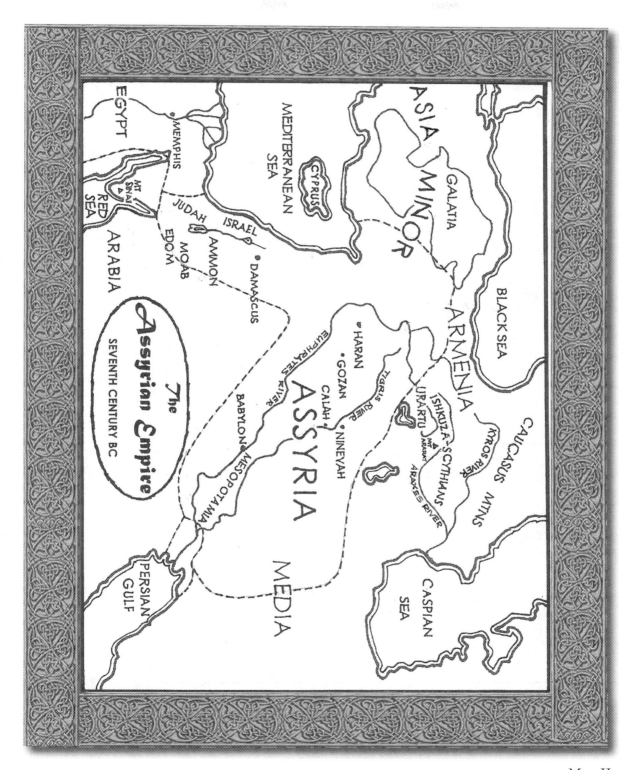

The Assyrian Empire
SEVENTH CENTURY BC

EGYPT
MEMPHIS
MT SINAI
RED SEA
ARABIA
JUDAH
EDOM
MOAB
AMMON
ISRAEL
DAMASCUS
MEDITERRANEAN SEA
CYPRUS
ASIA MINOR
GALATIA
ARMENIA
BLACK SEA
HARAN
GOZAN
CALAH
NINEVAH
EUPHRATES RIVER
TIGRIS RIVER
BABYLON
MESOPOTAMIA
ASSYRIA
URARTU
MT ARARAT
ISHKUZA-SCYTHIANS
ARAXES RIVER
KYROS RIVER
CAUCASUS MTNS
CASPIAN SEA
MEDIA
PERSIAN GULF

Map II

xix

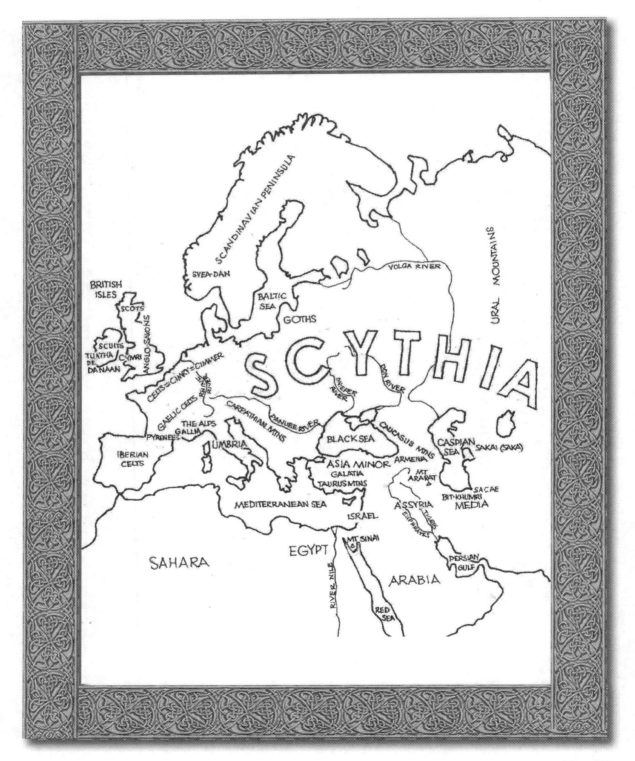

Map III

CHAPTER I

GOD CONTROLS DESTINIES OF ALL NATIONS

What are the historical and archaeological KEYS which unlock the racial origins of the people of North-west Europe? The main emphasis in this thesis will be on "secular" history rather than on "sacred" history! We must, however, briefly consider Biblical history before we can rightly understand the mountain of evidence available from the uninspired historical accounts.

For over three thousand years, the Scriptures have given detailed prophecies concerning the various races and nations of this earth.

Throughout the centuries many scores of prophecies have predicted accurately the fates of many of the smaller nations like Egypt, Libya, Syria, Greece, Italy, Spain, Arabia and Ethiopia. But are such modern, mighty nations as France, Britain, Germany, America and Russia excluded in these prophecies? Would God ignore these major nations?

Most students of Biblical prophecy know that the Russian nation and peoples are mentioned under such names as Meschech and Tubal (Moscow and Tobolsk), and Gog and Magog (Ezek 38:2). But would not the same Being who inspired these prophecies also mention America, Britain and France? God has not ignored these nations. They are all mentioned in the Bible—not under their present-day names—but under their ancient Biblical names!

Before one can know the names under which these nations are mentioned in the Bible, he must understand the names by which those nations were called in Bible times. The great FAMILY TREE from which every nation of this earth has sprung must be thoroughly understood.

Bear in mind that God makes and unmakes nations (Job 12:23). "Behold the nations are as a drop of a bucket, and are counted as the small dust of the balance" (Isa. 40:15). God reveals that He sets the boundaries of the nations—He reduces one nation and enlarges another. It is God Almighty (the Controller of the destinies of all nations) who does all these things, none can thwart His will.

Nebuchadnezzar, King of Babylon, after seven years of insanity inflicted on him because of his great pride, said, ". . . He (God) doeth according to His will in the army of heaven, and among the inhabitants of the earth: and none can stay His hand or say unto Him, What doest thou?" (Dan. 4:35).

EVOLUTION—THE BIG HOAX

Before we can intelligently trace the racial origins of the peoples of North-western Europe, it is imperative that we see why the conclusions of this thesis are all based on the concept of SPECIAL CREATION rather than the theory of EVOLUTION!

Firstly, Evolution is a hypothesis which is neither proven nor provable! Secondly, there is not one scintilla of proof to substantiate the Evolutionary Theory. Science can produce nothing to show that Evolution has ever occurred; neither can Science offer anything to show that Evolution is now occurring on this earth—or anywhere in the Universe!

Let us now thoroughly analyze this subject of SPECIAL CREATION versus EVOLUTION from (1) Science, (2) intelligent reason and (3) from the revealed Word of the Creator—the Bible!

It is important to bear in mind that there is no conflict (neither indeed can there be) between the facts of Science and the revealed Word of God! Any real conflict between "Science" and those who believe in God is always a result of (1) misinterpretation of scientific knowledge, resulting in erroneous deductions which lead to fallacious conclusions; or (2) misinterpretation of the revealed Word of God which always results in the formulation of erroneous doctrines.

There are some who try to reconcile the beliefs of Evolution with the Bible. These "Theistic Evolutionists" are willing to compromise the truth of the Bible in order not to appear ridiculous or uninformed in the eyes of those who hold the cherished theories of Evolution. But it is impossible to believe in the divine inspiration of the Bible and also Evolution—according to its true meaning!

The Bible and Evolution are just as incompatible and unmixable as water and oil!

According to the theory of Evolution, all life on this earth (from the one-celled amoeba up to the most complicated life forms) evolved from dead matter! This supposed evolution of life from dead matter, we are told, was from the simple to the complex—first one-celled amoebas, invertebrates, vertebrates (fish, fowl, animals and finally man)! The following order of Evolution of the vertebrates is often given—fish, amphibia, reptiles, mammals, then man!

ANTIQUITY OF EVOLUTIONARY THEORY

It will undoubtedly come as a surprise to many to learn that the old Greek philosopher, Thales (640?-546 B.C.) believed that water or moisture was the primordial (or primary) germ from which all life evolved. Another Greek philosopher, Pythagoras (circa 6th century B.C.) thought that "number" was the primordial germ.

A disciple of Thales, Anaximander (611-547 B.C.) taught that all plant and animal life evolved from the earth by heat and moisture. And Anaxagoras (500?-428 B.C.) believed that both plants and animals were the products of germs carried in the air which, by some unknown process, gave fecundity to the earth. He believed that "animals and man sprang from warm and moist clay." So the atheistic concept of Evolution is by no means a new theory!

In modern times, however, Charles R. Darwin (1809-1882) is the man who, more than anyone else, popularized the Evolutionary hypothesis. It was he who propounded (in 1858) the theory of the origin and perpetuation of new species by a process which he called "natural selection" and "the survival of the fittest." (See his "On the Origin of Species by Means of Natural Selection" and "The Descent of Man."). He considered natural selection as the most important single factor in Organic Evolution.

According to Webster's New Collegiate Dictionary (2nd ed.) NATURAL SELECTION is defined as, "The natural process tending to cause the 'survival of the fittest' (that is, the survival of those forms of animals and plants best adjusted to the conditions under which they live) and extinction of poorly adapted forms. Darwin considered natural selection as the most important factor in organic evolution."

Before examining this doctrine of "the survival of the fittest" and "natural selection" more thoroughly, let us consider another important hypothesis which is accepted by many Evolutionists. Even before Darwin, the French naturalist, Lamarck (1744-1829), postulated the theory of "organic evolution"—that changes in the environment cause changes in the structure of plants and animals, and that such changes ("acquired characteristics") are transmitted to the offspring. He received great acclaim for his hypothesis; but this fanciful theory has now been completely discredited by Science.

The hypothesis simply stated is as follows: If a creature of the sea needs to swim, fins will sprout. But if it finds itself on the land and has a need to walk, legs will appear; if it needs to fly, wings will spontaneously form; if it needs to see, eyes appear; if it needs to hear, ears will develop; if it needs to smell, a nose will emerge; if it needs to eat or talk, a mouth will appear.

There can be no doubt that there is a certain amount of continued multiplicity of characters or characteristics of plants and animals of every kind producing infinite varieties. There is, however, not one scintilla of fact to support the theory that: (1) life originally evolved from simple to complex life forms, or (2) that Evolution has been or is occurring anywhere in the world today!

EVOLUTION—THE ATHEIST'S RELIGION

Just what is Evolution? The Theory of Evolution is perhaps the most pernicious and widely-accepted lie being palmed off on today's gullible world. It is, however, an erroneous concept based upon false deductions without the support of any scientific facts!

In reality, Evolution is the religion of atheists! The Theory of Evolution is merely a modern form of atheism dressed up in the deceptively respectable-appearing garb of pseudo-science. Most (if not all) atheists believe in Evolution.

Though the Atheistic Evolutionist ridicules the Christian for his supposed "blind faith" in a Creator, yet the Evolutionist has a remarkable faith in the Theory of Evolution—his particular form of religion! The chief exponents of the Evolutionary Theory are the "high priests" of their new-found faith—Evolution. They preach and teach their sinister doctrine.

The Evolutionist has only two tools at his disposal—observation and reason. Those who believe in Special Creation not only have these tools at their disposal, but they have a third tool—God's revelation to man—the Bible!

Let us consider from "observation" to see what Science has been able to reveal regarding the origin of matter and life.

"Just where did all of the matter in the Universe come from?" The Evolutionist believes matter has always existed. The Bible, however, teaches that God created the Universe (Genesis 1:1) and that this material, physical, tangible Universe was created out of the invisible, unseen world of spirit essence. "Through faith we understand that the worlds were framed by the Word of God, so that things which are seen were not made of (or from) things which do appear" (Heb. 11:3).

The Evolutionist denies the existence of a Creator, of spirit beings, of miracles or of anything supernatural. There is, however, a mountain of metaphysical evidence accessible to Science today, proving there is an unseen world of the supernatural.

God Almighty created the material world out of His own dynamic energy—from the Spirit of the living God!

POINTS WHICH BAFFLE THE EVOLUTIONISTS

(1) The Evolutionist bases his theories on the hypothesis that matter has always existed. But the facts of Science disprove this theory. If matter had always existed then all radio-active elements such as uranium, radium and strontium, would have disintegrated and have become non-radio-active—countless ages ago! All radio-active elements continue to disintegrate (according to the "half-life period" law) at a uniform, but measurable rate.

There is no scientific evidence to show that any radio-active elements are being brought into existence by any process known to man. And certainly the Evolutionist will not admit that there is a Creator who could create new radio-active materials. The inescapable conclusion (if one rejects a Creator) is that THERE HAS BEEN NO PAST ETERNITY OF MATTER! Evolutionists are only guessing when they say that matter has always existed! They have no proof—they don't know!

(2) The Evolutionist postulates the ridiculous theory that life evolved from dead matter by the hypothetical means of "spontaneous generation." But there is not one shred of scientific evidence to show that any form of life ever evolved by any process known to man, including that of "spontaneous generation." One of the most inexorably binding

"Laws of Nature" is the "Law of Biogenesis"—that life can only come from life! The inanimate cannot product the animate!

The Bible shows that God created life, but the Evolutionists say it just evolved by "spontaneous generation." They don't know how this may have happened; neither is there any way they or anyone else can prove their theory. They freely admit there is no such "spontaneous generation of life" occurring today. They are merely guessing—they have not one proof that life evolved by "spontaneous generation."

(3) We see in the world tremendous powers, energies and forces. Where did this dynamic power and energy originate? The Evolutionist does not know. Again, he can merely guess. He cannot account for the existence of the incalculable forces and energies which exist in the Universe today.

(4) The material world is governed by certain inexorably binding laws. These laws (the Laws of Gravity, Inertia, Thermo-dynamics, Biogenesis, Motion, Heredity and all of the LAWS OF NATURE) are not able to be accounted for by the Evolutionist. He cannot explain who or what established these so-called "Laws of Nature" which govern the whole Universe! Neither can the Evolutionist explain what or who sustains these "Laws of Nature."

(5) The world in which we live is inhabited by myriads of forms of animal life—all possessing varying degrees of intelligence. Where did this INTELLIGENCE come from? Dead matter has no intelligence whatsoever. (Intelligence cannot come from non-intelligence).

The Evolutionist admits that intelligence exists, but by what power or through whom it came into existence—he does not know! Again, he must acknowledge he does not know how intelligence came into being, neither is there any scientific proof whatsoever to show that intelligence evolved by any known laws.

(6) The earth and the entire Universe is laid out or constructed according to a marvellous plan, an awe-inspiring DESIGN! The countless forms of life among fishes, fowl and mammals (including man) manifest not only varying degrees of intelligence, but they also reveal infinite wisdom, knowledge and understanding of the principles of design. In fact, man designs and patterns almost everything he makes after something in nature.

Many volumes could be written explaining and extolling the marvellous design and function of the human body—the most perfectly designed in all the universe!

The Bible reveals that God Almighty designed the human body after His own image—in His own likeness! Mankind was made in the general form and shape of his Creator, and therefore his bodily form possesses the most perfect design found in the Universe.

There is no way that the basic, over-all design of the human body could possibly be improved! Every member in the body is put in the right place, and functions perfectly. One would not want two noses with one being located in the back of his head. Neither would one want and extra eye, or perhaps a couple of extra eyes, placed on any other location in the body. Not only would such innovations in the human body look odd, but they would impair and confuse the basic single-track functioning of the human brain.

Admittedly, there are times when one feels it would be a distinct advantage to possess several eyes, arms, hands, legs or feet. Even though it would on occasions be advantageous to have extra members, yet for the over-all functioning of the human body, we would neither look as comely as we do, nor would it be an over-all advantage to possess such added members. One could go on indefinitely to describe the functioning of the human body, and then show from reason that there is no way the basic design of the human body could ever be improved!

Now consider the marvellous designs which one finds in the plant kingdom—such infinite variety of design and beauty! Did all this arise by mere blind chance, through "spontaneous generation," "use and disuse," or through any theoretical process of Evolution?

(7) The Evolutionist believes life developed gradually through the various life forms—beginning with a primitive, one-celled type all the way up to man. He then hopes to prove his theory from archaeological data as found in the fossil layers of this earth. According to this theory, the most simple life forms should be found in the earliest fossil layer of the earth, the more complex life forms appearing as one proceeds upwards through the various strata. Evolution teaches that life forms as found in this layer should be: simple, few in number, and should develop step by step.

But here are the facts: (a) In the first fossil layer (the Cambrian stratum) 455 different species of life are found instead of a "few forms of life" which we are supposed to find in this layer. (b) Complex life forms are found in this stratum instead of simple life forms. (c) Giant forms of life are found instead of more diminutive specimens. (d) Instead of very early or "primitive" types of life, large numbers of the life forms are found in this "Cambrian" stratum which are identical (or in other instances almost identical) with living representatives. (e) Instead of finding natural deposits of life forms such as one would find today along beaches or deltas, in the "Cambrian" stratum there is evidence of life forms having been buried alive by a sudden, great catastrophe!

These archaeological findings prove that life forms did not evolve—from the simple one-celled amoeba to the more complex types! The facts as recorded in the fossil layers all over the earth disprove Evolution—disprove the theory that life developed gradually from simple to complex types.

(8) God, through the Bible, has given many prophecies, explaining in great detail what would happen to mighty nations and cities. The fulfillment of these prophecies continues, and there is no valid human explanation how these prophecies could have been written thousands of years ago, and yet are being fulfilled precisely to this very day.

(9) The Evolutionist has denied one further proof of the Creator since he does not believe in prayer—for answered prayer is but one more proof to the BELIEVER in God that there is a living, prayer-answering Creator, sitting at the controls of this Universe, who hears and answers prayer.

Now let us consider some of the laws governing life and all living creatures! Remember, according to the Law of Biogenesis, life can only come from life. Dead matter can by no process known to Science give rise to either plant or animal life. The theory of "spontaneous generation" is not supported by any facts of Science. Thus all PHYSICAL life has come from God—the great Life-giver.

MUTATIONS—BUT NO TRANSMUTATIONS

Next, let us notice Lamarck's childish theory. He formulated the theory that acquired characteristics are transmitted to the offspring of plants and animals. But what are the facts? If one acquires a tan, is it ever transmitted to one's offspring? Never! Though Jewish males have been circumcised for about four thousand years, yet Jewish boy babies are always born uncircumcised.

Science is so replete in furnishing irrefutable and overwhelming proof verifying the fact that acquired characteristics are never transmitted to one's offspring that it is unnecessary to give further proof of this fact in this thesis.

Another very important law governing all life on this earth is that all life-forms can only reproduce "after their own kind"—"Like always begets like!" (Gen.1).

There are many different forms of plant and animal life on this earth today. Though there are infinite varieties found among every "GENESIS KIND" of plants and animals, yet two different "genesis kinds" can never interbreed. Though sudden changes or MUTATIONS are commonly found among all different "genesis kinds" of both plants and animals, yet such mutations are always contained within the "genesis kind." Such mutants always reproduce (if at all) after the same kind as their own parent kind. In nature, there are many mutations (changes), but there are no transmutations!

Examples of mutations are: tailless dogs and cats, a black sheep suddenly cropping up in a herd of white sheep where there has not been any "dark blood" for many hundreds of generations; short-legged sheep (Ancon sheep) descended from a long-legged ram by mutation; hornless calves being born from livestock whose forebearers have always possessed horns. We are surely all familiar with examples of men (or even animals) developing (through mutations) extra fingers or toes, or two heads, etc.

It is also well to point out that mutations are nearly always harmful or undesirable!

Though many mutations occur according to the natural laws existing in "nature," yet man has also learned to produce mutations through the use of radiation, heat or chemicals. But man must always work in conformity with certain definite laws of nature, in order to produce such mutations.

One of the most firmly established and best known laws of nature pertains to the "fixity of the kind" or "fixity of the species (meaning kind)." This simply means that a particular "kind" or "species" of plant or animal can never reproduce except within its own kind. As an example, the bovine (ox) family or "kind" could never reproduce or interbreed with the equine (horse) family. Likewise, the canine (dog) family could never interbreed with the feline (cat) kind. Also, the perverted mind of man has learned that mankind (homo sapiens) cannot be crossed with any other animal.

Almighty God set the laws of nature in such a way that within any one "kind" infinite variety is possible. No two human beings have ever been alike. Human variation ranges all the way from giants to pygmies. Also in the human family we see the black, yellow and white "races" with straight, wavy, curly, kinky, frisly or peppercorn type of hair. There are many other ways in which an infinite variety of differences are found in the human family. This is true of all types of animal life.

Through natural reproductive processes, infinite "species" or "varieties" within the "genesis kind" are possible, yet each kind can only reproduce "after its kind." Like always begets like. This is one of the firm laws of genetics. There are many other laws governing genetics and heredity, but space does not permit a thorough examination of these in this thesis.

Through experimentation, man has developed many thousands of generations of FLIES, but even though mutations appeared and different varieties developed, the end product was always a fly! Likewise, man has developed infinite varieties of species of GARDEN PEAS, but the offspring of these garden peas was always simply more garden peas. Botanists have developed thousands of different species of ROSES (and other types of flowers). But the end product is always a rose. The rose cannot be crossed with a water lily, any more than garden peas can be crossed with potatoes. One of the firm laws that God has set in nature is that like can only beget like. This is another proof that there is no crossing between any of the various "kinds" or "families" in either the plant or the animal kingdom. There are many varieties within each "kind," and occasional MUTATIONS which cause further varieties within the kinds, but SCIENCE HAS NEVER YET RECORDED ONE TRANSMUTATION—such as the cross-breeding of the bovine and the equine families or the crossing of the oak tree with the cedar.

We have seen that life can only come from life. We have also observed that like always begets like. Furthermore, we have seen clearly demonstrated that though there are mutations in all varieties of plant and animal life, Science has yet failed to produce one TRANSMUTATION. Therefore the theories of "spontaneous generation," "natural selection" (as explained by Evolutionists), "inheritance of acquired characteristics" and all of the basic theories of Evolution are scientifically unproven, unprovable and unscientific!

Let us also observe some of the basic laws governing all life (plant and animal) on this terra firma.

(1) The Creator God Almighty, created all of the various "kinds" of plant and animal life upon the earth.
(2) All present-day varieties or species of plant and animal life are the descendants of the same "genesis kind" of plants and animals which God originally created.

(3) In each of these "kinds," God put within their reproductive processes the ability to produce infinite varieties or species (through mutations, etc.)—but through such mutations new "kinds" would never evolve.

(4) Such physical changes (or mutations) which have appeared since the creation of the original "genesis kinds" of plants and animals have always occurred in accordance with the principles of the laws in nature which God ordained from creation.

(5) All of the natural or physical laws governing life and the whole physical Universe were set in motion to sustain the physical Universe and life upon this earth by the power of an omniscient (all-knowing) and omnipotent (almighty) Creator!

We have now seen from Science and from the Bible that Evolution is not only an uproven and unprovable theory, but it is totally unscientific. One could never prove that life evolved through "spontaneous generation," "natural selection," "inheritance of acquired characteristics," or through any of the fancied theories of Evolution.

EVOLUTION—IS IT REASONABLE?

Now let us observe from reason, as well as from God's Word, why it is more scientifically reasonable to believe in Special Creation, rather than Evolution.

(1) Evolutionists and Special Creationists alike agree that the material Universe exists. Evolutionists say it always existed; those who believe in Special Creation say that the invisible God (who is Himself composed of Spirit) brought the visible Universe into existence out of the invisible substance of the unseen world—out of spirit essence.

Exactly how God did this, the human mind cannot fully fathom, any more than the human mind can fully grasp how a black cow can eat green grass and produce white milk and yellow butter! Neither can the human mind fully understand exactly what light, or electricity really are, though we know a great deal about them.

(2) The Evolutionist and the Christian (with few exceptions) likewise agree that life exists! The Evolutionist says life evolved by "spontaneous generation," the Christian believes God created all life. Remember, one of the laws of nature (the Law of Biogenesis) is that life can only come from life! All life came from God!

(3) The fact that there are myriads of laws in this earth and throughout the Universe proves that there had to be something or someone to set these laws in motion. In order for there to be laws, there must have been a Law-maker or a Law-giver—God. Furthermore, we see those laws are continually operated, kept in motion, made to function. This functioning or upholding of all existing laws proves there must be a great Law-sustainer—one who sustains, operates, upholds His laws!

(4) Throughout the Universe (and especially on this earth) are infinite DESIGNS that stagger the imagination. Such designs must have had a Designer—they couldn't just have happened!

(5) The world about us contains infinite varieties of animals possessing varying degrees of INTELLIGENCE. This intelligence could not have come from dead matter. Intelligence can only come from intelligence.

(6) God Almighty is able to foretell the future and then to bring such predictions to pass. Fulfilled prophecy is a further proof of God.

(7) Answered prayer is a further proof of God to those who believe in prayer, and who have consequently had their prayers answered. The atheist is usually ignorant of this proof of God's existence.

The author was recently asked by an atheist why he believed in God. One example which baffled this young atheist will now be given. The writer took off his watch, handed it to the young atheist, asking him if he believed it was possible for the watch to have designed, made and wound itself up! The young atheist promptly replied that he didn't believe it was possible, and that anyone who would hold such a belief would be a little off in the head! He was then asked which was greater—the watch or this Universe. Of course, the young man had to acknowledge that the Universe was infinitely greater than the watch.

Then the writer pointed out to him the error of his own reasoning: If the watch could not design, make and wind itself up, neither could the Universe design, build and "wind itself up." No creature existing in the whole earth was able to (1) create or make itself, (2) give itself intelligence or (3) bestow upon itself life!

The Evolutionist is right in believing that something has always existed! God Almighty reveals, through the Bible, that something has always existed. But He reveals that that "Something" is God Himself—the Self-Existent or Eternal One. The Evolutionist believes that the material Universe has always existed, but God shows that the physical world or Universe has not always existed. Rather, it is the unseen world of spirit which has always existed.

ONE CANNOT PRODUCE ANYTHING GREATER THAN ONESELF

Another law or "truism" is that though a creature or being can make or build something INFERIOR to itself, yet no creature in all the Universe can create or make anything SUPERIOR to itself!

According to the Christian concept of God, even the Creator cannot create a being greater than Himself—with more intelligence, power, or glory. Yes, life can only come from life, and like always begets like.

It is true that those who believe in Special Creation can no more fathom how God has always existed, than the atheist can explain how matter could always have existed. The answer to this is very simple. In Deuteronomy 29:29 we read, "The secret things belong unto the Lord our God: but those things which are revealed belong unto us and to our children for ever, that we may do all the words of this law." So Moses knew that there were certain secret things which only God could understand, but man could not.

King Solomon, the wisest man who ever lived, was inspired to write, "Then I beheld all the work of God, that a man CANNOT FIND OUT the work that is done under the sun: because though a man labour to seek it out, yet he shall not find it; yea farther; though a wise man think to know it, yet shall he not be able to find it" (Eccl. 8:17).

David, King of Israel, was also inspired to reveal that certain knowledge is so "high" that he could not "attain unto it" (Psa. 139:7-17). Those who accept the concept of Special Creation have the humility to realize their limitations—to see that their minds are finite; and that they are not able to fathom everything.

GOD INFINITE—MAN FINITE

Notice Psalm 147:4,5 "He (God) telleth (counts) the number of the stars; He calls them all by their names. Great is our Lord, and of great power: His understanding is INFINITE." Yes, God's understanding is unlimited, but man's understanding is very finite—very limited! Also read Isaiah 40:12-31.

Man's puny little mind is so finite in comparison with the mind of God that there really is no true comparison. One might compare man unto an ant, and God unto the man. God's intelligence is infinitely greater than man's, even more so than man's intelligence is infinitely greater than the intelligence of an ant.

If someone had the power to give immortality to an ant and cause that ant to sit upon the face of a watch, listening to the ticking of the watch, observing the movement of its hands—for a billion years—then that little ant's mind could not comprehend any more about the watch at the end of that period than when it began its observation a billion years earlier. In other words, the ant's mind is so finite that it could never comprehend who designed and made the watch, why it was made, what kept it going, or from what it was made. So there are a number of questions which man cannot yet fully fathom and will never be able to completely understand in this life. Let us be humble and honest enough to admit our limitations!

BIBLE AND TRUE SCIENCE AGREE

Before concluding this section, let us observe a few Scriptures which clearly show that the Bible and true Science always agree!

One so-called stumbling block to Science has been that many Christians have maintained the Bible says God created the Universe six thousand years ago (Gen. 1:1). Careful study of this verse (by checking the original Hebrew) reveals the following: "In the BEGINNING God created the heaven and the earth." But this does not say how long ago that "beginning" actually was. It may have been billions of years ago!

Genesis 1:2 says, "The earth became without form and void (Hebrew 'tohu' and 'bohu'—waste and void)."

The Hebrew word translated in this verse as "was" is the same verb which is used in Genesis 19:26, where it says that Lot's wife looked back and "became" a pillar of salt. Also, read carefully Isaiah 45:18. Here it says that God did not create the earth "waste and void" (Hebrew "tohu" and "bohu"—meaning waste and chaotic). Thus we see that Genesis 1:2 shows the earth became "tohu" and "bohu", but Isaiah 45:18 shows that God did not create it this way.

The earth became chaotic and waste as the result of a cataclysmic destruction which Almighty God brought upon the earth because of the sin of angelic beings who had originally been placed on this earth. (For scriptural proof of this, study Isa. 14:12-15; Ezek. 28:12-17; Luke 10:18; Rev. 12:4,10; Jude 6 and II Peter 2:4). These scriptural references show conclusively that God brought a great physical devastation upon the earth as a result of the sin of the angels, just as He later brought a great physical catastrophe upon the earth as a result of the sins of the ante-Deluvians in the time of Noah; and just as He later brought a physical destruction upon Sodom and Gomorrah in consequence of their loathsome, degraded sexual deviations.

So no atheist or Evolutionist can truthfully accuse God or the Bible of saying the earth was created six thousand years ago. The Bible does not say that, but rather implies Creation of the earth occurred in the far distant past (aeons ago)! The Bible and Science agree on this point. But the creation of man occurred about 6,000 years ago.

The Bible, in three different places, shows that the earth is a sphere (see Isa. 40:22; Prov. 8:27 and Luke 17:24-36). Also notice Job 26:7 which says that God "hangeth the earth upon nothing." Yes, the earth is literally suspended in space—held in orbit by the gravitational pull of the sun.

The Bible is truly scientific though it was not intended to be a scientific textbook. None the less, every statement made in the Bible is completely accurate from a scientific standpoint.

EVOLUTIONISTS BELIEVE IN MIRACLES

Most Evolutionists are atheists. They claim they do not believe in a God, but we have seen that they, too, have a religion—that of Evolution!

But do they believe in miracles? Absolutely!

(1) They believe in the existence of the physical world—of this created Universe. To have a creation without a Creator (something made without a Maker) is certainly a miracle!

(2) We have seen that Evolutionists believe in life without a Life-giver. They set aside the Law of Biogenesis—that life can only come from life.

(3) They believe in Laws without a Law-giver!

(4) They believe those laws are sustained, upheld and kept in motion without a Sustainer. Another miracle!

(5) They believe in the myriads of designs without a Designer—still another miracle!

(6) They believe in intelligence coming from non-intelligence. Yet another miracle!

The Apostle Paul was inspired to write: "For the invisible things of Him from the creation of the world are clearly seen, being understood by the things that are made, even His eternal power and Godhead; so that they (the atheists) are without excuse" (Rom. 1:21).

Paul then showed that these infidels by "Professing themselves to be wise, they became fools" (v.22).

Yes, truly God's physical creation reveals that there had to be a Designer, Creator and Sustainer of this vast Universe!

What does God's Word thunder at today's atheists—the modern Evolutionists? "The FOOL has said in his heart, There is no God . . ." (Psa. 14:1).

The wise know there is an All-wise, All-powerful Creator-Sustainer God whose marvelous works are truly awe-inspiring!

"O the depth of the riches both of the wisdom and knowledge of God! How unsearchable are His judgments, and His ways past finding out" (Rom. 11:33).

Because the anthropologists have built their theories upon the shifting sands of EVOLUTION, they are going more and more into hopeless confusion! No books on anthropology or ethnology can have much real truth in them if they base their conclusions on Evolution—which has already been exposed to be simply a cult pretending to explain the origin of things on the basis of mere conjectures. If one will count such expressions as "apparently," "perhaps," "possibly," and similar words found in the books based on Evolution, he will be amazed to see how many assumptions there are masquerading under the name of "Science."

Does one dare base his beliefs on such a shaky foundation? The Bible is the only reliable foundation upon which one can reconstruct history!

THE THREE PRIMARY BRANCHES OF MANKIND

God inspired Moses to write: "These (the progeny of Shem, Ham and Japheth—v.1) are the families of the sons of Noah, after their generations, in their nations: and by these were the nations divided in the earth after the flood" (Gen. 10:32).

Note carefully that the three main branches of mankind have descended from Noah through his three sons—Shem, Ham and Japheth. Many modern ethnologists do not agree with God on this point; but they have gone into hopeless confusion as a result of their rejection of this simple truth!

The Apostle Paul was inspired to affirm: "And God hath made of one blood all nations of men for to dwell on all the earth, and hath determined the times before appointed, and the bounds of their habitation" (Acts 17:26).

The following statement is a verification of this Biblical fact: "Most physical anthropologists accept modern man as one genus, and one species" (Ency. Amer., 1960 ed., Vol. II, p.20d).

Dr. Wylie explains this point very well:

> When Noah comes forth from the Ark we see him accompanied by three sons—Shem, Ham and Japhet. These are the three fountain-heads of the world's population.

> "These are the three sons of Noah, and of them was the whole earth overspread." . . . and after four thousand years . . . the population of the world at this day . . . is still resolvable into three grand groups, [or four groups—if we include the brown people as a separate race], corresponding [roughly] to the three patriarchs of the race, Shem, Ham and Japheth." (History of the Scottish Nation, Vol. I, P. 10).

Let us have the courage to deny the theories of atheism, agnosticism and so-called "higher criticism" which exalts itself above God, and makes gods out of its own pet theories. Let us believe the truth (which until a few years ago was commonly believed and taught) that mankind has been scattered over the face of the earth since the Flood; and that the nations of this earth have descended from Noah's three sons. There are many historical proofs which substantiate this three-fold source or division of mankind.

Let us now examine a few quotations which will verify the above statements from secular sources.

In the very latest edition of the Encyclopedia Americana, we find the following statements:

> Most physical anthropologists accept modern man as one genus, and one species; Reginald R. Gates, alone, suggests that there are five species. The majority viewpoint recognizes THREE MAJOR "DIVISIONS" or "stocks" which taxonomically occupy the level of sub-races. These groups are CAUCASOID or "white," MONGOLOID or "yellow," and NEGROID or "black." (1960 ed., Vol. II, P. 20d).

Then the Encyclopedia Americana proceeds to group the various people of the earth under the afore-mentioned divisions.

Keane also divides the races into (1) "Negroes," (2) "Mongols" and (3) "The Caucasic Peoples." (Man Past and Present).

"The Living Races of Mankind," by Johnston and Harry, likewise divide humanity into three chief stocks or types.

It is essential, however, to a right understanding of the subject that a few paragraphs should be devoted to a consideration of the THREE leading types, or stocks, into which the human race is obviously divisible.

These THREE primary types, which have been in existence throughout the historic period and are probably of much greater antiquity, are familiar to all of us under the respective designations of the white man, the yellow or red man, and the Negro or black man." (Vol. I, p. 1, Introduction).

Not everyone, however, classifies the human race into this three-fold division. The Encyclopedia Britannica illustrates these three "divisions" or "stocks" of humanity (Caucasoid, Mongoloid, Negroid) and also adds a fourth—Australoid. But the Australoid type is clearly just a branch of (or sub-division of) the Negroid "race" of mankind! (Encyclopedia Britannica, 1960 ed., Vol. II, Anthropology).

Hammerton, in his Peoples of all Nations, likewise uses the same four stocks as does the Encyclopedia Britannica—except that he says the Caucasoid, Mongoloid and Negroid races have all descended from the AUSTRALOID "race." Both Scripture and secular history show that he is merely guessing when he says the three main divisions of mankind have descended from the "Australoid" stock! (J.A. Hammerton, Peoples of all Nations, Vol. I, p. XI).

Ripley divides the human species into "four groups" so far as skin colour is concerned: (1) "Jet or coal black colour," (2) "Brownish colour," (3) "Yellow," (4) "White." There are many shades or gradations of the "dark" branch of humanity. But if we include the "brown" people as a sub-division of the "black" stock of mankind then there are just three branches of the human family.

There is nothing in the Scriptures or in Science to prove that man just evolved (perhaps 1,000,000 or more years ago) and has roamed around in primitive infancy virtually ever since.

The Scriptures tell us that HAM (Heb. "burnt" or "hot") is the father, generally speaking, of the "Black" or burnt-appearing (Negroid or African-type) dark races. We are further told by the inspired writers that JAPHETH (Heb. "enlarging" or "stretching out") is the father of the prolific Mongoloid, the so-called "Yellow" Asiatic races. (Japheth is also the father of some fair-skinned people). SHEM (Heb. "name" or "renowned") is the father of most of the "White" Caucasian "races."

Every race or nation of this earth will fall into one of these three major divisions of mankind (Shem, Ham and Japheth), or else can be proven to be a cross-breed between two or more of these three main branches of the human family.

This does not mean that all of the races were fully developed immediately after the Deluge. It took some time before the three primary branches of mankind (White, Yellow and Dark) were fully developed (probably through mutations) as we know them today.

Remember, some classify humanity into four groups or branches: (1) White, (2) Yellow, (3) Brown, and (4) Black. Since, however, most of the brown people have descended from Ham, it simplifies things if we class them with the "dark" races. They are a sub-division of the "dark" or "Negroid" branch of Ham's descendants.

The peoples of each of the three great branches of man must have intermarried with members of their own "racial type" in order to produce a true type of race. Such interbreeding would, over a period of several generations, tend to produce a distinct racial type.

The Hebrew word for Ham ("burnt") shows that he was a dark or burnt-appearing person. Secular history is also very clear in showing that Nimrod, a descendant of Ham, was certainly a dark man.

Shortly after the Deluge, Nimrod, a grandson of Ham, organized the first man-ruled dictatorship in defiance of God, and in defiance of Shem, who was successor to Noah in teaching mankind the ways of God (Gen. 10:6-11).

Nimrod and his harlot wife, Semiramis, started the old mystery religion of Babylonia which has permeated the whole world today—even including modern "Christianity."

Because of Nimrod's idolatry and also because of his despotic rule over his fellow man, Shem finally organized enough God-fearing men to destroy Nimrod and his power. History shows that Nimrod had fled to Egypt, and it was there that Shem and his followers finally put an end to the life of that wretched man.

Even at that early date, the Egyptians were an idolatrous people, and had been easily swayed by Nimrod. They had looked upon him as a great benefactor—a Saviour. After the death of Nimrod, his followers began to deify him. They looked upon Shem (and all who were sympathetic with him) as tyrants!

According to Alexander Hyslop's The Two Babylons, one of the names by which the Egyptians knew Shem was "TYPHO" or "TYPHON"—meaning the Desolator or Destroyer. In other words, since Shem had killed Nimrod, their leader, they spoke of Shem as "Typhon" meaning Devil. (The Two Babylons, pp. 65, 276, 277).

> We have seen that Shem was the actual slayer of Tammuz [another name for Nimrod]. As the grand adversary of the Pagan Messiah, those who hated him for his deed called him for that very deed by the name of the Grand Adversary of all, Typhon, or the devil" (ibid., pp. 276,277).

Hyslop illustrates (in The Two Babylons) a picture or likeness of Nimrod (ibid., p. 44) and the features are very clearly those of a black man—thick lips, etc. **[Editors note: this has been reconstructed from the passage quoted on page 34 of Hyslop's 'The Two Babylons']**

[Editors Note: Fig 18 above is the illustration referred to. This has been incorporated for the benefit of the reader, it was not reproduced in the original text]

"Now Nimrod, as the son of Cush, was black, in other words, was a Negro" (ibid., p. 34).

The prophet Jeremiah was inspired to write "Can the Ethiopian (Cushite) change (the color of) his skin . . . ?" (Jer. 13:23). The Hebrew word for "Ethiopian" is Cushite. So this verse should read "CAN THE CUSHITE CHANGE HIS SKIN . . . ?"

There can be no question that the present day Ethiopians (who are the descendants of Cush) are very dark skinned. Nimrod (son of Cush) was certainly a dark-skinned person!

Now let us notice some quotations from Plutarch which show that not only was Nimrod a black man, but Shem (the father of the majority of the Caucasians) was a fair person with a red complexion. "TYPHON HAD RED HAIR." (ibid., p. 73). "Osiris, on the other hand, according to their legendary tradition, was dark . . ." (ibid., p. 81). (Only fair-skinned people are truly "red in complexion").

Yes, Nimrod was a dark or black man, but Shem (Typhon—a derogatory name applied to him by the Egyptians) "was red in complexion" and "had red hair."

For a further account of Nimrod's death at the hands of Shem (Typhon) see Diodorus of Sicily, Vol. I, Book 1, para. 21, and para. 88. Notice the following interesting quote: "RED oxen, however, may be sacrificed, because it is thought that this was the colour of TYPHON (Shem), who plotted against Osiris [another name for Nimrod] and was then punished by Isis [Semiramis] for the death of her husband. Men also, if they were of the same colour as Typhon, were sacrificed, they say, in ancient times by the kings at the tomb of Osiris; however, only a few Egyptians are now found RED in colour, but the majority of such are non-Eqyptians . . ." (Diodorus of Sicily, Book I, para. 88).

Thus we can clearly see that secular history shows Nimrod was a black man, and Shem (Typhon) was a person with a ruddy complexion, having red hair! These historical accounts show that Ham's descendants were "dark" (not all necessarily black) and that Shem's descendants were fair with "red" or ruddy complexions!

Some of the brown race and other sub-races are directly descended from Ham; while others developed as a result of intermarriage between members of the three primary "divisions" or "stocks" of mankind.

Two examples of sub-races are the Arabs and the Philippinos. Both of these "races" are a mixture of two or three of the primary divisions of mankind.

HISTORY ATTESTS TO THE THREE RACES

Here is a very enlightening quotation from Myers:

> The Races of Mankind in the Historic Period.—Distinctions in bodily characteristics, such as form, color, and features, divide the human species into THREE chief types or races, known as the Black or Ethiopian Race, the Yellow or Mongolian Race, and the White or Caucasian Race. But we must not suppose each of these three types to be sharply marked off from the other; they shade into one another by insensible gradations (Myers, The Eastern Nations and Greece, p. 14).

The BLACK "RACE" inhabits primarily Africa south of the Sahara, parts of India and many of the islands. The YELLOW (Mongoloid) "RACE" lives mainly in Eastern, Northern and South-eastern Asia. Myers says the "ARYAN or INDO-EUROPEAN" and also the "SEMITIC" peoples belong to the so-called WHITE "RACE" which inhabits Europe, Western Asia, North America, South Africa and Australia (ibid., pp. 15,16).

Of course, members of these three branches of humanity are scattered in many other areas of the world.

It should be pointed out here that the "Semitic" (Shemitic) peoples constitute, in the main, the White Race.

Today the term "Semitic" is generally misunderstood and is consequently misused. Most people think that the Jews and Arabs comprise about all of the true Semitic peoples. The Anglo-Saxon-Keltic peoples who today inhabit North-western Europe are definitely Semitic and will later in this work be proven to be Shem's descendants. The Germans and other Europeans are also descendants of Shem.

Some of the descendants of Japheth, however, have light skins, but many of these Japhetic light-skinned peoples have a yellowish or olive tint to their skins. This can be witnessed in the Mongoloid peoples as well as in the original-type Greeks, and some of the Italians and Spaniards—who are descendants of Japheth through his son, Javan. Also, Japheth is the father of bronze—or red-skinned Indians inhabiting North, South and Central Americas.

After the Patriarch Noah and his three sons, Shem, Ham, and Japheth and their wives came forth from the Ark, they descended from the Mountains of Ararat—in present day Armenia. Their progeny settled in the regions of the Tigris and Euphrates rivers. They were still in this area at the time of the Confusion of Tongues when all of the families of mankind were scattered abroad on the face of the whole earth (Gen. 11:1-9).

HOW TO DETERMINE RACE

Before we can trace the racial origins of the peoples under consideration in this thesis, we must clarify certain words and terms which are commonly used by ethnologists and anthropologists. Let us first define the word "race."

> The descendants of a common ancestor; a family, tribe, people, or nation, believed to belong to the same stock . . . Ethnology. A division of mankind possessing constant traits, transmissible by descent, sufficient to characterize it as a distinct human type (Webster's New Collegiate Dictionary, Art. Race, p. 696).

Let us next see how this word "race" is defined by Myers:

> Distinctions in bodily characteristics, such as form, color, and features, divide the human species into three chief types or races, known as the Black or Ethiopian Race, the Yellow or Mongolian Race, and the White or Caucasian Race (Myers, The Eastern Nations and Greece, p. 14).

Beside the three (four—if the Brown "race" included) chief types or "races" just mentioned there are many other "races" or sub-races, with which most people are at least vaguely familiar.

> The simplest division of the human family is into the three races, the Yellow Man, the White Man, and the Black Man . . . (Anderson, Extinct Civilizations of the East, p. 14).

In recent years, ethnologists have tended to invent more and more names for all sorts of races and sub-races until the average student finds himself quite confused by such a labyrinth of names. One would need to possess a prodigious memory in order to remember all the names for the various races and sub-races as defined by some modern ethnologists.

CEPHALIC INDEX—HELPFUL IN DETERMINING RACIAL AFFINITIES

The CEPHALIC INDEX is the main key, used universally by most, if not all, present day ethnologists, to ascertain racial affinities FROM SKELETAL REMAINS!

One can readily determine "race" on the living populations by such tests as: Skin color, stature, nasal indices, general build, color of hair and eyes, head shape, and by mental and personality traits.

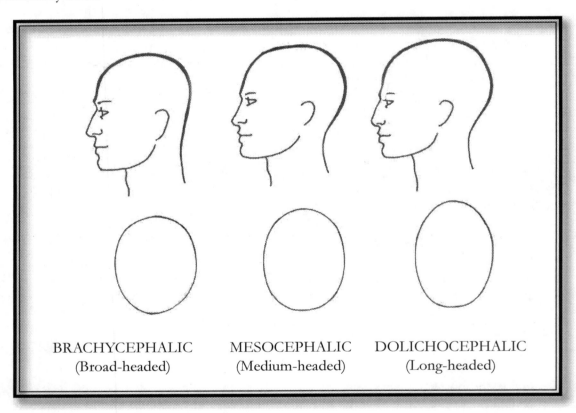

BRACHYCEPHALIC (Broad-headed)   MESOCEPHALIC (Medium-headed)   DOLICHOCEPHALIC (Long-headed)

Fig. I

Classification of CEPHALIC INDEXES:

1. Brachycephalic   Above 80
2. Mesocephalic   Between 75 and 80
3. Dolichocephalic   Below 75

[Ripley, The Races of Europe, pages 37 and 38]

But such tools elude the anthropologist who must determine the racial connections of a by-gone people from skeletal remains alone. With these silent men of yesteryear one can only judge their racial type by such measurements as general height, bodily proportions (from bone measurements), and the cephalic index.

Since the C.I. (cephalic index) is of utmost importance in determining the racial affinities of people from their skeletal remains, we shall examine this subject thoroughly, explaining the C.I. directly from the works of well-known ethnologists.

We shall have reason to rely heavily upon the cephalic index on numerous occasions to assist us in determining which racial type a particular people belonged to.

Professor Ripley, who was considered one of the world's foremost authorities on "race", has some interesting remarks on this subject:

> The shape of the human head—by which we mean the general proportions of length, breadth, and height, irrespective of the "bumps of the phrenologist—is ONE of the best available tests of race known" (The Races of Europe, Chap. III, p. 37).

Ripley then shows that the best way to measure the head form is by using the "cephalic index." He says:

> This is simply the breadth of the head above the ears expressed in percentage of its length from forehead to back. Assuming that this length is 100, the width is expressed as a fraction of it. As the head becomes proportionately broader—that is, more fully rounded, viewed from the top down—this cephalic index increases. When it rises above 80, the head is called brachycephalic; when it falls below 75, the term dolichocephalic is applied to it. Indexes between 75 and 80 are characterized as mesocephalic. (ibid, p. 37).

See The Passing of the Great Race, page 19, for the same view, as expressed by Grant. Ripley points out that a broad head is usually accompanied by a rounded face, and that a long head usually has an oval face (The Races of Europe, Chap. III, p. 39).

The cephalic index measurements are all "dependant upon the boney structure of the head," and he says that the C.I. (cephalic index) must be accurately taken, not including the "superficial fleshy parts" (ibid., p. 39).

Ripley shows that the general shape of the head seems to bear no direct relation to the intellectual power or to the intelligence of any particular individual (ibid., p. 40).

He mentions that the absolute size of the head of the individual is very unimportant to the anthropologist. ". . . popularly, a large head with beetling eyebrows suffices to establish a man's intellectual credit; but, like all other credit, it is entirely dependant upon what lies on deposit elsewhere. Neither size nor weight of the brain seems to be of importance" (ibid., p. 43).

The reader will observe that Ripley places a great deal of importance upon, not the size, but the general shape of the skull as the chief factor in determining the racial connections of a people from their skeletal remains. He shows the color of the hair, the eyes and the stature are open to modification by local circumstances (ibid., p. 52).

> "On the other hand the general proportions of the head seem to be uninfluenced either by climate, by food supply or economic status, or by habits of life; so that they stand as the clearest exponents which we possess of the permanent hereditary difference within the human species [from skeletal remains]" (ibid., p. 52).

CRANIOMETRY VERSES PHRENOLOGY

It should be pointed out here that craniometry, which includes the study of THE CEPHALIC INDEX, is an accurate science, and HAS NOTHING WHATSOEVER TO DO WITH THE SO-CALLED "SCIENCE" OF PHRENOLOGY, which contains much error and a little truth. Nearly all modern anthropologists and ethnologists utilize the cephalic index. Most of them agree that it is one of the most important single factors in determining "race" or racial affinities.

The value of the cephalic index can, therefore, hardly be overstressed. As we have already observed, the C.I. is of especial value when classifying skeletal remains. When trying to determine the racial type to which an individual belongs, one is at a distinct disadvantage when working with skeletal remains.

In such cases, he cannot judge the color of the hair, eyes, or the shape of the nose or lips. Here is where the C.I. is of utmost assistance. By this means one can classify skeletal remains to a fairly accurate degree.

MEANS OF DETERMINING RACE—ACCORDING TO HADDON

Let us notice how Haddon, another well-known ethnologist defines "race."

"The term 'race' is employed in various senses, but usually to connote a group of people who have certain well-marked characters in common" (The Races of Man and Their Distribution, p. 1).

Haddon indicates that the main physical characters which he employs to determine race are: hair, skin-color, form of the head, stature, the characters of face, nose, and eyes (ibid., p. 5).

He then proceeds to mention the various kinds of hair—straight, smooth, wavy, frizzly, curly, and woolly. The hair varies in shades from black, and dark browns, to red and different shades of blond.

This author proceeds to show the different skin colors—white, yellow, brown, and black. He shows clearly that the pigmentation of the skin has nothing whatsoever to do with the environment! In other words, the dark races are not dark-skinned because of their having lived for many years in the hot, tropical regions; neither are the light-skinned people fair complexioned because of having lived many years farther north in the colder, cloudier and more temperate zones (ibid., p. 8).

Haddon next mentions a number of points relative to stature, showing that some races are naturally taller than others, but that environmental factors can definitely increase or retard the height of the members of any race (ibid., pp. 8,9).

In regard to the form of head, Haddon says:

> A very valuable character is the general form of the head. When looked at from above some heads are seen to be long and others short, the former are also generally narrow and the latter broad. This distinction is illustrated by the cephalic index (C.I.), which is the ratio of the breadth of the skull or of the head to its length, the latter being taken as 100 (ibid., p. 9).

Haddon shows that a skull with a C.I. of "below 75" is dolichocephalic; but if it is "between 75 and 80," it is termed as mesocephalic; if "it exceeds 80" it is brachycephalic (ibid., p. 9).

Then Haddon proceeds to describe such characters as the face, nose and eyes. Faces may be classified as long and narrow, broad, square, round, oval or "disharmonic."

There are many different classifications of faces and noses, and a lengthy discussion is not necessary. Let it suffice to say that some noses are long and narrow, others are broad and thick, some are hooked or aquiline, others are up-turned, while still other types are straight.

Eye colors range from black through brown, steel blue, light blue, grey and green. There are other differences in the eyes. There is the horizontal and more-or-less wide-open eyes of the Europeans and the North Asiatics, the almond-shaped eye of South Europe, South Africa and Near East, and the "Mongolian eye" which is called the slant-eye, slit-eye, or the oblique-eye. Haddon also mentions the epicanthic fold or the Mongolian fold, as it is sometimes called, which covers the inner angle of the eye of Mongoloid peoples and of some Negroes (ibid., pp. 10,11).

There is one more very important point which must be stressed regarding the C.I. It must be understood that some ethnologists use only two cephalic indexes—dolichocephalic (long-headed) and brachycephalic (broad-headed). With such ethnologists all cephalic indexes below 80 are classed as dolichocephalic, and all over 80 as brachycephalic.

This method of classifying all head forms as either dolichocephalic or brachycephalic is clearly explained in the Encyclopedia Britannica.

> Cephalic Index . . . if the shorter or transverse diameter falls below 80 the skull may be classed as long (dolichocephalic), while if it exceeds 80 the skull is broad (brachycephalic) (Ency. Brit., 11 ed., Vol. V, Art. Cephalic Index, p. 684).

Note carefully that "if it exceeds 80" the skull is considered brachycephalic, but if the C.I. "falls below 80" the skull is considered long.

Webster's New Collegiate Dictionary uses the same method of measurements for classifying brachycephals ("80 or above") and dolichocephals ("less than 80").

Most ethnologists use the term "dolichocephalic" for a C.I. of less than 80, and "brachycephalic" for a C.I. of 80 or more. Haddon uses only two—dolichocephalic and brachycephalic (The Races of Man and Their Distribution, p. 9).

Later, we shall see abundant evidence proving that North-west Europeans are overwhelmingly a dolichocephalic (C.I. 80 and under) people.

It can further be proved beyond question that the long-headed Scythian (or Sacae) skulls which were formerly found on the Steppes all across South Russia and Northern Europe from the Danube to the Don River (and even farther east) are today found in type only among North-west Europeans. These long-headed folk who formerly inhabited South Russia have been succeeded by a round—or broad-headed "Slavic" or "Alpine" type of people. The long-heads were pushed further west by successive waves of Eastern invaders, until today they are only found in appreciable numbers in North-west Europe and, of course, in the countries colonised by these peoples. There are Negroid and Latin type long-heads, but other factors such as general bone proportions make it very difficult to confuse the Nordic long-heads with the Latin and African type of long-heads.

Grant shows that the use of the cephalic index is "the best method" of determining the particular type of race of the European populations:

> In dealing with European populations the best method of determining race
> has been found to lie in a comparison of proportions of the skull, the so-called
> cephalic index. (Grant, The Passing of the Great Race, p. 19).

From the standpoint of the C.I., Europe is divided into two types—dolichocephals and brachycephals. The broad-headed people are, with few exceptions, found in the inland and mountainous districts. The long-heads are almost invariably located on the coastlands and islands of Europe.

The dolichocephals (long-heads) are further divided into two main groups: (1) The Nordics who inhabit North-west Europe, and (2) The Mediterraneans who inhabit the southern regions of Europe, and are mainly found in the countries contiguous to the Mediterranean Sea.

The Scythians (or Sacae), who formerly lived in South Russia, were of the Nordic branch of the dolichocephals. The foremost authorities on the Scythian question are generally agreed on this point. Other characters enable a trained ethnologist to clearly differentiate between the skeletal remains of Nordics and Mediterraneans. The Nordics are longer-limbed, have typically larger skulls, and are generally larger-bodied than are the Mediterraneans.

The difference between Nordic and Mediterranean skeletal remains is as easily discernable as is such difference readily noticeable between the living North-west European Nordics and the South or South-east European Mediterraneans.

We have seen from a number of foremost authorities on the "race" question that the cephalic index is of utmost importance to the ethnologist when sorting out and classifying skeletal remains. The general shape of the skull remains more constant than any other tangible racial character. Height, weight and other minor characters are sometimes altered by environment.

However, there is as yet no scientific proof that the basic shape of the skull of any race has ever yet altered noticeably except by intermarriage with a race having a different skull type, or by deformations. The skulls of ancient Egyptians are identical with those of the unmixed modern Coptic Egyptians.

Some, however, fail to distinguish and rightly interpret skeletal findings. To illustrate this point, it is well to show that in some countries the skulls found in the ancient cemeteries indicate that the population at one time was that of a long-headed type. Skulls from modern cemeteries or skulls from the living population, however, may generally be of the broad-headed type. Some anthropologists hastily jump to the conclusion that the general shape of the skull of this particular population has changed from that of a long-headed race to that of a broad-headed people.

But the truth is that a long-headed people at one time lived in that country and were buried in the older cemeteries. Subsequent invasions by round—or broad-heads supplanted the older population so that the modern population, and consequently those interred in the later cemeteries, are those of a broad-headed type of people.

There are instances where this has been reversed—where a broad-headed people had formally inhabited a certain territory, and were later driven out by a long-headed race.

Our final remarks in this chapter regarding the C.I. are from Professor Sayce. He adds enough points to help completely clarify this subject.

> One of the most important characteristics that distinguish races one from another is the shape of the skull. Certain races are what is called dolichocephalic or long-headed, while others are brachycephalic or round-headed. These terms relate to the proportion of the length of the skull to its breadth . . . Stature often corresponds to the form of the skull, a tall stature accompanying a long skull, and a short stature a round skull. (The Races of the Old Testament, Chap. I, pp. 26-28).

Sayce says that a skull with a C.I. between 70-80 is dolichocephalic, and one which is between 80-90 is brachycephalic.

He points out, however, that stature is largely dependant on food and nourishment, and is, therefore, not a sure test of race.

Stature by itself cannot be regarded as one of those physiological traits which separate race from race. It may be a racial characteristic, and is so in some instances; but in other cases it is dependant on the nourishment given to the growing child (ibid., pp. 26,27).

One should bear in mind that craniology is not always a safe guide. Skulls are sometimes artificially distorted from their natural form. In fact, there have been tribes in which distortions have been customary. When dealing with ancient skulls, therefore, the craniologist must be on his guard against any such deformations. One must be sure he has enough specimens to give a true representation of the subjects he is studying. It is nearly always unsafe to argue from a "single instance." (ibid., p. 27).

Here is a most important statement which bears remembering.

Apart from artificial distortions, however, the shape of the skull is one of the most marked and permanent characteristics of race. It is startling to see how unchangeable the same type of skull is reproduced, generation after generation, in the same race. (ibid., p. 28).

Did you notice that Sayce is very specific in showing that apart from "artificial distortions" the general skull type of a particular race is reproduced unchanged in generation after generation.

Sayce then shows that the shape of the skull is due to "physiological causes" which act from the moment one is born. (ibid., p. 28).

WHICH IS THE SUPERIOR TYPE?

Which is the superior racial type—the dolichocephals (long-heads), or the brachycephals (broad-heads)? According to Isaac Taylor, the superior type is that of the brachycephalic races. He says:

Virchow, Broca, and Calori agree that the brachycephalic or (Turanian) skull is a higher form than the dolichocephalic. The most degraded of existing races, such as the Australians [aborigines], Tasmanians, Papuas, Veddahs, Negroes, Hottentots and Bosjemen, as well as the aboriginal forest tribes of India, are typically dolichocephalic; while the Burmese, the Chinese, the Japanese and the natives of Central Europe are typically brachycephalic (The Origin of the Aryans, p. 241).

Most books written in the English language point out that the long-headed people are the superior type of human being. They reason that it has been the long-headed Nordics of North-western Europe who have been the ones to "make history."

Madison Grant expresses this view very well in the following words:

"The English, Flemings, Dutch, North Germans and Scandinavians are descendants of the Nordic race while the dominant class in Europe is everywhere of that blood." (The Passing of the Great Race, pp. 61,62).

Grant explains that the Nordics all over the world are a race of adventurers and explorers, soldiers and sailors, "but above all, of rulers, organizers and aristocrats in sharp contrast to the essential peasant and democratic character of the broad-headed Alpines." (ibid., p. 228).

"The English," says Ripley, "are distinctly long-headed." (The Races of Europe, p. 41).

Which is the superior type? The answer to this question seems to depend more upon the shape of the head of the particular writer, or upon his personal fancy or prejudice than anything else.

The fact that the North-west Europeans (who are generally classed as long-headed Nordics) have been the dominant peoples of Europe, and of the world, is undoubtedly more dependant upon the blessings of the God of Israel than upon the particular shape of their heads.

The fact, as mentioned earlier, that the aboriginal Australians, the native Africans and other backward peoples are decidedly long-headed should prove that long-headedness alone is not synonymous with greatness. The North-west, "Nordic," dolichocephalic Europeans have become great because of the blessings they received from Almighty God.

ACQUIRED CHARACTERISTICS—NOT INHERITED

There is another misunderstanding which should be cleared up at this point. Some ethnologists, who, unfortunately, believe in the THEORY OF EVOLUTION, believe that the light races are light-skinned because of their having resided in the cold, cloudy regions of the earth for a long period. Likewise they foolishly assume that the darker races are darker in skin color and pigmentation as a result of having lived in or near the tropical zones for many thousands of years. A more absurd and unscientific theory is hardly conceivable!

One of the best known and most inexorably binding laws of science shows that "acquired characteristics are never inherited!" Such a theory is quite unscientific, to say the least. Haddon (according to Sayce) completely refutes any such ideas!

"The dark colour," says Haddon, "which is characteristic of race has nothing to do with climatic influences" (Sayce, The Races of the Old Testament, Chap. I, p. 37).

Sayce then goes on to show that the fair-skinned Kabyle and swarthy Bedouin who live side by side and in the same manner and under the same general conditions, in the same climate, eating the same food—these two contrasted peoples who live in North Africa are totally different in skin pigmentation.

The Egyptians and the Nubians, as another example, have lived in the Nile River valley for several thousands of years. Though they have lived side by side under the same general conditions, there is still a vast difference between the Egyptian and his darker neighbor the Nubian—except, of course, where there has been intermarriage.

> The dark colour of the black races is due to a pigment which is spread under the true skin immediately beneath the epidermis or scarf-skin (Sayce, The Races of the Old Testament, Chap. I, p. 37).

Professor Sayce discusses the subject of the sun-tan. He points out that:

> Such tanning, however, is never permanent and cannot be inherited. It is wholly distinct from the dark tint which distinguishes the skin of the Italian or Spaniard, and still more from the brown hue of the Mali or Polynesian (ibid., p. 38).

With the points which have been mentioned in this chapter regarding "race" firmly in mind, we shall now be able to discuss with comprehension terms commonly employed in the describing "race" such as the cephalic index. With these various means of determining racial affinities, we are now able to trace the racial origins of the peoples of North-west Europe through both history and archaeology.

CHAPTER II

EARLY HISTORY OF ISRAEL

Although the nations of Egypt, Assyria and Babylon were founded long before the Kingdom of Israel was established, the history of Israel is the most fascinating of all!

The nation of Israel has descended from SHEM through the Patriarchs—(1) Abraham (2) Isaac and (3) Jacob.

JACOB, whose name was later changed to ISRAEL (Gen. 32:28), was the father of the TWELVE sons who became the founding fathers of the TWELVE TRIBES comprising the nation of Israel.

During the lifetime of Israel (or Jacob) severe drought and famine gripped the land of Palestine. Joseph, one of Jacob's twelve sons, had become the second in command under the Pharaoh in the land of Egypt. He was, in fact, Egypt's Prime Minister! Joseph invited his father, Israel, and his whole family to come down and dwell in the very choicest part of the land of Egypt—the land of Goshen (Gen. 46:28-34). The total number of all the house or family of Israel (if we include Joseph and his two sons) who went down to Egypt (circa 1731 B.C.) was SEVENTY souls (Gen. 46:27).

The sons of Israel and their descendants lived in Egypt for about two hundred and forty years. See Dr. Torrey's Comments on Exodus, Chap. XII, for a clear explanation of the exact numbers of the years of Israel's sojourn in Egypt (The Treasury of Scripture Knowledge, p. 46).

In 1491 B.C., Moses (a man of great ability) was given the charge of leading the infant nation of Israel from Egypt to the Promised Land.

How many Israelites were there at the time of the Exodus from Egypt? According to Dr. Adam Clarke there were "upwards of three millions" (Clarke's Commentary, Vol. I, pp. 357-358). Jamieson, Fausset and Brown in their Critical and Experimental Commentary say there were "2,400,000" Israelites who took part in the Exodus (Vol. I, p. 317). There were undoubtedly between 2,500,000 and 3,000,000 who left Egypt under Moses!

If this phenomenal population increase seems incredible, consider the following facts!

In 1800 England had a population of about 8,000,000; the United States had circa 7,000,000. A century and a half later, England had nearly 50,000,000 (not including the millions who emigrated to the Commonwealth countries)! The U.S. grew to about 170,000,000 in the same period. The population of any country (if unchecked by warfare, famine or disease epidemics) increases very rapidly!

Notice what God said concerning the people of Israel: "The Lord did not set His love upon you, nor choose you, because ye were more in number than any people; for you were the fewest of all people: But because the Lord loved you, and because He would keep the OATH which He had sworn unto your fathers . . ." (Deut. 7:7,8). God had solemnly sworn unto the Patriarchs that He would bless Israel so that they would become a very prolific people.

Notice God's oath which was repeated to all of the patriarchal, founding fathers of the nation of Israel! To Abraham, God had said: "I will multiply thy seed as the STARS of heaven, and as the SAND which is upon the seashore" (Gen. 22:17). Unto Isaac's wife, Rebekah, it was said: "Be thou the mother of thousands of millions . . ." (Gen. 24:16). Unto Jacob (or Israel) God had solemnly promised: "And THY SEED shall be as the DUST of the earth, and thou shalt spread abroad to the WEST, and to the EAST, and to the NORTH, and to the SOUTH" (Gen. 28:14).

These are only a few of the many promises which God made to the Patriarchs concerning their children. God truly had solemnly sworn that the descendants of Abraham, Isaac and Jacob were to become as the "stars," as the "dust" and as the "sand."

Notice another very important promise which the Almighty God made to Israel (or Jacob): "And God said unto him, I am God Almighty: be fruitful and multiply; a nation and A COMPANY OF NATIONS shall be of thee and kings shall come out of thy loins" (Gen. 35:10,11).

Yes, the descendants of Jacob were prophesied to become a "COMPANY ('MULTITUDE'—Gen. 48:19) of nations." The JEWS have never comprised more than ONE small nation! But all of the descendants of Israel collectively were to become a multitude or company of nations!

Because of faithlessness, outright rebellion and gross iniquity, the people of Israel who took part in the Exodus were all denied entering the Promised Land—except Joshua and Caleb, who, as a reward for their faithfulness to God, were commissioned to lead the nation of Israel across the Jordan river and into the Promised Land (Num. 14:30)! There were about THREE MILLIONS of Israelites who occupied the Promised Land under Joshua in circa 1451 B.C.

In the Promised Land Israel was ruled over by Judges for about three and a half centuries.

From the time Joshua led the Twelve Tribes of Israel into the Promised Land (in 1451 B.C.) until the time that the Ten-Tribed House of Israel was taken captive (in 721 B.C.) was a total of about 730 years (The Cambridge Companion to the Bible, p. 182).

But in the time of Samuel (about 1092 B.C.) the people of Israel wanted a human king. God granted them their desire, but protested—showing them the tragic consequences of their action (I Sam. 8).

Saul was the first king of Israel, but because of his refusal to rule Israel according to the laws and ways of God, he was rejected and David was chosen as his successor. David ruled Israel wisely, and when he died his son, Solomon (Heb: "peaceable") ascended the throne and ruled the Twelve Tribes of Israel. He governed Israel judiciously during his lifetime, and as a result there was great peace and prosperity throughout the land during his reign.

When King Solomon died, his son, Rehoboam, ascended the throne. Because of his unwise policies and exorbitant taxes, the northern Ten Tribes of Israel revolted (in 972 B.C.) from the leadership of the throne of David and formed a separate kingdom under the leadership of their newly elected king, Jeroboam (I Ki. 12).

After the revolt of the Ten-Tribed House of Israel from the leadership of the kings of Judah, we thereafter read of "Israel" and "Judah" as being distinct nations though they were closely related. The term "Israel" thereafter referred to the northern Ten-Tribed House or Kingdom of Israel (whose capital was Samaria), and the term "Judah" referred to the Kingdom of Judah which was comprised of the tribes of Judah, Benjamin and most of the Levites. The capital city of the Kingdom of Judah was Jerusalem.

What is the origin of the name "Israel"?

The first use of the name Israel in the Bible is found in Genesis 32:28, where the angel who wrestled all night with Jacob says: "Thy name shall be no more called Jacob, but Israel: for as a prince hast thou power with God and with man, and hast prevailed."

"Israel" is derived from a Hebrew root which literally means "he that strives (or prevails) with God."

> As Jacob became Israel, so his descendants through his TWELVE SONS became the tribes of Israel and the ISRAELITES . . . When Israel was divided by civil war in the time of Rehoboam and Jeroboam, the NORTHERN kingdom alone retained the name ISRAEL, while the SOUTHERN kingdom was called JUDAH. From that time on we read of the kings of Israel and the kings of Judah, although the inhabitants of both kingdoms continued to be called Israelites in the older and broader sense of the inhabitants of the old land of Israel (Stimpson, A Book About the Bible, pp. 235,236).

When Israel was rent by civil war under Rehoboam (king of Judah) and Jeroboam (king of Israel), "the Northern kingdom alone retained the name Israel," after which the Southern kingdom was called—not Israel—but Judah.

The Encyclopaedia Britannica also shows that the name of Israel was for some centuries "applied to the northern kingdom as distinct" from the nation and the peoples of Judah.

> ISRAEL (Hebrew for "God strives" or "rules"; See Genesis 32:28 . . . Israel was a name borne by their ancestor Jacob the father of the 12 tribes. For some centuries the term was applied to the NORTHERN KINGDOM, as DISTINCT

from JUDAH, although the feeling of national unity extended it so as to include both (Ency. Brit., 11th ed., Art., Israel, p. 885, par., 1).

THE ORIGIN OF "JEW"

The inhabitants of the Southern kingdom as the author just quoted pointed out, were sometimes called Israelites; but they were never called the "House of Israel" or the "Kingdom of Israel." However, not one Scripture can be produced to prove that the inhabitants of the Northern Ten-Tribed Kingdom of Israel were ever called JEWS! Throughout the histories of Israel as found in the books of the Kings and of the Chronicles of Israel and Judah, you will notice that there was intermittent strife between the Kingdom of Israel and the Kingdom of Judah.

In fact on one occasion, the army of the Ten-Tribed Northern Kingdom of Israel entered Jerusalem as the victor (II Kings 14).

The first mention of the word "Jews" in the Bible is also found in this same book.

> Then Rezin king of Syria, and Pekah son of Remaliah, king of ISRAEL came up to Jerusalem to war: and they besieged Ahaz, but could not overcome him. At that time, Rezin, king of Syria recovered Elath to Syria and drave the JEWS from Elath (II Kings 16:5,6).

In verses 7 and 9 you will notice that King Ahaz of Judah, in order to get out of this dilemma, sent messengers and silver and gold from the very Temple of the Lord to the Assyrian King, Tiglath-Pileser to secure the aid of the Assyrian monarch against his enemies, Rezin King of Syria, and Pekah King of Israel.

The Assyrian king, Tiglath-Pileser, in response to this letter invaded the Ten-Tribed House of Israel and carried them into captivity.

We have observed the origin of "Israel", but we have not seen the origin of this word "Jew" even though we have seen the first place in recorded history where it is used.

How did the word "Jew" originate? It is derived from Judah (Yehuda), the fourth of Jacob's twelve sons. The territory occupied by the tribe of JUDAH was called Judah and its inhabitants were denominated JEWS, or the children of Judah. After Israel was split into two kingdoms, the southern section, comprising Judah, Benjamin and most of the Levites, was called the Kingdom of Judah, while the northern tribes were called the Kingdom of Israel. In 604-585 B.C. this southern Kingdom of Judah was destroyed and its people were deported to Babylon, where they remained for 70 years. At the end of this 70-year-period under Persian protection, a remnant of this Babylonish captivity returned to Palestine and established the Jewish nation and the Temple worship once again. "This state, like its predecessor was called Judah" (Stimpson, A Book About the Bible, p. 236).

Notice how the word "Jew" developed through the centuries. Stimpson says:

> The inhabitants of Judah (Yehuda) called themselves Yehudim in Hebrew and Yehudaye in Aramaic. To the Greeks and Romans Yehuda became Iouda and Judea and the inhabitants Ioudaios and Judaei. The name of the inhabitants of the Hebrew commonwealth passed through the following successive linguistic stages: Hebrew, Yehuda, Greek, Ioudaios, Latin, Judaeaus, Old French, Juieu, and English, Jew. One of the earliest known uses of the English form Jew is dated 1175 A.D. (ibid., p. 236).

These are a few of the many different forms or ways of spelling this word "Jew." For still further interesting spellings of "Jew" see Encyclopedia Britannica, 11th ed. Notice the following interesting statement: "For centuries adherents of the Mosaic faith who lived in Judea were called JEWS, while those of the dispersion were called ISRAELITES" (ibid., p. 237).

Stimpson has clearly shown that for centuries those who adhered to the "Mosaic faith" in Judea were called by the name of "Jews" while the TEN TRIBES of Israel in the DISPERSION were called ISRAELITES. He showed that the word "Jew" finally came to denote "any adherent of the Mosaic faith."

Notice this significant statement from Josephus:

> "So the Jews prepared for the work: that is the name they are called by from the day that they came up from Babylon, which is taken from the tribes of Judah, which came first to these places, and thence both they and the country gained that appellation" (Antiquities of the Jews, Book XI, p. 274).

It is superfluous to quote from any more authorities showing what has already been clearly pointed out in this chapter—that Israelites are descendants of Israel, and that Jews are either the physical, fleshly descendants of Judah or else those who have taken up the Jewish faith and have consequently been termed as "Jews" because of their Jewish beliefs.

Reuben was the firstborn son of Israel (Gen. 49:3), and was therefore the first "Israelite" (son of Israel). The Jews were the sons of Judah, but we do not know when the sons of Judah were first called Jews.

ISRAEL'S CAPTIVITIES AS MENTIONED IN THE CUNEIFORM INSCRIPTIONS

A very important archaeological discovery bearing upon the history of the people of Israel in their pre-captivity period is the Black Obelisk. Kinns, quoting from the front of the Black Obelisk, says: The tribute of Yaua (Jehu), son of HUMRI (Omri): silver, gold, a golden cup, golden vases, golden vessels, golden buckets, lead, a staff for the hand of the King, and sceptres, I received (Kinns, Graven in the Rock, p.494).

A footnote referring to this incident says: "It is possible that the writer of this inscription did not know who Jehu's father was, or he might have meant that he was a royal son or successor to Omri, whom he knew to have been a prominent sovereign."

> Jehu. On the Black Obelisk, 'Jehu' (=Yaua), 'the son of Omri' (=Khumri), is represented as giving tribute to Shalmaneser II . . . He was 'son' only as a successor to the throne of Omri the late king. He was the son of Jehosaphat and grandson of Nimshi (Norton, Bible Students' Handbook of Assyriology, pp. 105,106).

The Black Obelisk is a black alabaster stone which was set up by Shalmaneser III at Nimrud. On its four sides is inscribed an account of the expeditions undertaken by Shalmaneser during the thirty-one years of his reign, and depicts scenes representing the paying of tribute by the kings whom he had conquered. "The description 'son of KHUMRI' is thought merely to show that Jehu was an Israelite, because Israelitish territory was called 'BIT KHUMRI'" (A Guide to the Babylonian and Assyrian Antiquities of the British Museum, pp. 46,47).

IMPORTANT ASSYRIAN INSCRIPTIONS

"(Sargon) the conqueror of the Thamudites, the Ibadidites, the Marsimanites, and the Khapayans, the remainder of whom was carried away and whom he transported to the midst of the land of BETH-OMRI" (Sayce, Assyria, pp. 178-179).

Another extract from this same work, from fragments of the Annals of Tiglath-Pileser IV, says:

> The town of Gil(ead) and Abel-(beth-Machah?) on the frontier of BETH-OMRI [Samaria], the widespread (district of Naphtali) to its whole extent I turned into the territory of Assyria. My (governors) and officers I appointed (over them) . . . The land of BETH-OMRI . . . a collection of its inhabitants (with their goods) I transported to Assyria (ibid., pp.176,178).

Here is a further translation from the inscriptions of Tiglath-Pileser, Luckenbill cites a notable instance of the use of the name OMRI ("BIT-HUMRIA") in The Ancient Records of Assyria and Babylonia:

> Gala'za(?), Abilakka, which are on the border of BIT-HUMRIA (House of Omri, Israel) . . . the wide land of Naphtali, in its entirety, I brought within the border of Assyria. The land of BIT-HUMRIA . . . all of its people, together with their goods I carried off to Assyria. Pakaha, their king they deposed, and I placed Ausi (Hoshea) over them as king (Series 1926, Vol. I, par. 815,816).

We know the English word for the Hebrew name of the people of Israel as recorded in the Scripture was just simply "Israel," "House of Israel," or the "land of Israel" and similar names.

But what name or names did the Gentile nations (the neighbors of Israel) use when referring to the land or to the House of Israel?

This question is very ably answered by Dr. Schrader, in his remarks concerning the Assyrian inscriptions.

> Israelites. The name Israel does not occur in the inscriptions as a general term for the Israelites. Nor does it, as a rule appear as the name for the Northern Kingdom. Instead of this the name that is usually employed is mat BIT-HUMRI i.e. land of the House Omri . . . (Schrader, The Cuneiform Inscriptions of the Old Testament, Vol. I, pp. 137, 138).

Israel came into contact with Assyria at a much earlier period, and was in fact tributary to Assyria in the ninth century B.C. (ibid., p. 144).

> Israel . . . The usual term for the Kingdom of Israel in the Assyrian inscriptions is not this, as we have already observed. The ordinary designation was rather MAT BIT-HUMRI or MAT HUMRI "LAND OF THE HOUSE OF OMRI," or "LAND OF OMRI," or merely "LAND OMRI" (ibid., p. 177).

The translations just cited from Dr. Schrader's book will, it is hoped, suffice to give the reader ample knowledge of the most important cuneiform inscriptions bearing upon the history of the nation of Israel.

ISRAEL'S FIRST INVASION

We have seen a number of quotations taken directly from the cuneiform writings excavated in the Middle East, proving the absolute veracity of the scriptural account. Thus again we find the Bible stands completely verified. Let us now go to the historical accounts of the invasions and the deportations of Israel as found in the Scriptures.

The Kingdom of Israel was invaded on three different occasions by the Assyrian monarchs. First in 771 B.C. Pul, also called Assurbanipal, in the reign of Menahem, king of Israel, invaded the northern outskirts of the Kingdom of Israel. Menahem bribed the king of Assyria with a huge sum of 4,000 pounds of silver (II Ki. 15:19). This bribe temporarily, at least, averted the greed of the Assyrian monarch, and he thereupon retired from the land of Israel not having occupied the northern portion of the land of Israel which he had invaded: neither did he carry away any Israelitish captives at that time.

The prophet Isaiah was inspired to refer to this First Invasion as a "light affliction" on the land of Zebulon and the land of Naphtali (Isaiah 9:1).

The land of these two tribes lay immediately to the west of the Jordan River extending from the northern extremity of the border of Israel down to a point just southwest of the Sea of Galilee. You will find this First Invasion of the land of Israel described clearly in II Kings 15:19,20.

> And Pul the king of Assyria came against the land: and Menahem gave Pul a thousand talents of silver, that his hand might be with him to confirm the kingdom in his hand. And Menahem exacted the money of Israel, even of all the mighty men of wealth, of each man 50 shekels of silver, to give to the king of Assyria. So the king of Assyria turned back, and stayed not there in the land.

But the kings of Israel who ruled over the Northern Ten-Tribed Kingdom of Israel (called Samaria) paid little attention to this "light affliction." They still continued in the sins of Jeroboam.

ISRAEL'S SECOND INVASION

Shortly after this, God sent the Assyrian ruler, Tiglath-Pileser back to the land of Israel, this time to afflict the people of Israel with greater severity. A new king had arisen over the nation of Samaria by the name of Pekah.

> And he did that which was evil in the sight of the Lord: he departed not from the sins of Jeroboam the son of Nebat, who made Israel to sin. In the days of Pekah, king of Israel, came Tiglath-Pileser, king of Assyria, and took Ijon and Abel-beth-maachah and Janoah and Kedesh, and Hazor, and Gilead and Galilee, all the land of Naphtali, and carried them captive TO ASSYRIA (II Ki. 15:28,29).

This brief historical, scriptural account of the Second Invasion of Israel (their first captivity) occurred (according to Ussher) in the year 741 B.C.

Notice all of the towns and territories described in the above reference were located in the general territories of the tribes of Naphtali, Gad, Reuben, and the half tribe of Manasseh lying east of the Jordan. The tribe of Naphtali was situated in the extreme northern part of the Kingdom of Israel, and lay immediately to the west of the Jordan River, the Sea of Galilee and Lake Hulah. The one-half tribe of Manasseh, and the tribes of Reuben and Gad were all located immediately east of the Jordan River. This territory had been known as the land of Bashan and Gilead.

Numerous Scriptures show that the half tribe of Manasseh, the tribe of Gad, and the tribe of Reuben all had their inheritance on the east side of the Jordan River (Deut. 29:7,8; Josh. 1:12-15; 12:1-6; 13:7-8).

It is also interesting to note that Moses had given this land to these tribes before his decease (Josh. 12:1-6).

If one will follow this Second Assyrian Invasion, he will see that the Assyrian king, Tiglath-Pileser, swept down from the north through the northern tribes of Naphtali going south to the Sea of Galilee where he turned eastward and conquered the three afore-mentioned tribes lying to the east of the Dead Sea, in the region called Trans-Jordania.

We are informed that the tribe of Reuben prior to the Assyrian invasions had extended its territory all the way to the Euphrates River (I Chron. 5:6-9).

Another account of the Second Invasion of the Ten-tribed Northern Kingdom of Israel, or Samaria, is found in the fifth chapter of the book of I Chronicles.

> And they [referring to the three tribes living east of the Jordan—i.e. the half tribe of Manasseh, the tribe of Gad, and the tribe of Reuben] transgressed against the God of their fathers, and went a whoring after the gods of the people of the land, whom God destroyed before them. And the God of Israel stirred up the spirit of Pul, king of Assyria, and the spirit of Tiglath-Pileser, king of Assyria, and he carried them away, even the Reubenites, and the Gadites, and the half tribe of Manasseh, and brought them unto Halah, and Habor, and Hara, and the river Gozan, unto this day (I Chron. 5:25,26).

Before going to the cuneiform inscriptions for verification of the Second Invasion of Israel, let us again recall that this Second Invasion of the land of Israel was a more grievous affliction than the former.

Now let us read again the inspired account of this Second Invasion of Israel: "Nevertheless the dimness shall not be such as was in her vexation, when at the first He [God] lightly afflicted the land of Zebulon and the land of Naphtali, [referring to the First Invasion] and afterward did more grievously afflict her [the Second Invasion] by way of the sea, beyond Jordan, in Galilee of the nations" (Isa. 9:1).

CUNEIFORM ACCOUNT OF THE SECOND INVASION

Again we return to the cuneiform inscriptions where Israel's First Captivity (the Second Invasion) of 741 B.C. is mentioned:

> "The cities of . . . Gala'za(?), Abilakka, which are on the border of BIT-HUMRIA . . . the wide land of Naphtali, in its entirety, I brought within the border of Assyria. My official I set over them as governor . . ." (Lukenbill, The Ancient Records of Assyria and Babylonia, Vol. I, p. 292).

ISRAEL'S THIRD AND FINAL INVASION

The Assyrian account of the Third Invasion (the second and last captivity) of the land of the Ten-Tribed Kingdom of Israel in the year 721 B.C. is as follows:

> The land of BIT-HUMRIA . . . all of its people, together with all their goods I carried off to Assyria, Pakaha, their king they deposed, and I placed Ausi (Hoshea) over them as king (ibid.).

The Assyrian name for Pekah was Pakaha, and their name for Hosea was Ausi.

Despite these two invasions by the Assyrian monarchs—the first light affliction of Israel, and the second more severe affliction, when a number of the tribes were carried captives to Assyria—the kings of Israel and their people still turned a deaf ear to their God. They could not see the handwriting on the wall. They went on blindly as though no calamity could overtake them. How could such a disaster befall them? Were they not God's "chosen" people?

But whether they knew it or not, the Assyrian king was already plotting the culminating defeat, the complete overthrow of the Ten-Tribed House of Israel, called Samaria.

The account of this final deathblow to Israel, her Second Captivity dealt by Assyria, is recorded as follows:

> Then the king of Assyria came up throughout all the land, and went up to Samaria, and besieged it three years. In the ninth year of Hoshea, the king of Assyria took Samaria, and carried Israel away into Assyria, and placed them in Halah and in Habor by the river Gozan, and in the cities of the Medes . . . There was none left but the tribe of Judah only . . . He . . . cast them out of His sight. For He rent Israel from the house of David . . . the Lord removed Israel out of His sight . . . So was Israel carried away out of their own land to Assyria unto this day (II Ki. 17:1-23).

What was the date of this final captivity? The commonly accepted date of this second and final captivity is 721 B.C.

Observe closely who it was that was brought into the land of Israel (Samaria). These Gentiles were still residing there in the time of Christ.

> And the king of Assyria brought men from Babylon and from Cuthah and from Ava, and from Hamath, and from Sepharvim, and placed them in the cities of Samaria instead of the children of Israel: and they possessed Samaria, and dwelt in the cities thereof (II Ki. 17:1-24).

In the sacred account just quoted, there are a number of important points which should be brought to the attention of the reader. Notice why God let Israel be taken into captivity. They had become very sinful, had degenerated into loathsome and sensuous Babylonish and Phoenician religious practices, and had even caused their sons and daughters to "pass through the fire" (II Ki. 17:17).

THE AREA TO WHICH ISRAEL WAS DEPORTED

Another very important point that should be brought to the reader's attention is mentioned in verse 6 of the previous reference.

"The king of Assyria took Samaria and carried Israel away into ASSYRIA, and placed them in Halah and in Habor by the river Gozan, and in the cities of the MEDES."

In connection with this also note verse 23:

"So was Israel carried away out of their own land to Assyria unto this day." The expression "unto this day" refers to the time of Ezra and Nehemiah who directed the final canonization of the Hebrew Scriptures. This statement proves that the Ten Tribes were still in exile in about 400-450 B.C.

Notice the places to which Israel (the Ten-Tribed Northern Kingdom) was carried! These people were deported "to ASSYRIA," and to "the cities of the MEDES," to Gozan, Habor and Halah.

If you will consult an accurate map of these times, you will note that the people of Israel were deported to the lands lying immediately SOUTH OF THE CAUCASUS MOUNTAINS and south of the Caspian Sea. Keep this location in mind as it has a most important bearing upon points which will be mentioned later. (See The International Standard Bible Encyclopedia, Vol. I, pp. 569-571; The Imperial Bible Dictionary, Vol I, pp.347-350.)

Here is another interesting point worth noting:

"And the Lord rejected all the seed of Israel, and afflicted them, and delivered them into the hand of spoilers, until He had cast them out of His sight" (II Ki. 17:20,23).

What is meant by the expression "cast them out of His sight"? Speaking of the Promised Land, the land Israel was to inherit, God had revealed His concern for it in the following words:

"A land which the Lord thy God careth for, the eyes of the Lord thy God are always upon it, from the beginning of the year even until the end of the year" (Deut. 11:12).

Notice that this Scripture shows the eyes of God are always on the Promised Land. When Israel was removed from this land, God spoke as though they were removed out of His sight.

Ezekiel was inspired by God to write the following comment concerning Israel's captivity.

I scattered them among the heathen, and they were dispersed through the countries: according to their way and according to their doings I judged them. And when they entered unto the heathen, whither they went, they profaned My

Holy name, when they said to them, these are the people of the Lord, and are gone forth out of His land (Ezekiel 36:16-20).

The nineteenth verse just quoted is of especial importance. It says that God had "scattered Israel among the heathen" and "dispersed them through the countries." Keep this fact in mind as we later go through some of the historical sources following the footsteps of Israel from the time they left their ancient homeland in Palestine until they reached their modern-day lands.

We have already observed that the people of the Northern Ten-Tribed Kingdom of Israel were in the biblical account called "Israel," "Kingdom of Israel," or "House of Israel," whereas the people of the Southern Kingdom of Judah were called "Jews," "Judah," or the "Kingdom of Judah."

The people of the Northern Kingdom were never called Jews! The people of the Southern Kingdom were, however, sometimes still called Israelites. But there is not one instance in sacred or secular history where the Northern Ten Tribes of Israel were (as a nation) ever called Jews.

THE POPULATION OF ISRAEL IN 741-721 B.C.

The population of Israel at the time of the Exodus from Egypt was undoubtedly somewhere around three millions. The Twelve Tribes of Israel inhabited the Promised Land circa 1451 B.C. They remained in this land for about 730 years before finally being taken captive. (Remember also that they were a very prolific people.)

How many Israelites were in Palestine when the Assyrian kings began the captivities or deportations of this people? (For further comments regarding Israel's population in 741-721 B.C., see: The Expository Times, Vol. IX, p. 168.)

Let us now notice a few significant statements from Salo Baron in regard to the population of the Jews.

During the Eichmann trial held in Israel in 1961 Baron testified against Eichmann by giving some astounding figures regarding the Jewish population and their slaughter by the Nazis in World War II.

The London Daily Express of April 25th, 1961, had this to say regarding Salo Baron.

"Professor Salo Baron, reputed to be the world's greatest living authority on Jewish history . . ."

Notice that Professor Baron is reputed as "the world's greatest living authority on Jewish history."

In his book, A Social and Religious History of the Jews, Baron, speaking of the Israelitish captivity by Assyria, says:

The 27,290 deported from Samaria in 721, mentioned in the well-known inscriptions of Sargon, represent only a fraction of the Israelitic exiles. We must add not only a number of women and children who accompanied them but, in all probability, unrecorded further groups deported in 734;733, and perhaps in 720. Similarly Sennacherib's boast about the effects of his campaign against Judah in 701, "200,150 people, small and great . . . I brought out of their midst and counted as booty," whether or not absolutely accurate, reflects a large-scale involuntary expatriation (ibid., Vol. I, p. 95).

Professor Baron says, "There were not less than four hundred settlements classified as towns" in the land of Israel prior to the Assyrian Captivity of 721 B.C. (ibid., Vol. I, p. 72).

Since Sennacherib deported "200,150 people small and great" in "his campaign against Judah in 701" this proves that there must have been a few million Jews at that time, for it would appear that the bulk of the Jewish population was left intact and was carried into captivity over 100 years later by Nebuchadnezzar, king of Babylon.

Recall that this Assyrian invasion of Judah occurred in 701 B.C., or 20 years after the remnant of Ten-Tribed Israel had gone into captivity. And yet after myriads were slaughtered and 200,150 were deported there must have been many hundreds of thousands of Jews living in Palestine at the time of the Babylonish invasions of 604-585 B.C.

This further proves that the small Southern kingdom of Judah must have had at least two or three millions of inhabitants prior to the Assyrian invasions. Consequently the Northern Kingdom of Israel (composed of not two, but Ten Tribes) must have easily contained a population of 5,000,000 or more at the time of the beginning of the overthrow of Israel by Assyria in 741-721 B.C.

According to reliable estimates there were somewhere around 7,000,000 or more people in Israel and Judah prior to their captivity. The Promised Land was formerly a "land flowing with milk and honey" and could have easily supported this number (Ex. 3:8; Lev. 20:24). Also remember that the population of the United States increased from 7,000,000 to about 170,000,000 in a period of circa 150 years—1800-1950 A.D.

It was after this land vomited out these rebels that God turned it into a desolation. Since the small family of Israel grew from 70 people to about 3,000,000 in a short period of 240 years while in the land of Egypt, it is probable that there were even more than 7,000,000 people in the land of Palestine just before Israel's deportations. From the time that Israel occupied the Promised Land until the captivity encompassed about 730 years.

THE LAND OF ISRAEL'S CAPTIVITIES

We have seen from the Scriptural account that the people of Israel were taken into captivity by the Assyrians to the land of the MEDES, and the ASSYRIANS. Any reliable map showing the lands of Media and of Assyria for this period, will reveal that these two territories were located south of the Caucasus Mountains, southeast of the Black Sea, and south to southwest of the Caspian Sea. It is very important to keep the general location of this territory in mind because later it will be shown that all of the modern nations of North-west Europe comprising most of the so-called "Nordic races" came from this very area of the Caucasus in S.W. Asia.

Also bear in mind that the remnant of the Northern Ten-Tribed House of Israel were finally invaded and conquered in the year 721 B.C., or perhaps as late as 718 B.C. The exact date is not of any great importance in this instance.

But the Southern Kingdom of Judah was not conquered and deported to Babylon until circa 585 B.C., when Nebuchadnezzar at last beat down the walls of Jerusalem and completely demolished the city, killed many of the Jews and took the remainder, except the poorest of the land, to Babylon. Remember, Babylon lay to the EAST of Palestine. Israel had been taken to an area NORTH of Babylon 130 years before the Jewish captivity. The Bible and secular history both show that the Ten Tribes of Israel never mingled to any great extent with the exiles of Judah. The peoples of these two distinct captivities remained separate.

The Jews remained in the Babylonish captivity for 70 years. After this time God stirred up the hearts of the Persian kings, Cyrus and Darius the Great and others who issued three different decrees (536 B.C., 457 B.C., 444 B.C.) permitting the Jews to go back to Jerusalem to build their Temple and to re-establish the Jewish nation (Halley, Bible Handbook, p. 312).

There were about 50,000 Jews who returned from the Babylonish captivity (Ezra 2:64; Neh. 7:66), plus about 1,000 priests and Levites who returned with Ezra to set up the Temple worship.

ONLY JUDAH AND BENJAMIN RETURN

Did any from the Ten Tribes of Israel return to Judah in the time of Ezra and Nehemiah? Here is the answer from the Bible:

> Now when the adversaries of Judah and Benjamin heard that the children of the captivity builded the Temple of the Lord God of Israel, then they came to Zerubbabel, and to the chief of the fathers, and said unto them, Let us build with you: for we seek your God, as ye do; and we do sacrifice unto Him since the days of Esar-haddon, King of Assur, which brought us up hither (Ezra 4:1,2).

Did you notice that only Judah and Benjamin were mentioned as having returned to Jerusalem?

"Then all the men of Judah and Benjamin gathered themselves together unto Jerusalem within three days" (ibid., 10:9).

Notice again that only the two tribes of Judah and Benjamin were mentioned as having returned to the Holy Land at that time. Does this not prove that there were no other tribes present, except as we shall see later some of the Levites? In the book of Ezra, the Levites are mentioned about twenty-one times; and in the book of Nehemiah they are mentioned over forty times. These numerous references to the Levites prove that many of the Levites returned with their Jewish brethren from the Babylonish captivity to the land of Judah.

A casual perusal of all the biblical and historical material regarding those who returned from Babylon, will show that only a small portion even of the Jews returned to Palestine at that time. Most of the Jewish people remained either at Babylon, Alexandria, Egypt, or else were left scattered throughout the provinces of the Persian Empire.

The Apostle Peter was inspired to write:

"The Church that is at Babylon, elected together with you, saluteth you" (I Pet. 5:13).

The Apostle Paul shows that the gospel of (or to) the circumcision had been committed to Peter, whereas the gospel of the uncircumcision had been committed to him (Gal. 2:7). Peter was the one in charge of the dissemination of the gospel to those who were circumcised, that is, he was sent primarily to the Jews. Paul was commissioned to oversee the preaching of the gospel to the Gentiles.

We know from historical sources that many Jews remained in Babylon. Some estimate the Jewish population to be over 1,000,000 at Babylon in the time of Christ. The church which Peter mentioned at Babylon was undoubtedly a Jewish church primarily.

Since there must have been at least 7,000,000 Israelites inhabiting the territories of the kingdoms of Israel and Judah just prior to their deportations, just how many were there in the Northern Ten-Tribed House of Israel at that time?

The Southern Kingdom of Judah, remember, was comprised of the tribes of JUDAH, BENJAMIN, and undoubtedly the majority of the LEVITES. Taking all of these things into account, the Kingdom of Judah may well have contained two million inhabitants at the time of the Jewish captivity (585 B.C.), and the Northern Kingdom of Israel must have had a population of at least 5,000,000 at the time of her captivity by Assyria.

Such a computation seems well justified judging by David's census (I Chron. 21:5). According to that census, there were 1,570,000 "MEN-AT-ARMS" (Moffatt translation) in Israel and Judah, and this did not include the tribes of Benjamin and Levi!

Since there were ONE MILLION, FIVE HUNDRED AND SEVENTY THOUSAND able-bodied "men-at-arms" in Israel and Judah in David's time, there may have been 15,000,000 people living in all Israel at that time. It would be rare indeed for any nation to have one-tenth of its total population eligible for military service at any given time! And remember, this was about 300 years BEFORE Israel was taken captive!

Putting all of these points together, one cannot help but conclude that Israel's population (excluding the people of the Kingdom of Judah) must have been at least five millions by 741 B.C.—the beginning of Israel's captivities!

THE DISPERSION

In the 7th chapter of the gospel of John is recorded a very interesting conversation between Christ and the Jews. Christ had spoken about going to a place which would be inaccessible to the Jews. He was, of course, referring to heaven. But the Jews, misunderstanding Him, said: "Will He go unto the dispersed among the Gentiles, and teach the Gentiles?" (v. 35).

Who were the dispersed (Gk. diaspora)?

Dr. Bullinger gives the following note regarding the diaspora. "Dispersed (The) diaspora, dispersion, (occ. James i,1, and I Pet. i,1) . . . John vii, 35." (A Critical Lexicon and Concordance to the English and Greek Testament, 8th ed., p. 228).

Remember, we have already seen that when Israel sinned against their God, He solemnly declared, "Wherefore I poured my fury upon them for the blood that they had shed upon the land, and for their idols wherewith they had polluted it: and I scattered them among the heathen, and they were dispersed through the countries" (Ezek. 36:18,19).

Who were the ones who were to be "dispersed through the countries?" Only the Jews? No, God says Israel had been scattered and dispersed among the Gentile peoples. The Jews only comprised the people inhabiting the small Southern Kingdom in Palestine; whereas the Ten-Tribed House of Israel inhabited the northern part of the Promised Land. Also bear in mind that the House of Israel were carried into captivity, some in 741, and the remainder in 721 B.C. The Jews were taken captive to Babylon circa 604-585 B.C.

This Greek word "Diaspora" referred to all of the Israelites which were dispersed or scattered throughout the whole world. The overwhelming majority of the dispersed ones at this time were Israelites from the "House of Israel."

THE TWELVE TRIBES SCATTERED ABROAD

Few have ever noticed that the Apostle James wrote an epistle to the dispersed tribes of Israel. "James a servant of God and of the Lord Jesus Christ, to the twelve tribes which are scattered abroad, greetings" (Jas. 1:1). The Revised Standard Version and the Moffatt translation render this verse as follows: "To the twelve tribes in the dispersion."

The epistle of James was not addressed to an individual, or a church, or the "Elect," or the "Saints," but it was written to "the twelve tribes in the dispersion." Nearly every other epistle in the entire New Testament is addressed to a particular church, or to the "Saints" of a particular city such as Rome, Corinth, or Ephesus, or to some particular individual, such as Timothy, or Titus. The epistle of James was not written to the Saints primarily, but to the unconverted Twelve Tribes of Israel.

"From whence come wars among you? Come they not hence, even of your lusts that war in your members" (Jas. 4:1). Notice that James is not speaking of Saints warring among themselves. They would not have been "Saints" had they literally been fighting among themselves! He was referring to carnal-minded Israelites!

SHOULD WE SEEK THE "LOST SHEEP"?

Some express the erroneous opinion that it is wrong to be concerned about the present-day whereabouts of the people of Israel. They would not hold such a view if they realized how much of the Bible is devoted to prophecy directly concerning the Lost Ten Tribes of Israel—whoever they may be! The Bible clearly reveals that certain blessings were to accrue to these "lost sheep" in the "last days," only to be followed by a great national calamity of unparalleled proportions brought on them because of their ingratitude and disobedience (Jer. 30:7).

Let us see what Christ thought about this subject. In the great commission to the twelve disciples, as recorded in Matthew, chapter 10, we find Christ giving the following charge: "Go not into the way of the Gentiles, and into any city of the Samaritans enter ye not. But go rather to the lost sheep of the house of Israel" (Matt. 10:5,6).

THE TWO-FACED SAMARITANS—ISRAELITES?

Who were the Samaritans? Huxley and Haddon show that "the blood-groups of the Samaritans show no affinity to those of the Hebrews" (We Europeans, p. 186.).

The present-day Samaritans, according to their blood groups, are not closely related to the Hebrews. Who were the Samaritans who lived in Samaria in the time of Christ?

According to II Kings 17:24, they were Gentiles, who had replaced the Israelites. We are informed that the King of Assyria brought men from Babylon, Cuthah, Ava, Hamath, and from Sepharvaim, and placed them in "the cities of Samaria instead of the children of Israel."

Josephus informs us that these Samaritans were two-faced. They claimed kinship to the Jews only when it would be to their advantage. When the Jews fell into disrepute, the Samaritans disclaimed any racial affinity with them.

> But now the Cutheans, who removed into Samaria . . . are called in the Hebrew tongue Cutheans, but in the Greek tongue Samaritans. And when they see the Jews in prosperity, they pretend that they are changed, and allied to them, and call them kinsmen, as though they were derived from Joseph, and had by that means an original alliance with them; but when they see them falling into a low condition, they say they are no way related to them, and that the Jews have

no right to expect any kindness or marks of kindred from them, but they declare that they are sojourners, that come from other countries . . . (Ant. Bk., IX, Chap. XIV, Sec. 3).

In Christ's day, the Jews had "no dealings with the Samaritans" (Jo. 4:9).

Now let us return to Matthew 10:5,6. Notice Christ told the disciples not to go into any city of the Samaritans (because they sometimes claimed they were Israelites even though they were not)—neither were they to go into the way of the Gentiles.

Who were the Gentiles? The word "Gentile" in the Hebrew and Greek languages simply means "nations"—including, of course, all of the nations outside of "the nation of Israel."

Also notice that Christ told the apostles to go to "the lost sheep of the House of Israel."

The Palestinian Jews were not lost. Neither were their Jewish brethren lost who were scattered through the world. The Jews have always retained many of their customs traditions and laws, such as the observance of the weekly and annual sabbaths, and their dietary regulations which prohibit the use of blood, fat, or unclean meats. (See Lev. 3:17; 11:1-31). Their observance of the sabbath has kept them from being lost wherever they have gone (Ex. 31:13-17). Remember, the Jews have been scattered, but never have they been "lost" so far as their racial identity is concerned.

The "lost sheep of the house of Israel" referred to by Christ, meant the Lost Ten Tribes of the Northern Kingdom of Israel. Christ told His disciples to go to these "lost sheep." How could they go to the lost sheep, unless they knew where they were? There is every reason to believe—in fact we know—that Christ (and possibly the apostles) knew the whereabouts of the dispersed people of Israel at that time, even though they were undoubtedly lost so far as most people were concerned. The apostles would have to find the "lost sheep" before they could go to them and teach them.

In the 34th chapter of Ezekiel, God solemnly indicts the "shepherds (pastors or ministers) of Israel" for a number of things which they neglected to do:

> Son of man, prophesy and say unto them, Thus saith the Lord God unto the shepherds. Woe be to the shepherds of Israel that do feed themselves! Should not the shepherds feed the flocks? Neither have ye sought that which was lost; but with force and with cruelty have ye ruled them. My sheep wandered through all the mountains, and upon every high hill: yea, my flock was scattered upon all the face of the earth, and none did search or seek after them (Ezek. 34:2,4,6).

In verses 9 and 10 God shows that He is "against the shepherds." "I, even I, will both search my sheep, and seek them out" (v. 11). When will God seek out His sheep? This will occur at the Second Coming of Christ. God shows that at that time David will be resurrected to become their shepherd (v.23).

The clergy stand foremost in the ranks of those who oppose the truth regarding the identity of modern-day Israel. They are often intolerant toward anyone who does have the concern, or the zeal to seek out the "lost sheep of the House of Israel."

Now we should clearly understand the importance of tracing historically the people of Israel from the time of their captivity in 741, 721 B.C., throughout their dispersion and wanderings through the countries; and finally to their present-day national homelands.

WHAT BECAME OF THESE TEEMING MILLIONS?

We have seen that there must have been at least 5,000,000 Israelites dwelling in the Northern Kingdom of Israel at the time when the Ten Tribes were taken into captivity.

We now come to the most important question of all—"Just what happened to those 5,000,000 (or more) Israelites who were taken bodily from their own homeland in Samaria and were transported into the lands of MEDIA and ASSYRIA—just south of the CAUCASUS MOUNTAINS, to the area of the southern shores of the CASPIAN SEA? Yes, just what happened to these teeming millions of prolific Israelites?"

This is a question which has perplexed countless millions down through the ages and has baffled Catholic, Protestant, and Jewish theologians as well.

Let us notice what Graetz, a prominent Jewish historian, has to say on this question of the "Lost Ten Tribes of Israel."

> The kingdom of the Ten Tribes, of Israel, had existed for two centuries and a half . . . but in one day it disappeared, leaving no trace behind. The country vomited out the Ten Tribes, as it had vomited out the Canaanitish tribes. What has become of them? They have been looked for and believed to have been discovered in the distant East as well as in the far West. Cheats and dreamers have claimed to be descended from them. But there can be no doubt that the Ten Tribes have been irretrievably lost among the nations (Graetz, History of the Jews, Vol. I p. 265).

Do not millions erroneously hold the same view which Graetz has expressed? Many believe that "the Ten Tribes have been irretrievably lost among the nations." Such a view, however, is incompatible with the facts!

Next let us notice what the Jewish Encyclopedia has to say on this most vital question of just what happened to the myriads of Israelites who were deported from the Northern Kingdom of Samaria in 741-721 B.C.

> TRIBES, LOST TEN . . . As a large number of prophecies relate to the return of "Israel" to the Holy Land, believers in the literal inspiration of the Scriptures have always labored under a difficulty in regard to the continued existence of the

tribes of Israel, with the exception of those of Judah and Levi (or Benjamin), which returned with Ezra and Nehemiah. If the Ten Tribes have disappeared, the literal fulfillment of the prophecies would be impossible: if they have not disappeared, obviously they must exist under a different name (ibid., p.249).

First, note carefully the significance of the foregoing statements. It is true that (as stated) many prophecies speak of Israel and Judah (Ezek. 37:15-22; Jer. 3:17,18; 51:15).

Secondly, note that God's word is at stake on this matter of whether the Ten Tribes still exist: "If the Ten Tribes have disappeared, the literal fulfillment of the prophecies would be impossible." But remember, the Scripture cannot be broken (Jo. 10:35; Tit. 1:2).

Thirdly, notice that "If they [the Lost Ten Tribes] have not disappeared, obviously they must exist under a different name." And that is precisely the case—they do "exist under a different name!" How else could they be "lost" if everyone knew their identity?

> In the Apocrypha it is presumed that the TEN TRIBES still exist as tribes. Thus Tobit is stated to be of the tribe of Naphtali, and the Testaments of the Twelve Patriarchs assume their continuous existence. In the Fourth Book of Ezra (xiii. 39-45) it is declared that the Ten Tribes were carried by Hosea, king in the time of Shalmaneser, to the Euphrates, at the narrow passages of the river, whence they went on for a journey of a year and a half to a place called Arzareth. (Jewish Ency., p. 249).

The article then mentions all of the places or countries where the Lost Ten Tribes have supposedly been located: North Arabia, India, Abyssinia, Persia, Yemen, Armenia, Afghanistan, South Russia, China, the Sahara, Japan, Australia, Peru, Mexico, North America (the aborigines), and Denmark. According to this article, the Lost Ten Tribes are identified with the "English", the "Teutonic race", with the "Sacae," (or Scythians), and with the "Tuatha da Danaan" of Irish Tradition (ibid., pp. 249-252).

In fact, there is hardly any people who have not, at one time or another, been identified with the "Lost Ten Tribes." The great arch-deceiver, Satan, has caused this confusion in order to keep this knowledge lost to modern-day Israel. Also much confusion on this vital subject has caused people to scoff at the real truth.

> G. Moore, indeed, attempts to prove that the high-class Hindus, including all the Buddhists, are descendants of the Sacae, or Scythians, who again, were the Lost Ten Tribes (ibid., p. 250).

Later, we shall see conclusive proof that the Sacae and the Scythians were included in the dispersed tribes of Israel. We will see that the Sacae and Scythians settled in North-west Europe—and not in the Orient!

> The identification of the Sacae, or Scythian with the Ten Tribes because they appear in history at the SAME TIME, and very nearly in the SAME PLACE,

as the Israelites removed by Shalmaneser, is one of the chief supports of the theory which identifies the English people, and indeed the whole TEUTONIC RACE, with the TEN TRIBES, Dan is identified sometimes with Denmark, and sometimes with the Tuatha da Danaun of Irish Tradition (ibid., p. 250).

This last admission is of utmost importance. One of the "chief supports" of the "identification of the Sacae, or Scythians with the Ten Tribes" is that these Sacae or Scythians "appear in history at the same time, and very nearly in the same place."

All history confirms the fact just mentioned. The Sacae or Scythians do not appear in history before Israel's captivity, but they do appear in the areas of the Black and Caspian Seas, shortly after Israel was deported to those same general regions.

The Scythians are generally found a little further north than Israel was located at the time of her deportation to Assyria and Media, and the Sacae (a Scythian branch) had moved from the southern shore of the Caspian Sea (the land of their captivity) to the districts lying east of the Caspian.

Also bear in mind that this article in the Jewish Encyclopedia mentions that the "English people," "the whole Teutonic race," "Denmark," and the "Tuatha da Danaun" are all identified with the Lost Ten Tribes.

We shall shortly see abundant historical proof showing that the Anglo-Saxons, and the proper Teutons, the Celts, Gauls, Cimbri and the other peoples who settled North-west Europe are all descendants of the "dispersed" and "scattered" Lost Ten Tribes of Israel.

It will also be shown that the words "Teutoni" and "Germani" were first applied to Celtic tribes who were in no way Alpine-type of Germans. These true Teutoni and Celts are no longer found in Germany in any appreciable numbers!

This same article in the Jewish Encyclopedia then goes on to mention that more literature has been written on the identification of the English as Israel ("Anglo-Israelite") than any other. The second most publicised belief is that which identifies the American Indians as the descendants of the Ten Lost Tribes of Israel. Joseph Smith held this view, and propounded it in the Book of Mormon. (See 1920 ed., pp. 22, 429-432).

There are many reasons why we know the American Indians and the orientals, etc., are not descendants of Israel. They are descendants of Japheth, instead of Shem; and they had not been the recipients of the promises made to the Fathers, as have the Anglo-Saxon, Celtic peoples!

Speaking of the Lost Ten Tribes, Josephus says: "the entire body of the people of Israel remained in that country, wherefore there are but two tribes in Asia and Europe subject to the Romans, while THE TEN TRIBES are beyond Euphrates till now, and are AN IMMENSE MULTITUDE, and not to be estimated by numbers" (Ant. XI., v., sec. 2).

Josephus shows the Ten Tribes were "an immense multitude" in his day, and were not subject to the Romans. Only "two tribes" were subject to Rome. The Ten Tribes had certainly not returned to Palestine in Josephus' time. He was born in about 37 A.D. and died circa 100 A.D. (Webster's Biographical Dictionary, Art., Josephus, p. 795).

Keller, proceeds to express a personal opinion more-or-less commonly held by people concerning this question of just what happened to the so-called "Lost Ten Tribes" of the House of Israel. He says:

> The people of the Northern Kingdom and their Kings with them disappeared, were absorbed into the population of these foreign lands, and never emerged again in history. All investigation into what became of the TEN TRIBES who had their home there has so far come to nothing (The Bible as History, p. 247).

But is such a view tenable, even though it is accepted by countless millions—especially in the face of the overwhelming flood of archaeological and historical material which is at our disposal today?

Is it feasible to believe that this populous people of Israel lost their identity and became amalgamated among the nations where they went? Small nations such as Ethiopia, Lybia, Greece, Syria, Arabia, and other have continued to maintain their national identities throughout the centuries to the very present time.

Jerome shows the Ten Tribes inhabited the cities and mountains of the Medes ("Opera," vi, 780). Kitto also mentions that the Ten Tribes never returned.

> The captives of [the Ten-Tribed] Israel exiled beyond the Euphrates did not return as a whole to Palestine along with their brethren the captives of Judah; at least there is no mention made of this event in the documents at our disposal (Jewish Quarterly Review, Vol. I, p. 15).

> In fact, the return of the TEN TRIBES was one of the great promises of the Prophets, and the advent of the Messiah is therefore necessarily identified with the epic of their redemption (ibid., p. 17).

> The hope of the return of the Ten Tribes has never ceased among the Jews in exile . . . This hope has been connected with every Messianic rising (ibid., p. 21).

Edersheim says it is of the "greatest importance" to remember that only a "minority of the Jews" (about 50,000) returned from Babylon—in the time of Ezra and Nehemiah (The Life and Time of Jesus the Messiah, p. 8).

> In what has been said, no notice has been taken of those wanderers of the ten tribes, who trackless footsteps seem as mysterious as their after-fate . . . Josephus describes them as an innumerable multitude, and vaguely locates them

beyond the Euphrates . . . Still the great mass of the TEN TRIBES was in the days of Christ, as in our own, lost to the Hebrew nation (ibid., pp. 14-16).

These statements from leading Jewish and other authorities will suffice to show the utmost confusion in the minds of historians generally, whether they be of Jewish or Gentile origin, regarding the whereabouts of the "Lost Ten Tribes of Israel."

They are, however, pretty well agreed that Israel have been "irretrievably lost."

In the Jewish Chronicle of May 2nd, 1897, we read:

> The Scriptures speak of a future restoration of Israel, which is clearly to include both Judah and Ephraim (or Israel). The problem, then, is reduced to its simplest form. The Ten Tribes are certainly in existence. All that has to be done is to discover which people represent them.

ISRAEL TO BE SIFTED AMONG THE NATIONS

It is interesting to note how many different authors speak fo the Ten Tribes as being swallowed up in the other nations—amalgamated among them—so integrated, they think, among the Gentiles that they would be indistinguishable today. If this is true then God's Word definitely has failed.

> Behold the eyes of the Lord God are upon the sinful Kingdom, and I will destroy it from off the face of the earth; saving that I will not utterly destroy the house of Jacob, saith the Lord. For, lo, I will command, and I will sift the house of Israel among all nations, like as corn is sifted in a sieve, yet shall not the least grain fall upon the earth (Amos 9:8,9).

God revealed that He would destroy the sinful kingdom of Israel, but He promised that He would not utterly destroy the PEOPLE of the house of Jacob.

It was merely the kingdom of Israel as it was constituted in Palestine that God was going to destroy. But God could not destroy the people of Israel because He solemnly promised to Abraham, Isaac and Jacob that their seed would become as the stars in the heavens in number. God prophesied that the house of Israel would be "scattered," "dispersed," or "sifted" among "all nations"; yet He promised that not the least grain would fall to the ground.

The Bible clearly shows that the Jews look upon the Promised Land as belonging solely to them; they do not wish to share this and the Patriarchal blessings with the Lost Tribes of Israel.

Notice how clearly this Jewish reluctance to share the blessings with Lost Israel is brought out in the following Scripture: "Son of man . . . all the house of Israel wholly [the Lost Ten

Tribes], are they unto whom the inhabitants of Jerusalem [the Jews] have said, Get you far from the Lord: unto us is THIS LAND given in possession" (Ezek. 11:15).

But God's answer is very emphatic:

> Therefore say, Thus saith the Lord God; Although I have cast them far off among the heathen, and although I have scattered them among the countries, yet . . . I will even gather you from the people, and assemble you out of the countries where ye have been scattered, and I will give you the land of Israel (vv. 16,17).

Also compare this prophecy with the 48th chapter of Ezekiel which clearly shows that the Promised Land is yet to be divided among the Twelve Tribes of Israel.

When the true identity of the Lost Tribes of Israel is revealed, the Jews will at first be reluctant to acknowledge their long-lost brethren; and they will not wish to share the Holy Land with them—"unto us is this land given," they will say. But God will reveal to them that they are only co-inheritors with the rest of the tribes of Israel.

Ezekiel 11:19,20 and many other similar prophecies reveal that the time setting of this regathering of the Tribes of Israel, and the redividing of the Promised Land, occurs at the Second Coming of Christ.

The House of Israel and the House of Judah (two distinct peoples) will be joined in the not-too-distant future to become one forever-inseparable people (Ezek. 37:15-23). This chapter deals with the two sticks. One in the hand of Joseph, who was the leading tribe of the Northern Ten Tribes of Israel, and the other stick was in the hand of Judah, which was the leading tribe for the Southern Kingdom including the tribes of Benjamin, Judah and most of the Levites.

These two sticks, representing the entire Twelve Tribes of Israel, are to be joined or united in the land of Palestine once again. Many, many prophecies in the Bible relate this same thing. In Ezekiel 37:13-23, and also in Ezekiel 48:1-35, is given a description of the actual allotment or the re-apportioning of the land of Palestine among the Twelve Tribes of Israel after they are all gathered back to Paelstine—in the time when the Messiah will be ruling not only over Israel but over all the earth!

It is a great pity that Robert Ingersoll is said to have been led into atheism because he had seen in the Bible the staggering promises God had made to Abraham, Isaac and Jacob and their descendants—promises of material, physical and national greatness—promises which Ingersoll believed were never fulfilled. He certainly did not believe God kept His promises to Israel (see Some Mistakes of Moses, pp. 183-189).

Now let us seek out the Lost Ten Tribes of Israel from recorded secular history in order to see "which people represent them" today!

CHAPTER III

PHYSICAL CHARACTERISTICS OF EARLY ISRAELITES

Before we can trace the people of Israel from the land of their captivity to their present-day homelands, we need to answer this question—"Just what were the ancient Palestinian Israelites like?" Were they Nordics? Did they look like the "typical Jew" of today? In particular, we are concerned with the Ten-Tribed House of Israel, whose final captivity occurred, according to Ussher, in 721 B.C. Most people assume that the people of the Ten Tribes resembled the "typical Jew" of today.

Later, we shall see a couple of very interesting statements from Dr. Kephart, in which he seems to express a commonly held view regarding what the Israelites looked like. Let us notice a few very significant remarks by Dr. Kephart. In his recently published book, Races of Mankind, Their Origin and Migration, we find these interesting statements:

> In comparison with the most recent estimates of roughly 4.5 billion years as the age of this earth, man is a relatively late phenomena of nature. The humanoid stem from which he sprang probably arose on the earth only one or two million years ago, although much higher estimation have appeared recently... The leading authorities agree that all the existing races of mankind had a common origin (Chap. I, p. 1). [Emphasis mine].

He says that man roamed over this earth for many thousands of years before the beginning of recorded history. Dr. Kephart points out that we cannot be certain as to what happened to man "in his EVOLUTION during those ages" (ibid., p. 2).

He then makes a very profound and true statement:

"What is legend today may be history tomorrow, just as what is history today may be legend tomorrow" (ibid., pp. 2,3).

This author then proceeds to advance his explanation along the lines of Evolution. He uses the words "theory," "estimates," "probably," and such words quite often. He speaks about the Azoic, Archeozoic, Proterzoic, Paleozoic, Mesozoic, Cenozoic and Pleistocene ages. The author of this book, who obviously espouses the theory of Evolution, arrives at many false conclusions.

One cannot build a house which will stand upon the shifting sands. Likewise those who try to build their theories on the origins of the races upon the shifting quicksands of Evolution are starting from a false basis and much (if not most) of what they believe, write and teach will be in error.

Again let it be firmly stated that the veracity of the Scriptures has been proven in so many ways, that there is absolutely no doubt whatsoever that the Bible is accurate historically, as well as an infallible guide revealing to man what his ultimate destiny is to be.

The Scriptures as originally given (of course minor errors have crept into existing manuscripts, consequently no particular translation is 100% accurate) were inspired by Almighty God (II Tim. 3:15,16) and were, therefore, perfect. The Scripture cannot be broken (John 10:35); consequently if one bases his research and his beliefs upon the solid foundation of the Scripture, his work is sure to have at least an unshakable foundation.

"LOST TEN TRIBES"—WERE THEY ARYAN NORDICS?

Now we shall notice a flagrant error which the author of this book would have us believe—an error which is based on the theory of Evolution.

> Variation of color of skin is dependant mainly on climatic conditions, the darkest races having become so by long habitation in low, moist, hot places near the equator and the lighter races having lost skin and eye pigmentation by long habitation in the rigorous dark or hazy climate of the north . . . (Kephart, Races of Mankind, Their Origin and Migration, Chap. I, p. 66).

Dr. Kephart does, however, realize the importance of the cephalic index in seeking to ascertain racial origins from skeletal remains. He speaks of the cephalic index as "One of the most useful methods of segregating people . . ." (ibid., p. 66).

Notice how many authors realize the importance of the cephalic index in determining racial affinities.

Now let us notice a statement of Kephart's regarding what the "original Hebrews" were like. Also note carefully what is said concerning the "lost Tribes of Israel."

> Since the original Hebrews were Kassites of typically Turkic build, i.e., with tawny complexion, of medial height and stocky build, with prominent nose, and brachycephalous [broad-headed], all efforts to identify Aryan Nordic people of Europe as descendants of the Lost Tribes of Israel are doomed to failure. A more futile task is inconceivable (ibid., fn. p. 150).

WERE THE ORIGINAL ISRAELITES LIKE THE "TYPICAL JEW"?

Where did Dr. Kephart learn that "the original Hebrews were Kassites," and of "Turkic build?" How did he come to the conclusion that the original Hebrews had a "tawny complexion," and were of a "medial height," and "stocky build," that they had "prominent nose," and "brachycephalous" (broad) type of head? Yes, just where did Dr. Kephart learn all of these fables?

Notice the author of this book has already revealed his lack of understanding on a number of points and now he propounds the belief that seems to be common among so many people today, that the Lost Tribes of Israel could not be identified with the Aryan, Nordic people of Europe.

Kephart dogmatically states that the people of the Lost Tribes of Israel were people "with tawny complexion, of medial height and stocky build, with prominent nose, and brachycephalous." In other words, Dr. Kephart would have you believe "the original Hebrews" looked like the so-called "typical Jew" of today. But this is merely a human assumption which we shall see exploded from Biblical and secular history!

"The peculiar notion advanced by some writers, chiefly religionists, that these dark-complexioned bracycephalic Turanian people were the ancestors of the blond mesocephalic Aryan Anglo-Saxons is too absurd physiologically to receive further notice." (ibid., p. 155).

We shall soon see from the Bible, and also from secular history that the "original Hebrews" (by which Dr. Kephart meant the Israelites) were primarily an Aryan or Nordic type people after all!

Speaking of the modern Jews, Dr. Kephart says that "Today there are JEWS of widely different physical types, many largely ARYAN in blood" (ibid., p. 157).

Yes, Dr. Kephart admits that many European Jews are Aryan in type or race, but he is puzzled as to how they could be "Aryan in blood."

If you were to ask the average man on the street to give you a description of what he thinks the people of the "Lost Ten Tribes" looked like, he would be sure to give you a description of the typical modern Jew. Such an individual would probably say that the Israelites were short, and of stocky build, with dark or olive-coloured complexion and with very dark (if not black) hair. And he would probably also add that the Israelites must have had prominent noses! This is what a "Semite" is supposed to look like. But is such a conception a true picture of the original pre-captivity Israelite?

Before we begin to accurately form a picture of what the original Israelite looked like, we must thoroughly examine the "Jewish question."

Most who have studied the Jewish question will generally admit that the present-day Jews are the descendants of Israel, and are, therefore, Israelites.

Are Dr. Kephart and others right in assuming that the people of the Twelve-Tribed House of Israel were all like the present-day Ashkenazic Jews, that is, "with tawny complexion, of medial height and stocky build, with prominent nose, and brachycephalous head . . . ?"

In other words, were the people of the Twelve Tribes of Israel like the present-day Ashkenazim Jews? Or were they not more like the Sephardic, Aryan or Nordic type of Jews? Also recall Dr. Kephart's statement, "The peculiar notion advanced by some writers, chiefly religionists, that these dark-complexioned brachycephalic [broad-headed] Turanian people were the ancestors of the blond masocephalic Aryan Anglo-Saxons is too absurd physiologically to receive further notice" (Races of Mankind, p. 155).

Ripley and many ethnologists and historians clearly point out that the Sephardic Jews are, in fact, Aryan or European in type.

Dr. Kephart seems to express the general notions of the average man-on-the-street in regard to the assumed appearance of the people of the ancient Kingdom of Israel. It seems that everyone automatically assumes that since many of the Jews today (the Ashkenazim) are in the main a dark-haired, dark-complexioned, broad-headed people; and since the Arabs are also a very dark people—everyone automatically assumes that the people of the Lost Ten Tribes of Israel must have been a dark-haired, dark-eyed, dark-complexioned, short type of people.

THE ISRAELITES WERE PREDOMINANTLY NORDICS

Now let us go to history and also to the Scriptures to prove what the pre-captivity people of the Twelve Tribes of Israel were really like.

Professor Sayce makes the following significant comment:

> The names of the Jewish towns captured by the Egyptian King Soshenk . . . recorded on the walls of the temple of Karnak are each surmounted with the head and shoulders of a prisoner. Casts have been made of the heads by Sir Flinders Petrie, and the racial type represented by them turns out to be Amorite and not Jewish (Sayce, Races of the Old Testament, pp. 115,116).

The Egyptian king who made these lifelike engravings of "Amorite" prisoners from the land of Israel was Pharaoh SOSHENK!

What does Professor Sayce mean when he states that these Palestinian prisoners turned out to be "Amorite" and not Jews after all? By "Amorite" he means they were a blond, Nordic type! He further states that "David . . . was blond and red-haired (ibid.)!

> It is plain that the Amorite belonged to the blond race. His blue eyes and light hair prove this incontestably. So also does the colour of his skin, when compared with that of other races depicted by the Egyptian artists. At Madianet Habu, for example, where the skin of the Amorite is pale pink, that of the Lebu or Libyan and the Mashuash or Masyes is red like that of the Egyptians, though we know that the Libyans belonged to a distinctively fair-complexioned race. In a tomb (No. 34) of the Eighteenth Dynasty, at Thebes, the Amorite chief of Kadesh has a white skin, and a light red-brown eyes and hair . . . (ibid., pp. 167,168).

Note carefully Professor Sayce's remarks, as they have a very important bearing upon the conclusions which will be drawn later. We shall see that Sayce and others call the Israelites "Amorites"—though the people of Israel were not Amorites in the true sense. The original Amorites were descendants of Ham (through his son, Canaan), and were dark-complexioned like all of Ham's descendants (Gen. 10:15-20).

Sayce then goes on to show that at that time a line of blonds extended all the way from the northern coast of Africa east to the corner of the Mediterranean, then north to Coele-Syria, and that this was only broken by the Delta of Egypt, where we know darker people have always lived.

BLOND ISRAELITES CALLED AMORITES

These statements show clearly that these Israelitish "Amorites" were a blond race. Now let us go back and analyze the statement made by Professor Sayce in regard to the campaign of SOSHENK, the Egyptian Pharaoh. According to Professor Sayce (and many historians give similar accounts), Pharaoh, in his campaign against Israel, took a number of prisoners. These so-called "Jewish" prisoners turn out to be "Amorite"—according to Professor Sayce! Also remember that a number of paintings, according to Professor Sayce and other sources, show that the Amorites were definitely a blond race. Their features were more like the North-west Europeans of today.

It should be pointed out, however, that the Pharaoh who took these Israelitish prisoners (called "Amorites") was the So mentioned in II Kings17:4. It was So, Pharaoh of Egypt, who recorded his conquests on the walls of the Temple at Karnak.

Whether these Israelitish prisoners were taken in the time of Rehoboam or at the later date (in the time of Hoshea—King of Ten-Tribed Israel), the fact remains that the prisoners were taken from the people of Israel. They were definitely a blond race!

This is just one more proof that the Israelites of the pre-captivity were a blond people!

Speaking of the busts of these "Jewish" prisoners, Professor Sayce says, "We must conclude, therefore, that even AFTER THE REVOLT OF THE TEN TRIBES, the bulk of the population in Southern Judah continued to be AMORITE [that is, blond and Nordic] in race though not in name" (ibid., p. 116). The "Jewish type" meaning the Ashkenazim was so scantily represented that the Egyptian artist failed to depict it at all. And remember by this expression "Jewish type," Professor Sayce undoubtedly means the short-statured, dark-skinned, broad-headed, Ashkenazic Jew familiar to most of us today.

Notice Professor Sayce says that these Jewish prisoners were not actually "Jewish" at all, but were Amorites. He says the "Jewish type" was so scantily represented that the Egyptian artist passed it over when depicting the prisoners who had been brought from Judah (ibid., p. 116).

But here is the real truth of the matter. After the Ten-Tribed Northern Kingdom of Israel rejected the rulership of the throne of David, forming a separate kingdom, only the tribes of Judah, Benjamin, and a portion of the Levites were left in the southern part of the land of Israel to form the kingdom thereafter known as the Kingdom of Judah.

MEN OF JUDAH AND BENJAMIN WERE NORDICS

These blond, long-headed prisoners taken captive by the Pharaoh of Egypt were undoubtedly typical of many of the Israelites.

It has already been clearly pointed out that many of the present-day Jews have a tendency towards blondism, and are of the long-headed type. These dolichocephalic Jews are found primarily among the Sephardic branch of the Jews, even though there are also quite a number of blond, long-headed Jews among the Ashkenazic Jews.

> The non-biblical material has markedly increased our knowledge of the Amorites . . . Egyptian illustrations of the New Kingdom show the Palestinian Amorites to have been a race much more like the northern Europeans than the Semites; long-headed, with blue eyes, straight nose and thin lips . . . The Amorites were inhabitants of a territory lying west of Babylonia, and the majority of them belonged (as forerunners of the Aramaeans) to the western Semitic race (Ency. Brit., 14th ed., Vol. I, Art. Amorites).

The Encyclopedia Britannica points out that the Amorites were "long-headed." It also mentions that the Babylonians called the people to the west of them "Amorites," meaning "Westerners." This term "Amorite" or "Westerner" was used by other peoples including the Egyptians, when speaking of the people living in the area of Palestine. The Babylonians called the people living in that area "Amorites" or Westerners without distinguishing one people from another. The Egyptians and others undoubtedly did the same thing. Many modern-day scholars do the same thing. They fail to differentiate between the true, original Amorites, mentioned in Genesis 10, and the other "Westerners" who lived in Palestine and who were also called "Amorite" by the Gentile nations.

"The profiles of the Amorites, as depicted on the monuments of the Nineteenth and Twentieth Dynasties, are practically identical with those of the figures at Karnak, which surmount the names of the cities captured by Shishak [SOSHENK] . . ." (Sayce, The Races of the Old Testament, p. 166). This shows conclusively that the blond Israelites were called Amorites!

In Genesis chapter ten, verse fifteen, we read that Canaan begat Sidon, Heth, and a Jebusite and an Amorite. The true, original Amorites (according to Biblical usage) were descendants of Canaan, and were therefore Canaanites. They were descendants of Ham—and were in no sense of the word "blonds." But, as already mentioned, undoubtedly this name "Amorite" was used by the Babylonians, Egyptians and others to denote generally the blond races which were living in the Palestinian area—races which had supplanted the original Amorites.

Let us notice a few interesting statements concerning the Palestinian Amorites, by Jessel. We shall presently see that he makes the grave mistake of thinking that the Jewish prisoners were Amorites.

> Sargon I., King of Agede, and first king of the Babylonian Empire describes PALESTINE on one of his monuments as a LAND OF THE AMORITES (Sayce, Patriarchal Palestine), and at a later period we find portraits of AMORITE PRISONERS on the wall sculptures of Egypt. The Egyptians depict them as a FAIR PEOPLE, WITH BLOND or REDDISH HAIR and BLUE EYES. (The unknown History of the Jews, p. 107).

Again note carefully that the Egyptians depict the "Amorites" as "a fair people" having "blond or reddish hair and blue eyes." This shows as we have seen proven that the Egyptians and others called the Israelites "Amorites."

Also remember that the true "Amorites" were Hamitic; and we know of no light-skinned, blond-haired, and blue-eyed descendants of Ham on this earth today, neither did such ever exist! All truly Hamitic peoples have dark skins, though this does not mean that they are all black or even dark brown.

> A study of ethnology leads to the conclusion that these people were the BLOND or RED-HAIRED WHITE RACE, of the Amurra or AMURRU we hear of occasionally in the Egyptian campaigns in the direction of the Amanus mountains. That the AMORITES were CAUCASIANS in appearance and physique leaves no room for doubt, and some of their habits and forms of worship point to their being A KELTIC SUB-RACE (ibid., p. 107).

Did you notice that Jessel plainly says the Amorites (these "Amorites" being beyond question Israelites) were "Caucasian" in physique and appearance. He says there can be no doubt that these Amorites were "a KELTIC sub-race."

Keep this important point in mind, for later on we shall see irrefutable proof showing that there are many connecting links to verify that the Kelts are definitely some of the dispersed peoples of the "Lost Ten Tribes of Israel"!

> In the accompanying illustrations [says Jessel] we reproduce, by permission of Professor W. Flinders Petrie, photographs of casts he has made from sculptures in the Egyptian tombs. These portraits of AMORITE [referring to Israelitish captives] prisoners of war belong chiefly to the period of Seti I . . . The shape of the head and the features generally remind us of the FAIR TYPE OF MODERN JEW, and have some resemblance to the Scotch, if we imagine a reddish colouring for the hair, and blue eyes . . . In Scotland, Sweden, Brittany, and Spain superstitions still survive which can be traced to Amorite forms of belief, and even the type of the Amorite can be distinguished in the population. These resemblances in Europe to certain forms of Jewish belief have led to the

vague notions about the "LOST TRIBES" which we sometimes hear . . . (ibid., pp. 107,108).

Notice that Jessel says the customs of the so-called Amorites (which in this case were beyond question Israelites) in Britain and elsewhere, were such as to cause some to think that the Lost Tribes are today found in such countries as "Scotland, Sweden," and Brittany.

"Here, then, may be the origin of those settlements," Jessel says, "on the shores of even the British Isles which introduced Amorite forms of worship; and we see in the cromlechs of THE DRUIDS the very same arrangement of stones which is characteristic of the Amorites of Palestine" (ibid., p. 110).

JUDAH AND BENJAMIN—CALLED "AMORITES"

Note carefully the following statements made by Jessel regarding the Jews and Benjamites:

> We find in the Bible many references to the fighting power of the Benjamin, and we find them also always in alliance with Yahuds [Jews]. Together these white races held in subjection the coloured people, the natives of Canaan.

> JUDAH and BENJAMIN are the Amurra ["AMORITES"] and the Kheta of the Egyptian monuments (ibid., p. 118).

Jessel thinks that the settlements in the British Isles which had built the cromlechs were the same people as the Palestinian Amorites. He plainly says that "JUDAH and BENJAMIN are the AMURRA" whom the Egyptians had depicted. Also, did you notice that Jessel spoke of the "YAHUDS" and the "BENJAMIN" as "these WHITE races"? He also spoke of the native CANAANITES as "the COLOURED people."

Truly, the native Canaanites were dark or colored in comparison with the people of the tribes of Judah (the Yahuds) and the Benjamin (Benjamites).

Furthermore, we have noticed that the Sephardic Jews are more "European" or "Nordic" than they are "Jewish"; and we have observed that there is a considerable degree of blondism among this branch of Jews. Many redheads are found among them. (For further verification of this, see the Jewish Encyclopedia, Volume XII, Art. Types, Anthropological, pp. 291-95).

We have seen that a number of casts were made of the busts of Israelitish prisoners and we noted that these prisoners from the land of Israel turned out to be "Nordic" in type. They are called "Amorites" by Sayce and others. They just can't believe that these blond and Nordic Israelitish prisoners (mistakenly called Amorites), captured by Pharaoh could be Israelites. They, like most, assume all Israelites would have to be a short, dark-skinned, broad-headed people like most of the Ashkenazic Jews.

All of these points lead us unerringly to the inescapable conclusion that the original Israelites were more "Nordic" in type than "Jewish." The bulk of them resembled their present-day "Nordic" descendants who inhabit North-west Europe!

We have seen abundant historical evidence proving that the original-type Israelites were not all short, olive-skinned, dark-haired, broad-headed people with prominent noses! Now let us see what RACIAL TYPE the ISRAELITES were—according to the Bible!

LABAN—THE BLOND SYRIAN

Just before Abraham died, he told his trusted servant to go to the city of Nahor to get a wife for his son, Isaac (Gen. 24:1-10). "And he arose, and went to Mesopotamia, unto the city of Nahor" (ibid., v. 10). "Mesopotamia" means "between the rivers"—Tigris and Euphrates.

Isaac did the same—before he died!

"And Isaac called Jacob, and blessed him, and charged him, and said unto him, 'Thou shalt not take a wife of the daughters of Canaan. Arise, go to Padan-aram, [the plain of Syria] to the house of Bethuel thy mother's father; and take thee a wife from thence of the daughters of LABAN thy mother's brother'" (Gen. 28:1,2). If one will read the rest of the 28th chapter of Genesis, and also the 29th and 30th chapters, he will see that Jacob obeyed his father, Isaac, and went to Padan-aram, "the plain of Syria," to the home of his uncle, Laban. Here he met and married Leah and Rachel, two of Laban's daughters.

But what does the name "Laban" signify? In the Hebrew language in which the Old Testament was written, "Laban" means "white." (Strong, The Exhaustive Concordance of the Bible, under "Laban").

Any good Bible dictionary will show that the word "Laban" means "white" and comes from the same Hebrew stem as does the word "Lebanon"—meaning "white." Strong's Exhaustive Concordance defines the word "Lebanon" in the Hebrew as "(the) white mountain (from its snow)." So we see that the Lebanon Mountain was named Lebanon because it was a white mountain.

Why, then, would Laban have been called "white" unless he was a fair, light-skinned or "white" person? He must have been a very fair person in order to have been called by this name, Laban. Judging from his modern descendants, one would conclude the same thing. See Genesis 49:12, "teeth 'white' with milk," and Numbers 12:10, where we read that Miriam became "white as snow." The word "white" in both of the references just cited is the same word in the Hebrew as the name translated "Laban."

NAMES ALWAYS HAD A MEANING

Also remember that in the time of the Hebrew Patriarchs, it was customary to always name a person with a significant name. There is hardly any example in the Hebrew Scriptures of the name of any individual being without some significance. Thus the name "Abraham" means "father of a multitude" (Gen. 12:1-5), "Isaac" means "laughter" (Gen. 21:1-6), "Jacob" means "heel catcher," i.e. "supplanter," or "deceiver" (Gen. 27:36), "Israel" means "overcomer with God" or "prevailer with God" (Gen. 32:28), and "Satan" means "adversary." These are just a few of many thousands of Hebrew words—all of which had a definite meaning. Laban, then, was named "Laban" or "white" because he was a white, fair-skinned person.

Jacob, also called Israel, went to the plain of Syria (Padam-aram) and married into his own family. He married two of his own cousins, Leah and Rachel. It was quite customary in Patriarchal times to marry a close relative. Even Abraham married his half-sister (Gen. 20:12); and Adam's children all had to marry their own brothers or sisters, since at that early stage in the development of "homo sapiens" there was no one else to marry.

Since Laban was a fair or "white" person, his two daughters, Leah and Rachel, whom Jacob married must have also been very fair; and since Jacob was their cousin, he must have had some of the blond, "Syrian" features of his uncle, Laban. This is also borne out by the modern-day descendants of Jacob, who have many blonds among them. Remember, we have seen that the Sephardic Jews have a great deal of blondism among them. Here is a list of Jacob's sons:

> The sons of Leah; Reuben, Jacob's firstborn, and Simeon and Levi, and Judah, and Issachar, and Zebulun: The sons of Rachel; Joseph, and Benjamin: And the sons of Bilhah, Rachel's handmaid; Dan, and Naphtali: And the sons of Zilpah, Leah's handmaid; Gad and Asher: these are the sons of Jacob, which were born to him in Padan-aram (Gen. 35:23-26).

Notice that these children were all born to Jacob while he was yet in Padam-aram, or the plain of Syria. Undoubtedly Leah and Rachel were quite fair-complexioned like their father, Laban.

Thus we see that the family of Abraham must have contained a considerable amount of blondism in their genes. This does not mean that there were no brunettes in the people of Israel. Remember, the word "blond" is used today to denote various shades of brown hair as well as to refer to "pure blonds" and redheads. A "brunet" is one who has very dark brown or black hair.

SARAH WAS "VERY FAIR"

Abraham says of his wife, Sarah, "Behold now, I know that thou art a fair woman to look upon" (Gen. 12:11).

And in verse 14 we read, "And it came to pass, that, when Abraham came into Egypt the Egyptians beheld the woman that she was very fair." Sarah was Abraham's half-sister (Gen.

20:12). The Hebrew word here translated as "fair" is "yawfeh." It is from a Hebrew root meaning "to be bright." The context shows that this word refers to the physical appearance, and is not here associated with mental aptitudes. There is every reason to believe that this word is to be understood according to its literal sense in regard to Sarah. She was not a dark-skinned person, but was a bright—or light-skinned person. Since Abraham was half-brother to Sarah (Gen. 20:12), he must also have been a fair-skinned person.

Rebekah was also "very fair" to look upon (Gen. 24:16; 26:7). The word used in this instance, however, is a different word and may not of itself prove that Rebekah was a light-skinned person. However, there is every reason to believe it is to be taken in this sense. The other many texts which we have cited show that Rebekah was from a family of fair-skinned people.

DAVID WAS RUDDY AND FAIR

We all know that David was a descendant of Judah, and was therefore a Jew. What did he look like? "For he [David] was but a youth, and ruddy, and of a fair countenance" (I Sam. 17:42). The word translated "fair" in this verse is the same word as was used in regard to Sarah. We have already noticed that this word in the Hebrew means "to be bright." It undoubtedly refers to the complexion of the individual.

Not only was David a fair person, but the Scripture shows that he was "ruddy." What is the meaning of the Hebrew word from which the English word "ruddy" was translated? The Hebrew word is "admoniy" and it means "reddish." It is the same word as is used in Genesis 25:25. "And the first [Esau] came out red, all over like an hairy garment; and they called his name Esau." The word here translated as "red" is the same as is found in I Samuel 16:12, which is translated as "ruddy." "Now he [David] was ruddy, and withal of a beautiful countenance, and goodly to look to."

So there can be absolutely no doubt about it—David was not the dark-skinned Ashkenazic type of Jew. He was a fair-skinned, ruddy-complexioned Jew—just as most blonds in North-western Europe have both light skins and ruddy complexions; and just as many Jews are, red-haired. They are, in fact, tribal relatives of King David, who was also "fair." This is the same word (yawfeh) as was used when describing Sarah; and means, in the Hebrew language "to be bright," and has to refer to a light or fair skin in David's case, for a "ruddy" complexioned individual is always a fair person.

SOME JEWS ARE RUDDY, WITH BLACK HAIR

In The Song of Solomon, chapter 5:10,11, we read, "My beloved is white and ruddy, the chiefest amongst ten thousand. His head is as the most fine gold, his locks are bushy, and black as a raven."

To whom does this refer? Does it refer to King Solomon? Or does it refer to Christ as some believe? This person was "white" and "ruddy," but his hair was "as black as a raven." Modern

Jews have both red and black hair. The word translated as "ruddy" in this verse is from the Hebrew word "awdome" meaning "rosy." It is the same word as is used in Isaiah 1:18, where it speaks of one's sins being "red like crimson." Also this is the same word used in a number of Scriptures when referring to "red wine."

Anyone who is "white and ruddy" is always a fair-skinned person.

There can be no question that this "Jewish type" referred to in the fifth chapter of The Song of Solomon was not an olive-skinned type of Ashkenazic Jew, but he must have been the Sephardic type of Jew, having a light skin with a pinkish or reddish cast to it.

The Jewess mentioned throughout this Song of Solomon is repeatedly called "fair" (Heb. "yawfeh") and indicates that the person alluded to here was a fair-skinned person.

ESTHER—A FAIR PERSON

Now let us notice that Esther, who became Queen of the Persian Empire, was a light—or fair-skinned person. She was of the tribe of Benjamin (Esther 2:5).

"He [Mordecai] brought up . . . Esther . . . and the maid was fair and beautiful" (Esther 2:7). This word "fair" is the same word that was used when speaking of Sarah. It means "to be bright" and is the only place in all the book of Esther where this word is used. We read that Vashti, the former haughty queen, was "fair" (ibid., 1:11). But the Hebrew word used here is a different word, and does not mean "to be bright," but it means to be beautiful. We read also of "fair young virgins" (ibid., 2:2,3). But the Hebrew word "yawfeh" is not used in regard to any of these women, but is used only in chapter 2, verse 7 in connection with Queen Esther. She had a "bright" or light skin. Esther was not only "fair," but she was also "beautiful." The Hebrew word translated as beautiful in verse 7 is "toar" and means "to delineate, outline, i.e. figure or appearance" (Strong, The Exhaustive Concordance of the Bible). Not only was Esther a fair—or light-skinned person, but she was also a person with a very beautiful figure.

The following facts should be borne in mind: Abraham, Isaac and Jacob and their children were all descendants of Shem, through his son, Arphaxad (Gen. 10:21-24). The people of Israel were, therefore, descendants of Arphaxad. All of Shem's descendants were fair-skinned. There is not one scintilla of historical (Biblical or secular) evidence to prove that any of the Semitic people were dark-skinned except by intermarriage.

JOB'S DAUGHTER—A BLONDE

Job was undoubtedly a descendant of Shem. "There was a man in the land of Uz whose name was Job" (Job 1:1). JOB WAS THE CHEOPS WHO BUILT THE GREAT PYRAMID. Cheops was the same person as Khufu, and Khufu, according to the Egyptian Manetho, "was of a different race" from the true Egyptians (Wathen, Arts and Antiquities of Egypt).

Now let us examine a very interesting quotation concerning Cheops proving that he was not of the dark-skinned, dark-haired Hamitic, Egyptian type.

> The pigmentation of the Egyptians was usually a brunette white; in the conventional figures the men are represented as red, the women often as lighter, and even white. Although the hair is almost inevitably black or dark brown, and the eyes brown, Queen Hetep-Heres II, of the fourth dynasty, the daughter of Cheops, the builder of the great pyramid, is shown in the coloured bas reliefs of her tomb to have been a definite blonde. Her hair is painted a bright yellow stippled with fine red horizontal lines, and her skin is white. This is the earliest known evidence of blondism in the world (Coon, The Races of Europe, p. 98). [Emphasis is mine].

We know, however, that Job was not an Egyptian, just as Joseph and his family were not Egyptians. Many foreigners have lived in Egypt throughout the ages. The Hyksos are definitely known to have been non-Egyptian in blood.

PEOPLE OF ISRAEL WERE WHITE AND RUDDY

Here is another interesting quote showing what the people of Israel were like. Speaking of Israelitish Nazarites, we read, "Her Nazarites were purer than snow, they were whiter than milk, they were more RUDDY IN BODY than rubies, their polishing was of sapphire" (Lam. 4:7).

To whom does this refer? Verse six speaks of "the daughter of my people" and verse twenty-two says, "The punishment of thine iniquity is accomplished, O DAUGHTER OF ZION." So the expression "Her Nazarites" must refer to the Nazarites of the people of Zion—Israel. Whether this refers to the Ten-tribed House of Israel or only to the Jews, or whether it is past, present, or a future prophecy is immaterial.

Notice, not only does it speak of her Nazarites being "purer than snow" and "whiter than milk," but it also says that "they were more ruddy in body than rubies."

This word "ruddy" is from the Hebrew word "awdome" and means "rosy." It is the same word used in The Song of Solomon 5:10 and Isaiah 1:18 ("red like crimson"). There can be no doubt that this word means ruddy, reddish, or rosy. This is another definite statement from God's inspired Word proving that the Israelites were a fair-skinned, ruddy-complexioned type of people.

Some think that this refers to the Church. But certainly no one can argue that the "spiritual Nazarites" are more ruddy in body than rubies. God's Church is made up of people of all racial types—white, black, yellow and brown. This verse shows that Israel's Nazarites had fair skins with a ruddy tint to them. These Israelitish Nazarites were white and ruddy. In fact, most fair—or white-skinned people, when in health, have ruddy skins; but when they are sick their skin becomes very white or pale as a result of a lack of red corpuscles.

These references should suffice to show any who are open-minded that the people of the ancient Twelve Tribes of Israel were not a dark—or olive-skinned people; but were primarily a light-skinned race, having a great element of blondism in their genes. This does not mean to imply that there were not some brown-, or even black-headed people among them. But judging by some of the modern blond Jews, and also from the Scriptures (both of which indicate that the Israelites were fair) we conclude that they were not primarily a short, dark and broad-headed people with prominent noses. But they were "Nordic" (North-west European) in type.

There is, however, a Biblical principle which should now be pointed out. The Bible does not say in most instances of what race of people the various wives of the twelve sons of Jacob were. We know that one of the three surviving sons of Judah (Shelah) was half-Canaanite since his mother was a Canaanite. We also know that of Simeon's six children, one of them was by a Canaanitish woman, and was therefore half-Canaanitish (Gen. 46:10).

It would appear that in every instance in the beginnings of the nation of Israel, when an Israelite married outside of the general family-stock of Israel, God always had it recorded in the Scripture for our benefit.

Here are the various instances of the Hebrew Patriarchs marrying outside of the family of Shem.

Abraham had a son by an Egyptian bond-woman named Hagar. This son, Ishmael, was half-Egyptian. Ishmael married an Egyptian wife (Gen. 21:21) which would mean that his descendants consequently would be three-fourths Egyptian. The Egyptians were relatively dark-skinned. Most of the present-day Arabs are the descendants of Abraham through Ishmael. They are about three-fourths Egyptian.

Later, Abraham's grandson, Esau, failed to marry into his own family and among his own people; but took a Canaanitish woman to be his wife. This proved to be a very great source of grief to his parents (Gen. 36:34-35). When Esau saw that his father, Isaac, was displeased because he had taken a Canaanitish wife, he then went to Ishmael, his uncle, and married one of that family. Remember, the people of Ishmael were now three-fourths Egyptian (Gen. 28:6-9; 27:46).

This shows that the descendants of Esau had mixed at an early period with the Canaanites and also with their Ishmaelitish kinsmen who were three-fourths Egyptian.

It would appear that the Bible always mentions it when the founding-fathers of the nation of Israel married foreign or Canaanitish daughters.

Remember, Canaan was under a great curse: "Cursed be Canaan; a servant of servants shall he be unto his brethren" (Gen. 9:25).

God did not wish "the Chosen People" to mix with the Canaanites, thereby coming under a curse. When we come to the Twelve Sons of Israel who founded the Twelve Tribes of Israel, the Bible only mentions that Judah and Simeon married Canaanitish daughters. Genesis 46:10, already mentioned, shows that one of Simeon's six children was by a Canaanitish woman—the inference being that the other five were not Canaanitish. The other five children must have been of the same race or people as the family of Abraham, Isaac, Jacob, Laban and the others.

They were from Padan-aram, ("the plain of Syria") in Mesopotamia ("between the rivers") i.e., the Tigris and Euphrates Rivers.

We have now seen clearly demonstrated from secular and sacred history that the original Israelites of old were not primarily a short, dark, broad-headed and prominent-nosed race!

The Scriptures speak of the historic Israelites as a "VERY FAIR" people with "RUDDY" complexions! Secular history also reveals the same thing. The Israelites of the Old Testament, pre-captivity times were called "Amorites" by the Gentile nations—and the Palestinian "Amorites" were definitely a blond, "Nordic" type of people. The Northwest European "Nordics" are descendants of these Palestinian Amorites! They are, in fact, the children of the dispersed Ten-Tribed Israel!

CHAPTER IV

THE IMPORTANCE OF THE DYNASTIC
NAME OF OMRI (GHOMRI)

We have already examined a number of quotations in which we have seen that the Gentiles used different names for the people of Israel than were used by themselves. Notice Dr. Schrader's comments on this subject:

> ISRAEL . . . the usual term for the Kingdom of Israel in the Assyrian inscriptions is not this, as we have already observed. The ordinary designation was rather . . . "Land of the House Omri," or "Land of Omri," or merely "Land Omri" (The Cuneiform Inscriptions and the Old Testament, Vol. I, p.177).

Dr. Schrader has shown very clearly that such names as "House of Omri," "Land of Omri" and "Land Omri" were the usual appellations which the Assyrians (and others) applied to the Northern Kingdom of Israel.

Notice what the Encyclopedia Britannica has to say regarding "Omri."

> The Dynasty of Omri.—Omri (q.v.), the founder of one of the greatest dynasties of Israel . . . Although little is preserved of Omri's history, the fact that the Northern kingdom long continued to be called by the Assyrians after his name is a significant indication of his great reputation (11th ed., Vol. XV, Art. Jews, p.377).

The Northern Kingdom of Israel continued to be called by Omri's name for over two centuries after the death of Omri, until after the final captivity of Israel in 721 B.C.

BIT-KHUMRI (THE HOUSE OF OMRI)

Many historians have recognised that Omri, king of Israel, had founded a great dynasty in the Northern Kingdom. He was known far and wide among the Assyrians, Moabites and other peoples as a great king.

The Scriptures also imply that he was a great legislator—not necessarily great in the scriptural sense, however. "The statutes of OMRI are kept, and all the works of the house of Ahab . . ." (Micah 6:16).

Notice further what The Encyclopedia Britannica says regarding Omri:

> Omri, in the Bible, the first great king of Israel after the separation of the two kingdoms of Israel and Judah, who flourished in the early part of the 9th century B.C. . . . and the fact that the land [of Israel] continued to be known to the Assyrians down to the time of Sargon as "HOUSE OF OMRI" indicates the reputation which this little-known king enjoyed (Ency. Brit., 11th ed., Vol. XX, Art. Omri, p.104).

Did you notice the last statement from this excerpt? It mentioned the well-known fact that the land of Israel continued to be known to the Assyrians, even down to the time of Sargon, as the "House of Omri"—indicating "the reputation" which the name of Omri had enjoyed.

> Payment of tribute by Iaua (Jehu), the son of Khumri (Omri) who brought silver, gold, lead, and bowls, dishes, cups, and other vessels of gold. The description "Son of Khumri" is thought merely to show that Jehu was an Israelite, because Israelitish territory was called "BIT-KHUMRI" (Luckenbill, The Ancient Records of Assyria and Babylonia, Vol. I, p.46).

Here is another translation of the same cuneiform inscription. Notice the spelling of "Omri" (Humri) is slightly different from the previous spelling as given by Luckenbill. "The tribute of Yaua (Jehu), son of HUMRI (Omri)" (Kinns, Graven in the Rock, p. 494).

But to whom did Jehu pay this tribute? This question is answered in the following quotation:

"Jehu. On the Black Obelisk 'Jehu' (=Yaua) 'son of Omri' (=KHUMRI), is represented as giving tribute to Shalmaneser II" (Bible Students Handbook of Assyriology, pp.105,106).

Following is an interesting statement, showing that the Assyrians became acquainted with the Northern Kingdom of Israel first in the time of Omri.

> Omri seems to have been an able soldier and he subdued Moab to Israel. This is acknowledged by the Moabite King Mesha in an inscription which has come down to us . . . The Assyrians first became acquainted with Israel in the time of Omri, and they call the country of the TEN TRIBES OF ISRAEL "the land of the house of Omri" even after the extinction of his dynasty (Hastings, Dictionary of the Bible, Vol. I, Art., Omri, p.668).

We shall later see that some of the Kelts were called by such names as "OMBRI" and "UMBRI".

God has not left us without historical proof to connect this name "Omri" (which we can definitely prove Israel bore before her captivity) with the present-day descendants of the House of Israel.

The most important key linking the House of Israel (Bit-Ghomri) with modern-day Israel is the famous Behistun Rock Inscriptions. These inscriptions, written in Cuneiform characters, are of utmost importance in unravelling the history of Israel.

BEHISTUN ROCK INSCRIPTIONS—KEY TO ISRAEL'S IDENTITY

Darius I had the famous Behistun Rock Inscriptions engraved (in cuneiform) on the steep face of a high rock beside the main road leading from Babylon (Baghdad) to Media. These important cuneiform inscriptions were written in three languages—(1) Persian, (2) Babylonian and (3) Susian (or Elamite).

> Above the inscription the picture of the king himself is graven . . . Nine rebel chiefs are led before him; . . . the ninth is Skunka, the chief of the Scythians (Sacae) whom he defeated . . . The inscriptions are composed in the three languages which are written with cuneiform signs, and were used in all official inscriptions of the Achaemenian kings (Ency. Brit., 11th ed., Vol. III, Art. Behistun, pp. 656,657).

It is interesting to note some of the particulars of the Behistun Rock inscriptions. Also notice that this Scythian chief "Skunka" is called "Sacae." The Sacae and the Scythians as we shall later prove, were basically the same people.

> In 1835 the difficult and almost inaccessible cliff was first climbed by Sir Henry Rawlinson, who copied and deciphered the inscriptions (1835-1845), and thus completed the reading of the old cuneiform text and laid the foundation of the science of Assyriology (Ency. Brit. 11th ed., Vol. III, Art. Behistun, pp.656,657).

Here follows excerpts from a translation of the Behistun Rock Inscriptions by L.W. King and R.C. Thompson.

"Thus sayeth Darius, the king: 'these are the provinces which are subject unto me, and by the grace of Auramazda became I king of them'" (The Inscriptions of Darius the Great of Behistun).

This translation translates all of the words on the Behistun Rock Inscriptions in three parallel columns. The first column contains the Persian, the second the Susian or the Elamite, the third contains the Babylonian translation.

These inscriptions mention twenty-two provinces. The nineteenth province listed by all three of these parallel columns is called in the Persian language "SCYTHIA (Phonetic: SAKA)," in the second column this same province is called, in the Susian language "Scythia (Phonetic: Sakka)," and the third column, in the Babylonian language, it is translated: "in the land of the CIMMERIANS (Phonetic: Gi-mi-ri)."

Professor Rawlinson, however, translated this 19th province as "the SACAE." Keep this in mind, for Saka (Sakka) and Sacae all refer to the same people.

Let us notice the three different names which are here used in these different languages to denote this nineteenth province: (1) SCYTHIA (Phonetic: Saka—or according to Professor Rawlinson, "Sacae"), and (2) Scythia (Phonetic: SAKKA), and (3) the land of the CIMMERIANS (Phonetic: GI-MI-RI).

The next question confronting us is who were these Scythians, Saka (Sacae), Cimmerians and the Gi-mi-ri? These are the various names which were applied to a people mentioned by Darius I and listed as the nineteenth of the twenty-two provinces which were subject to him.

VARIATIONS OF THE NAME "OMRI"

The Ethnic name of Gimiri first occurs in the Cuneiform records of the time of Darius Hystaspes, as the Semitic equivalent of the Arian name Saka (Sakai) . . . Whether at the same time these Gimiri or Saka are really CYMRIC CELTS we can not positively say . . . But . . . the Babylonian title of Gimiri, as applied to the Sacae, is not a vernacular but a foreign title, and . . . may simply mean "THE TRIBES" (Rawlinson, History of Herodotus, Bk. IV, Appendix, Note 1).

Notice Rawlinson appeared to believe that these Saka or Gimiri were CYMRIC CELTS. Also note that he says SACAE may mean "THE TRIBES." No nation or people have been spoken of so long and so consistently by the words "the tribes" as the people of Israel. One still hears about the Twelve Tribes of Israel, the "Lost Tribes" and similar expressions. Notice what Rawlinson says regarding these names:

As on the one hand, however, the termination of the name is certainly miri or mirri, while on the other, the identification of the Persian SACAE or SCYTHIANS with the people named by the Greeks KIMMERIOI . . . would seem highly probable, I venture . . . to read the entire name GIMIRI . . . (The Royal Asiatic Society, p.21).

Following are some important comments by Dr. Pinches regarding the name "Omri."

That Jehu, who destroyed the house of Omri, should be called "son of Omri" in the inscriptions of Shalmaneser II of Assyria is strange, and needs explanation . . . That Jehu may have been in some way related with Jehoram, and therefore a descendant of Omri, is possible and even probable. That he was not descended from him in a direct line is certain (The Old Testament in the Light of Historical Records and Legends of Assyria and Babylonia, 3rd ed., p.339).

It is well to point out that the Hebrews and other Semitics commonly spoke of one as being a "son of"—not only of the person's immediate father; but this expression was also applied to one who was a grandson, or a great-grandson, or a great-great-grandson, and so on, to any number of generations. Thus, Christ was a "son of David." The word "father" was also applied to one's distant parents as well as to one's own immediate father.

OMRI—PRONOUNCED AS GHOMRI

It is noteworthy that the Assyrian form of the name, Yaua, shows that the unpronounced aleph at the end was called him Yahua (Jehu). OMRI was likewise pronounced in accordance with the older system, before the ghain became ayin. HUMRI shows that they said at that time GHOMRI (ibid., p.339).

The statement just made by Dr. Pinches is of utmost importance. Did you notice that the word "HUMRI" was pronounced, according to the older way of pronouncing the Hebrew, as "GHOMRI"? In other words the names "Humri" and "Ghomri" of the ancient historians, refer to the same people. This is a most important point to keep in mind. The names Humri and Ghomri are synonymous and consequently refer to the same people. According to the Behistun Rock Inscriptions the Gimiri (GHOMRI) were the same people as the Sacae or Scythians, who gave birth to the Saxons, Celts, Cimmerians, Scots, Angles, Gauls, Cymri and other peoples who settled North-western Europe.

It is also important to point out that the Hebrew word "BETH" means house. "Bethel" means "House of God," "Bethlehem" means "house of bread."

The Assyrian language was also a Semitic language, closely related to Hebrew. But the Assyrian word for "house" is "BIT"—not "beth" as in the Hebrew. The expressions "Bit-Omri" or "Bit-Humri," or "Bit-Humria," or "Bit-Ghomri," (all of which meant the "House of Omri") referred to the Northern House of Israel, the House or Kingdom over which Omri and his dynasty had ruled for many years.

On the Behistun Rock Inscriptions we have seen that the words Scythia, Saka (Sakka), Cimmerians, Gimiri, all refer to the same people.

Later on we shall see a number of historical sources proving that the Cymry, Khumri, and the Cimmerians were all the same people and were always placed by all historians in the extreme western part of Europe.

Today we know the Welsh still call themselves Kymry or Cymry!

The Cimmerians according to the ancient historians were located in the extreme western parts of Europe, including the British Isles.

For further proof that the Cimmerians (or Cimbri) dwelt in the extreme western parts of Europe, check the following references: (Homer, Odyssey XI, 13-19), (Herodotus I. 6,15,16,103; and IV. 1,11 et seq). (Strabo, I. 20,61; 309; XI 494).

ISRAEL CALLED CIMMERIANS, GIMIRI AND CYMRY

The importance of the dynastic name of Omri (Ghomri) in connection with the later history of the people of Israel has been clearly demonstrated. We have seen Omri and the House of Omri (Bit-Humri) and the land of Omri (mat-Humri) as mentioned by the Assyrians. It has also been pointed out from a number of historical sources that the Assyrians continued to call Israel by the name of Omri for centuries after he had died. They were, in fact, still speaking of the people of Omri and the territory of Northern Israel as "mat Bit-Humri" and as "mat Omri" at the time of the captivity of Israel.

From the Behistun Rock Inscriptions, we have seen clearly pointed out that these inscriptions speak of the Gimiri (Ghomri) as being identical with the Cimmerians, who were also the same as the Scythians and the Sacae (Saka).

Since the Cimmerians are the same people as the Gimri, and these are the same as the people of Omri or Ghomri (according to Dr. Pinches), let us now trace these peoples from the land of their captivity in South-western Asia to their present lands.

Who were the Cimmerians, Gimiri and the Kymry?

The Encyclopedia Britannica gives the folowing account of the Cimmerians:

> Cimmerii . . . Herodotus (iv. 11-13), in his account of Scythia, regards them as the early inhabitants of South Russia (after whom the Bosporus Cimmerius [q.v.] and other places were named), driven by the Scyths along by the Caucasus into Asia Minor, where they maintained themselves for a century . . . Certainly it is that in the middle of the 7th century B.C., Asia Minor was ravaged by northern nomads (Herod. iv. 12), one body of whom is called in Assyrian sources GIMIRRAI and is represented as coming through the Caucasus . . . [the very region of Israel's captivity]. To the north of the Euxine their main body was merged in the invading Scyths. Later writers identified them with the Cimbri of Jutland, who were probably Teutonized Celts (11th ed., Vol. VI, Art. Cimmerii, p. 368).

According to the above account, the Cimmerii lived anciently in the vicinity of the Black Sea. They early had an encounter with the Scyths. It was about 650 B.C.—100 years after Israel's captivity—that this occurred. Remember, some of the tribes of Israel went into captivity south of the Caucasus in 741 B.C.!

Also note carefully that at least one body of these Cimmerii were called by the Assyrians Gimirrai, and also that they are represented as "coming through the CAUCASUS." This is the same area where Israel was taken captive. We are informed by this article that their main body was merged to the north of the Black Sea (Euxine) in the invading Scyths. We shall later see some of the Scythians were called Celto-Scythians.

These Cimmerians were also later "identified with the Cimbri of Jutland" and we are further told that they were "probably Teutonized CELTS." Observe that the names of Cimbri, Cimmerii and Celts are all inextricably connected and are in turn closely allied to the Scythians whom we shall later study in much greater detail.

We are further informed by the Encyclopedia Britannica that these Cimmerians or Cimbri wandered along the Danube for many years, and that the Cimbri later had an alliance with the Teutoni, and that they invaded northern Italy (ibid., Vol. VI, Art. Cimbri, p.368).

Robert Owen says:

> In leaving the far east, they [the Kimmerians or Kymry] must have occupied
> a country south of the Caucasus, extending from the river Araxes to the Palus
> Maeotis or Sea of Azof, where Herodotus remarks on the many places yet
> bearing the name of Kimmerian in his time (The Kymry p.11).

Did you notice that these Kimmerians had formerly occupied a country "south of the CAUCASUS"? This is the very territory to which Israel had been taken captive. So we see that these people must have moved northwards through the Caucasus Mountains about one century after going into captivity!

> I have sought in the nomenclature of rivers and mountains some grounds
> for inferring the occupation of the country east of the Euxine Sea [Black Sea]
> by Kelts or traces of their presence, which any temporary irruption in later times
> will never suffice to explain (ibid., p.12).

Owen then shows that the Kymry had long occupied this territory. He mentions some tribal displacements, so common in barbaric Asia. The Massagetae invaded the Scythians, and they in turn threatened the Kimmerioi, who chose to avoid an unequal conflict by fleeing. Thus early began the inveterate duel between the Kelts and the Teutons, the Kymry and the Saxons. "This established historic event occurred B.C. 635" (ibid., pp.14,15).

> I avoid dwelling on France or Gallia, because its Keltic origin is incontestable;
> the proofs are abundant; and my aim is to illustrate only a portion of the race,
> the Kymry, as the Welsh still call themselves. To them their Amorican brethren
> are still Britons (Brython) (ibid., p.25).

He then mentions that "The account of themselves rendered by the Kymry of Britain makes them to consist of three tribes of the same stock . . ." (ibid., p.26). These three tribes were the (1) the Kymry, (2) the Lloegrwys, and (3) the Brython.

> I cannot resist concluding that either the Kimbri were Kymry, or else that
> in remote times the tongues of Kelt and Goth agreed . . . It is not impossible
> that some of the Kimmerioi, who retired from their Asiatic home before the
> onset of the Scythians, took a northern course, which the pursuers afterwards

followed under the conduct of Odin from the Sea of Azov to the shores of the Baltic" (ibid., pp. 26,27).

Owen explains that before the Bretons reached England, they had invented or inherited the essentials of an earlier civilisation. "SOME OF THEIR TRADITIONS RESEMBLE SEMITIC RECORDS OF ANTEDILUVIAN PATRIARCHS" (ibid., p.33).

He continues: "Few of the modern Kelts, Kymry, Brezonet, and Gael, are aware that the apostle S. Paul addressed an epistle to a people of their blood and kindred" (ibid., p.43). Yet such is indubitably substantiated by the facts. It will be more appropriate to cover this subject in greater detail in a later chapter, but it is interesting to note that Robert Owen, in the preceding statements, mentioned that the Kelts, Kymry, Brezonet and the Gael are all the same people!

Lysons makes this very interesting statement:

> I confess but for the universal tradition which assigns our [BRITISH] descent to Japheth, I should have been rather inclined to attribute to the British Celts a SEMITIC origin, which we find in Britain, and also on account of the language, the traces of which we find still attaching to the names of those places where they carried on their religious ceremonies (Our British Ancestors, p.18).

In other words, what Lysons admits is that the facts prove that the British are, after all, Semitic in origin, and not Japhetic as tradition would have us believe. Lysons remarks:

> The Cimmerians seeming to be the same people with the Gauls or Celts under a different name; and it is observable that the Welch, who are descended from the Gauls, still call themselves Cymri or Kymry (ibid., p.23).

And on page 27 we read:

> The identity of the Cymri of Wales with the Cymbri of the Romans, seems worthy of being accepted as an historic fact, upon the ground stated by Niebuhr and Arnold (ibid., p.27).

Notice how Lysons identifies all of the following peoples, and makes them come from Armenia—the very place where Israel was first taken into captivity. Armenia is located in the area just south of the Caucasus Mountains. Lysons says:

> The chain of evidence seems to be complete. Appian (De Bell. Illyr., p.758) says the Cimbri were Celts. Diodorus says that the Cimbri were Gauls or Celts; the GAULS were GALATAE per syncope GELTAE or KELTAE: The names are synonymous (Caesar de Bell, Gall., lib. i). The way in which Mr. Rawlinson, in the Essay from which I have quoted, brings the Cymric Celts from Armenia to Britain is most masterly; it confirms all the traditions of the Welsh, the views of Nennius and the Anglo-Saxon Chronicles and all our earliest histories, and to anyone who has studied the question, seems most convincing (ibid., p.27).

Notice that Lysons shows that the name Geltae is the same as Keltae, and this name is related to Galatai, Galli and other cognate names. These points all show conclusively that these are all basically the same people.

It is interesting to note that according to Lysons the Anglo-Saxon Chronicle also shows that some of the early inhabitants of Britain had come from ARMENIA.

Here is the actual wording of this as it is found in the Anglo-Saxon Chronicle:

> The island Britain is 800 miles long, and 200 miles broad, and there are in the island five nations; English, Welsh (or British), Scottish, Pictish, and Latin. The first inhabitants were the Britons, who came from ARMENIA, and first peopled Britain southward (p.21, translated by James Ingram).

This statement clearly shows that the British (or the Britons) had their origin in Armenia. Bear in mind that the Lost Ten tribes were deported from the land of Israel into the district immediately south of the Caucasus Mountains, or to the vicinity of Armenia.

Lysons also shows that Gimiri were the same people as the Cimmerii (Our British Ancestors, p.26).

Sharon Turner, in his History of the Anglo-Saxons, mentions the following points regarding the Kimmerians. He shows that the Keltic language was the same as the Kimmerian language (ibid. Vol. I, p.23). He says the Kelts were the same people as the Kimmerians, and that they inhabited the far west of Europe (ibid., p.24). The Kimmerians and Kelts were the same as the Kimbri, or to be more exact, he says:

> That the Kimmerioi of the Greeks were the Kimbroi of the Greeks, and the Cimbri (Kimbri) of the Latin writers, was not only the opinion of Posidonius, whom Strabo quotes, Lib. VII, p.293 . . . Diodorus Siculus expressly says, that to those who were called Kimmeriois, the appelation of Kimbron was applied in the process of time . . . Plutarch, in his life of Marius also identifies the Kimbri with the Kimmerioi (ibid., fn. p.28).

Turner shows that the Kimbri were a branch of the Kimmerians (ibid., pp.28,30). The Kumri were the same according to Turner, as the Cymry, and they were the same people as the Kimbri. The Kymry were the "first inhabitants of Britain" (ibid., p.32).

He mentions that the Welsh Triads show that Hu Cadarn or Hu the Strong (or Mighty) led the people of the nation of Kymry through the Hazy, or the German Ocean, into Britain, and to Llydaw (Amorica) in France. Turner mentions that the Cymry came from the eastern parts of Europe—the regions where Constantinople now stands. This is mentioned also in Triad 4, p.57.

Another interesting point mentioned by Turner is that "The Kymbri swore by a brazen bull, which they carried with them" (History of the Anglo-Saxons, Vol. I, p.34).

Keep this fact in mind because a number of historical sources show that the early inhabitants of Britain swore by the brazen bull, and used the symbol of an ox or a bull commonly, as a representative figure for their people. This all ties in with the early history of Israel, who, even in the time of Moses and Aaron, set up the golden calf and worshipped it. At the time when the Ten Tribes of Israel revolted from the leadership of the throne of David, the first thing that Jeroboam, the ruler of the Northern Kingdom did was to set up two golden calves, one in Dan, and the other in Beersheba (I Ki. 12:28) The tribal emblem of Joseph was a bull and/or heifer according to various accounts. The people of Britain still use this symbol on the coat of arms. It is there called a unicorn. Also "John Bull" is symbolical for the nation or people of Britain.

Turner mentions that the Keltoi were the same people as the Galatai, and that the Galatai were the same as the Galli, and that the Keltoi were "one of the branches of the Kimmerian stock (ibid., p.36).

Grant says that the northern one-third of France in Caesar's time was inhabited by the Belgae, who were a Nordic people of the Cymric division of Celtic speech (The Passing of the Great Race, p.194). He mentions that the Cimmerians, the Sacae and the Massagetae all sprang from the Scythians (ibid.).

He also points out that the CIMMERIANS were Nordics who entered Asia Minor by the CAUCASUS ABOUT 650 B.C. (ibid., pp. 214, 258).

Again note that the Cimmerians came into Asia Minor by way of the Caucasus Mountains about 100 years after the first segment of Israel had been deported into that very region in 741 B.C.

Grant says:

> The Nordics [referring to Cimmerians etc.] also swept down through Thrace into Greece and Asia Minor, while other large and important groups entered Asia partly through the Caucasus Mountains, but in greater strength they migrated around the northern and EASTERN sides of the CASPIAN-ARIAL SEA (ibid. p.214).

Notice how this indicates the very territory to which Israel had been deported about 100 years earlier.

When the Assyrian power was beginning to wane, these captive peoples availed themselves of the opportunity to flee from under the oppressive yoke of their Assyrian overlords.

That the Cimbri and the Cimmerii were identical is also clear from the following statements:

"Cimbri, A Celtic people, probably of the same race as the Cymry . . . They appeared to have inhabited the peninsula which was called after them Chersonesus Cimbrica (Smith, Smaller Classical Dictionary, Art. Cimbri, p.150).

Speaking of these people, Smith says: "Cimmerii . . . The historical Cimmerii dwelt on the Palus Maeotis (Sea of Azov), in the Tauric Chersonesus, and in Asiatic Sarmatia" (ibid., Art. Cimmerii, p.150,151). In this instance, the Cimmerii are mentioned as living north of the Black Sea.

If we carefully piece together all of the various points which are clearly brought out by the different historians concerning the Cimmerians, the Gimiri and the Kymry, we are brought to the following conclusions:

(1) The Cimmerians appear in history in the same general vicinity to which Israel had been taken captive.

(2) They appear about one century after the first tribes of Israel were deported into the regions south of the Caucasus Mountains, near the Black and Caspian Seas—about 741 B.C.

(3) All of these peoples are closely related i.e. the Cimmerians, Gimiri, and the Kymry.

(4) They leave the area of Armenia, or the Caucasus regions, and arrive in North-west Europe. In fact, as we will see later, branches of these Cimmerians penetrated into Central Europe, North Italy, Spain, and into many countries of Europe, as well as into Britain and Scandinavia.

(5) We have also observed that these Cimmerian or Kymric peoples are also closely related to the Gauls and Kelts, but this particular phase will be covered more thoroughly in a later chapter.

(6) All of these peoples were sprung from the Scythian hoard, and mixed freely with them. The fact that they fought with the Scythians does not mean they were not close relatives of the Scythians. We have previously observed that the tribes of Israel even while still living in the Promised Land were continually warring among themselves, as is also mentioned in James 1:1; 4:1.

(7) The Cimmerians were the same as the Gimiri who were also the same as the Ghomri or the people of Omri. These peoples were different branches of Dispersed Israel.

CHAPTER V

THE PHYSICAL CHARACTERISTICS OF THE CELTS

Before concluding our study of the Cimmerian branch of the dispersed Israelites, let us examine more closely the people who were known in history as the "Celts." We have already seen that the Gauls, Cimmerians, Cymry and the Celts are all simply different offshoots of the CIMMERIAN branch of the great SCYTHIAN people.

The subject of the physical composition of the Celtic peoples is one of the most controversial on the study of European history (Coon, Races of Europe, p. 186). Some have argued that the Celts were tall and blond; others have maintained that they were dark and short. The truth of the matter, as we shall soon see, is that the celtic peoples contained both blond and brunette elements.

We are informed in the Encyclopedia Britannica that the ancient writers never applied the term "Celt" to any dark-complexioned person. They always spoke of the Celts as having (1) great stature, (2) fair hair, and (3) blue or grey eyes. The Greeks spoke of all fair-haired people north of the Alps as Kelts or Keltoi (11th ed., Vol. V, Art. Celt).

The Encyclopedia Britannica mentions that the Celts were of two types:

(1) N.W. European—with its chief seat in Scandinavia. This type of Celt has a long head, long face, narrow nose, blue eyes, very light hair and great stature. They are also known as Teutons.
(2) Alpines—who inhabit the mountainous districts of Europe. They have a broad head, broad face, heavy, broad nose, hazel-grey eyes, light chestnut hair, medium height, and thick-set body.

There is every reason to believe that the original Celts, like the early Teutons and Germani, were primarily of "Nordic" racial type even though a number of round—or broad-headed Alpine type were undoubtedly included among them. This name "Celt" has certainly been applied in later times to some Alpine types.

The Teutons are universally held to be Celts (Ency. Brit., Vol. V, Art. Celt). All of the Celtae or Galatae in France had come across the Rhine. The Belgic tribes in Northern France were Cimbri who had crossed the Rhine. We are also informed that the UMBRIANS were Alpine Celts. This article mentions that the CIMMERIANS were the same as the GIMIRRI mentioned in the Assyrian monuments (ibid.).

The ancient writers spoke of all the GAULS as CIMBRI and identified them with the CIMMERIANS of earlier date. The CELTS mixed freely with the SCYTHIANS and were called Celto-Scythians (ibid.).

The Celts had continued to move westward from the Black Sea and Caucasus region. We have already shown that all of these Celtic or Cimbric peoples had their origin in the vicinity of the Caucasus Mountains—the very place to which Israel were deported (ibid). We are informed in this same article that the Belgae were of Cimbric origin.

When did the Celts begin their period of expansion? According to the article just referred to in the Encyclopedia Britannica, we are told that the "general Celtic unrest" occurred in the 6th century B.C. This was about two centuries after the Ten Tribes were deported to the Caucasus Mountain region.

Dr. Guest mentions the following points regarding the Celts: He says that the early Greeks employed Kimmeriori as a general name for the Celtic races (Origines Celticae, Vol.1, p.7). These Kimmeriori lived "to the furthest limit of the deeply flowing Ocean" (ibid., p.8). By that, he meant that they lived in the western part of Europe near the Atlantic Ocean. He mentions that the Celts or Kimmeriori lived in Spain and named a town there "Kimmeris" (ibid., p.10). The Celts also lived in the countries lying along the Mediterranean (ibid., p.17). Dr. Guest says that Herodotus stated the Kimmeriori were living formerly in the Crimea and in the steppes, stretching from the Don to the Dnieper (ibid., p.17). He then shows that the Kimmeriori were invaded by the Skuthai; and he says this took place in the 6th century B.C.! (ibid., p.17). And remember that this would have been about two centuries after Northern Ten-tribed Israel was taken captive by Assyria to the Caucasus regions.

"Our most trustworthy authorities," says Dr. Guest, "agree in fixing these events in the LATTER PART OF THE SIXTH CENTURY B.C." (ibid., p. 17).

CELTS ALSO CALLED GAULS

The Romans called the Celtic race by the name Galli (ibid., p. 38). The Kimbroi (Kelts) were supposed to have emigrated, according to Dr. Guest, from the Pontic Scythia (Scythia north of the Black Sea) into Europe over a period of many years (ibid., p. 43). He also mentions that these Kelts were known as Kelto-Skuthai, or Kelto-Scythians. Dr. Guest says that Plutarch's (Marius II) employs this phrase "Kelto-Skuthai" to designate the Kimbric migration which had early passed from the Pontic Scythia to the western Ocean—to the territory of Jutland which we now call Denmark. He also informs us that the words "VOLCAE," "BOLCAE," and "BELGAE," all refer to the same people (ibid., p. 378). The GAELS were the same people as the GALLI, and the Belgae were a Gaelic race (ibid., p. 385).

Other points worth noting are mentioned by Dinan in his Monumenta Historica Celtica, Volume I. He states that the Adriatic Celts came to Alexander the Great for the purpose of establishing a treaty of good will and "guest friendship." Alexander asked them what they feared most, supposing that they would answer that he was the chief object of their dread. They replied that they feared most that the sky might fall upon them. Alexander made a treaty with them, but thought they were a bit arrogant.

It is interesting to observe that one of the Celtic tribes was called by the name "BRETTII" (ibid., p. 91). This tribe was undoubtedly related to the "BRYTHON" and other similar peoples who later came to the British Isles and gave their name to Britain.

There was a Celtic tribe, according to Dinan, called the "OMBRI"—"The land of the OMBRI" (ibid., p. 33); he mentions also a Celtic people known as the "UMBRI" who were supposed to have led a luxurious life (ibid., pp.35,53).

The "UMBRI" and the "OMBRI" were part of the Celtic division of the dispersed "land of Omri" or House of Omri or people of Omri (pronounced as Ghomri). They lived in North and Central Italy. One can easily see how these words are very similar in pronunciation. The Celts who lived in the far west (ibid., 43), were great admirers of the Greeks (pp. 45,51), and were on the most friendly terms with them.

Another point mentioned by Dinan proving the affinity of the Cimbri and the Celts is that Pytheas discovered that the Cimbri spoke a Celtic tongue (ibid., p.54).

Dinan says that according to Poseidonius of Apamea, the Galatae were of tall stature, had soft flesh and white skin, and naturally blond hair, which they often bleached still further (ibid., p. 313). Speaking of the women of Galatae, Dinan says: "Their children at birth are generally of fair hair, but as they grow up it assumes the colour of their fathers" (ibid., p. 323).

The Galatae (Celts) were famed for their courage (ibid., pp. 323,325). He also mentions that these Galatae were formerly known as Cimmerians, Cimbri, and as Gallo-Graecians (ibid.).

Lysons says that "The CELTS had a unvarying tradition that they CAME FROM THE EAST" (Our British Ancestors, p. 27), and we have observed earlier that these Cymric Celts came from Armenia to Britain (ibid., p. 27). Some think "Armenia" should read "Armorica," but we have seen from the Anglo-Saxon Chronicle that it plainly says "Armenia," and that is exactly what it means! These Cymric Celts and Gauls came from Armenia in the area of the Caucasus.

"In addition to the Keltic invaders of Anatolia . . . other tribes, such as the UMBRI, began about the same time to over run Italy along with the Kelts from Noricum" (Kephart, Races of Mankind, p. 284). And on page 302 we read ". . . other Keltic intruders, the UMBRI from Illyria, entered the Po River valley and pushed earlier arrivals ahead of them down the eastern coast and the Apennines." We also read of the etruscans invading Northern Italy from Tyre and "driving the UMBRI to Central Italy" (ibid., p. 302). We are further informed that ". . . the Volsci were a branch of the UMBRI in Central Italy . . ." (ibid., p. 304).

Who were these Celtic "UMBRI" or "Ombri"? Why, there can be no doubt whatsoever—they were people of Cymric or Cimmerian origin; and remember the Cimmerians were the same people as the Gimirri, mentioned in the Babylonian language on the Behistun Rock Inscriptions.

Sharon Turner, in his History of the Anglo-Saxons, Vol. I, mentions the following important points regarding the Celts. Firstly, he equates the Celts (or Kelts) with the following peoples—Keltoi, Kimmerians (Cimmerians), and Kimmerii, Kimbri, Cymry, Kymry, Kumri, Galatai, Galli, (pp. 23-41). Secondly, he shows that the Keltoi were "one of the branches of the Kimmerian stock" (ibid., p. 36). Thirdly, he mentions that the home-base of the Celts was France (ibid., p. 41), and from France and Belgium, they spread themselves virtually over the whole of Europe, including the British Isles. Fourthly, he shows that these Kymry (or Celtae) had come from the eastern part of Europe, from Constantinople. Fifthly, he mentions that the Keltic language was identical with the Kimmerian language, proving still further that the Celts and the Cymry were all the same people. They were all branches of the great Cimmerian stock which came from the Caucasus regions in the vicinity of present-day Armenia.

> The Celts were described by the ancient writers as men of large stature, of fair complexion, and with flaxen or red hair. They were long the terror of the Romans: once they took Rome, and laid it in ashes (B.C. 390) (Smith, A Smaller Classical Dictionary, Art. Celtae, p. 137).

Note that they occupied the western parts of Europe a few centuries before Christ. "Celtae, [were] a mighty race, which occupied the greater part of western Europe in ancient times" (ibid., p. 137).

After mentioning that the Celtae, Galatae, and the Galli were all the same people, Turner shows that the Kelts had spread themselves over much of Europe.

Besides the Celts of Gaul, we are informed that there were eight other different settlements of these Celtic peoples. There were:

(1) Iberian Celts who crossed the Pyrenees and settled in Spain. They were known as the Celtiberi.
(2) The British Celts who were the most ancient inhabitants of Britain, or Britannia.
(3) The Belgic Celts. They were the earliest inhabitants of Gallia Belgica.
(4) The Italian Celts. They had crossed the Alps at a fairly early period and settled in Northern Italy which was called after them, Gallia Cisalpina.
(5) There were Celts in the Alps and on the Danube who were known as the Helvetii, the Gothini, and a number of other tribes.
(6) The Illyrian Celts.
(7) The Macedonian and the Thracian Celts. They had remained behind in Macedonia while their Celtic brethren had invaded Greece, and
(8) The Asiatic Celts. They were known as the Tolistobogi, Trocmi, and Tectosages, who founded the kingdom of GALATIA (Smith, A Smaller Classical Dictionary, Art. Gatae, p. 137).

Deniker mentions that the Trans-Alpine Celts or Galatians invaded JUTLAND in the 5th century B.C. under the name of Celto-Belgae. Also, at this same time they invaded North Germany, the Low Countries and England. (The Races of Man, pp. 321, 322). He says that:

"The Roman conquest of Trans-Alpine Europe, effected in the 1st century B.C. and A.D. imposed the language of Latium on the majority of Celts, Iberians and Italo-Celts, and maintained the population within almost the same bounds during three centuries" (ibid., p. 322).

This shows when and how these Celts or Gauls came to speak a Latin tongue.

Dr. Wylie says:

"The new-comers brought with them the tradition of their descent. They called themselves Cymry or Kymbry. They are the GIMIRRAI of the Assyrian monuments. The Greeks, adopting their own designation, styled them Kimmerioi, and the Latins Cimbri" (History of the Scottish Nation, p. 15).

We have already seen that the "Gimirrai of the Assyrian monuments" are the same people as "Bit Humri"—the house of Omri, and we have also seen that Omri was a prominent king of Ten-Tribed Northern Israel!

Speaking of the Celts, he says:

"They are known in history by three names—the CELTAE, the GALATAE, and the GALLI. Their irruption from their primeval home in Central Asia was the terror of the age in which it took place. In the fourth century before Christ, after some considerable halt, they resumed their migrations westwards in overwhelming numbers and resistless force. They scaled the barrier of the Alps, rushed down on Italy, gave the towns of Etruria to sack, defeated the Roman armies in battle, and pursued their victorious march to the gates of Rome, where they butchered the Senators in the Capital, and had well nigh strangled the Great Republic in its infancy" (ibid., Chap. 5, pp. 47, 48).

The one Cimric family was divided into the NORTHERN and SOUTHERN branches. The NORTHERN branch inhabiting "from the shores of the German Ocean to the confines of Asia, and beyond, are known by the general name of SCYTHIANS. The SOUTHERN, who dwell in Belgium and France, and overflow—for their lands were fertile—into the mountains of Switzerland and the north of Spain, were the GAULS. Both peoples, as Tacitus informs us, spoke the same language, though differing slightly in dialect, and that language was the Gallic or Celtic.

"In process of time, the memory of their common parentage was lost, and the tribes or nations of later formation, of the Scythians and the Gauls, began to weigh heavily upon the earlier Kimbric races, by whom the various countries of Europe—empty until their arrival—had been peopled" (ibid., Chap. XX, p. 165).

The earliest population of Britain was Cimric, according to Dr. Wylie, but three new varieties, the Pict, the Scot and the Gaul finally all made their way to the British Isles where they settled. "There exists abundant evidence," he says, "to show that all the inhabitants of Britain, from this early period onward, were all sprung from the SAME STOCK, though they arrived in our island by different routes, and are known by different names" (ibid., p. 265).

He then mentions that the Bretons (or Cimri) and the Picts (the Caledonian Picts), the Belgae (or Gauls), and the Scots "were but four several branches from the same root, and that root was Gallic or Celtic" (ibid., pp 265,266).

Thus it is clear that all of the various tribes who have entered the British Isles at one time or another have all been of the great Scythian or Cimmerian branches of the human race; and that branch was composed almost completely of dispersed Israelites, who had lost their identity long before arriving in North-western Europe.

The Brut, or The Chronicles of the Kings of Britain also shows basically the same thing. Celtae, Galatai, Gaul and Gael are all considered as one people (p.250).

There can be no doubt that the Celts, the Cimbri, the Britons and the Cymri are identical (Mallet, Northern Antiquities, fn., p. 68.

Haddon says that the Belgae who occupied North-east Gaul and South-east Britain about the first century B.C. were not distinguished by Roman authors from pure Nordics (The Races of Man, p. 59).

We have noticed that the Belgae, and the Celts were mainly fair and Nordic in type. Now let us see what archaeology can do to enlighten us as to the racial affinities of these Celtic peoples.

We have earlier noted that Coon mentioned the confusion which exists over the subject of the Celts. He speaks of the CELTIC EXPANSION which began about 500 B.C.; he mentions that it was a rapid and extensive one (Races of Europe, p. 187), including Italy, Spain, Asia Minor and most of Continental Europe. The center of dispersion was Belgium and Northern France (ibid., p. 187).

The KELTS introduced trousers into Western Europe. This garment, he says, was Central Asiatic in origin and was typical of the SCYTHS (ibid., p. 187). This is just another link showing that the Celts and the Cymry were all sprung from the Scythian people.

Were the Celts long-headed, or round-headed? Coon says that both types were represented in the Celts (ibid., p. 188).

In Bohemia, out of 27 crania, we are told that most were "dolichocephalic" (long-headed), but that there was a "significant minority of brachycephals" (ibid, 188). It is well to bear in mind that the Keltic Boii, who once lived in Bohemia and who gave their name to it, are no longer found there in any great numbers. He says that the skulls from the Swiss and other series were primarily a long-headed type (ibid., p. 189).

The well-known "Dying Gaul" and similar statues are of mesocephalic or brachycephalic head form (ibid., p. 190). It may be well to add that some present-day Israelites living in the Low Countries, the Benelux countries, and in France and Switzerland are mesocephalic (medium-headed) or low brachycephalic (broad-headed).

The original Israelites must have been both round-headed as well as long-headed though modern day descendants of Ten-Tribed Israel have more long-heads than broad-heads.

Only the NORTHERN PART OF FRANCE, says Coon, received any great amount of KELTIC blood in the early populations of what later became the French nation (ibid., p. 191).

> Blondism was by no means characteristic of the Kelts as a whole. Rufosity was common, and the hair color was essentially mixed. Caesar himself noted the contrast between the ordinary Gauls and the partly Germanic Belgae, to whom he had to turn to find real blondes, for his triumph. Furthermore, the Romans noted the Keltic practice of bleaching the hair to simulate a blonde ideal, as in Greece" (ibid., p. 192).

According to this statement, we can see that it is not accurate to speak of all of the Celts as either blond or brunet. They were "mixed", but all historical references show that they tended more toward blondism.

When we consider all of the points which we have seen mentioned by all of the different authors, here is the picture which emerges: The Celts, Cymry, Cimmerians, Gauls, Galatians, Gaels and other peoples who ravaged and who finally populated much of Europe in past centuries were definitely a closely related people. They were all just different branches of the same Cimmerian stock; and we have seen that, though there were brunets among them, yet most historical sources show that blondism must have been predominant just as it is today in the countries which were finally settled by these Cymric or Celtic peoples. (Remember, the word "blond" also denotes varying shades of brown, whereas brunet simply means very dark brown or black hair.)

We have also noticed a number of references showing a very close racial connection between the Cimmerian and the Scythian branches of these peoples. They were, as we have had clearly pointed out, all of the same type or "race" of people. We have also noticed that all of these peoples trace their origin back to the region of the Caucasus Mountains—the very place to which Israel was taken in 741, 721 B.C. Most of these Celto-Scythians were different segments of Israel in exile.

We have seen the origin of the Celtic peoples, but we have not gone into the origin of the word "Celt" or "Kelt" in this chapter.

Let us again notice an interesting statement by Lysons regarding the Celts.

> "The chain of evidence seems to be complete. Appian . . . says the Cimbri were Celts. Diodorus says that the Cimbri were Gauls or Celts; the Gauls were

> Galatae per syncope Geltae or Keltae: The names are synonymous . . . The way in which Mr. Rawlinson, in the Essay from which I have quoted brings the Cymric Celts from ARMENIA TO BRITIAN is most masterly."

According to the above statement, the word "Galatae" was also spelled as "Geltae" or "Keltae." This is seemingly according to Lysons, the derivation of the word Celt or Kelt.

It is possible that this name "Kelt" is derived from the name of a rivulet or a brook just northeast of Jerusalem, very near Jericho. The Encyclopedia Britannica speaks of this brook and calls it "Wadi Kelt" (11th ed., Vol, XIX, Art. Palestine, p. 602).

This same Wadi is mentioned a number of times in the Rand McNally Bible Atlas, but it speaks of it as the "Wadi el Qelt" (Chap. XIX, p. 395).

It is highly possible that this name comes from "Wadi Kelt." The Ten Tribes of Israel would have been familiar with this Wadi since many of them from Northern Israel would have passed near it on their way to observing the annual festivals in Jerusalem.

Kelts have never in modern times lived in the area of Jericho, but it is now abundantly evident that the ancestors of the present-day Kelts did once live in the vicinity of the "Wadi Kelt."

MANY GAULS (AND SOME GALATIANS) WERE ISRAELITES

What is the origin of such words as "Gaul," "Gael," "Galatian"? These and other related words are connected directly with the people of Israel from the time of their captivity!

The tribes of Reuben, Gad and the half tribe of Manasseh, lying east of the Jordan River, in the land of Bashan, were among the first of the Israelites (the Bit-Humi or Bit-Ghomri) to go into captivity in the year 741 B.C.

In the territory inhabited by the half tribe of Manasseh lying east of the Jordan, there was a city named "Golan." The word Golan is a Hebrew word and means "exile" or "captive." (Strong, The Exhaustive Concordance).

DISPERSED ISRAELITES WERE "GOLAH" OR "GAULAH"

Spier mentions the name by which the exiles of Israel were known, at the time of the Second Temple. He says: "The second holidays were adopted by the entire GOLAH, the communities living beyond the confines of Israel—[meaning the exiled Ten Tribes]" (The Comprehensive Hebrew Calendar, p. 11).

This Jewish author uses the word "Golah" when referring to the dispersed Israelites who were living beyond the confines of the Promised Land. Note the similar pronunciation of the words "Golah" and "Gaul." Speaking of the territory east of the Jordan River and the Sea of Galilee, Hurlbut says, "Decapolis . . . embraced no less than five sections as may be seen upon the map: (1) Gaulonities, the ancient Golan now Jaulan, east of the Jordan" (A Bible Atlas, p. 94).

This is speaking of New Testament Palestine. The city which was anciently called "Golan" had by New Testament times given its name to the district called "Gaulonities." (Ency. Biblica, Art. Golan, pp. 1747, 1748).

The word "Golan" had been slightly changed in spelling to Gaulon-itis, the land of the Gaulon, meaning the land of the dispersed. On pages 100, 101, 104, and 105 of Hurlbut's A Bible Atlas are maps illustrating this area lying immediately to the east of the sea of Galilee.

The celebrated Jewish historian, Josephus, speaks of a territory in the inheritance of Israel known as Gaulonitis. "He also gave Gaulonitis . . . to Philip, who was his son . . ." (Ant. Bk. XVIII, Chap. VIII par. I). See map IX.

We now know that the people of Israel who lived in the area of GAUL-on-itis or Golan went into their captivity in 741 B.C. Those "Gaulonites" from Gaulonitis were the first to be dispersed among the nations. Since they spoke Hebrew at the time of their exile, they must have called themselves "Golah" or Gauls meaning "Captives." These East-Jordanic Gauls, the exiles, or captives, who had been taken out of their land by the Assyrians, had probably ceased to pronounce the "h" sound by this time.

We shall see later on that these same people afterward bore the name "Gauls" in Europe and some of their kindred brethren also bore the name "Galatians," and lived in Central Asia Minor—in the heart of modern-day Turkey. The true Galatians (or Gauls) only comprised about one-tenth of the population of the territory of "Galatia."

THE ORIGIN OF "GAUL"—AN ENIGMA

The reader will search in vain, however, to find one historian who will give the true derivation of the word "Gaul" though there are different conjectures. The reason why seemingly nobody has understood the derivation of this word is that Israel was to be lost and scattered among the nations. Their identity was not to be revealed until these last days.

WHO WERE THE GAULS?

Speaking of the Gauls and Kelts, Funck-Brentano in his work, The Earliest Times, states that the Celts came from the north—from Jutland, Friesland and from the coasts of the Baltic. He says: "They were the Normans of the century before our era" (ibid, p. 27).

They called themselves "CELTS," but they were also known by the name of "GALATES," and the Romans called them "GALLI." To the ancients, the designations, Galli, Galates, and

Celts were synonymous. But he says that these three names may have designated three different branches of the same race originally (ibid, pp 27, 28).

A fourth branch was the Volcae—Walah, Wallachians, Wallons, and Welsh, all being derived from this Celtic name Volcae. The Celtic branch were tall and fair with pink and white skin. The Greek artists in the third century B.C. used the Gauls or Kelts as their ideal in sculpture and paintings (ibid., pp. 27,28).

The Gauls conquered Rome in 390 B.C. They conquered Great Britain, France except the Rhone basin, the whole of Spain except its Mediterranean coast, and north of Italy, parts of Germany, Russia, Switzerland, Hungary, Romania, and Silesia. Their empire was greater than either that of Charlemagne or of Napoleon—reaching from the Straits of Gibraltar to the Black Sea at the time when Alexander the Great was engaged in his conquest of Asia in 334 B.C. (ibid., 46, 47).

He mentions another interesting point. "They [the Gauls] loved bright and varigated colours in their clothes, coloured stripes and checks" (ibid., p. 67). Here we can see the tartan or "Scotch Plaid" which is still used by some of the present-day descendants of the Kelts who now live in Scotland.

There were two Roman Gauls: (1) Gallia Cisalpina (Hither), included North Italy between the Alps and Apennines, and (2) Gallia Transalpina (Further), encompassed modern France, Belgium, and parts of Holland, Germany, and Switzerland.

"The Greek form of GALLIA was GALATIA, but Galatia in Latin denoted another Celtic region in Central Asia Minor, sometimes styled Gallograecia" (Ency. Brit., 11th ed., Vol. XI, Art. Gaul p. 532).

It is interesting to note that Livy and the elder and younger Pliny were Celts.

Julius Caesar in his Commentaries says that Gaul in his day was divided into three peoples—(1) Aquitani, (2) Gauls or Celts and (3) Belgae.

THE ORIGIN OF THE GALATIANS

Who were the Galatians? All history shows that they were a Gaulish tribe who had come from European Gaul, and had gone to Asia Minor where they finally settled. The territory in which they settled was known as Galatia. This territory was an inland district in Asia Minor, occupied by these Gaulish tribes in the 3rd century B.C. The 20,000 invading Gauls who finally settled this district were divided into three tribes: (1) Trocmi, (2) Tolistobogii and (3) Tectosages.

This was one of the peoples and the territories with which the Apostle Paul was directly connected. But how many of the people living in Galatia were of Gaulish or Keltic descent?

The Galatian (or Gaulish) overlords were naturally very few in number, and hardly lived in the towns at all (Ency. Brit. 11th ed., Vol. II, Art., Galatia, pp 393, 394).

"According to the majority of scholars, it [the term Galatians] denotes the people of Galatia Proper, a mixed population, consisting of A MINORITY descended from the three Gaulish tribes . . ." (Hastings, Dictionary of the Bible, Vol. II. Art. Galatians).

We are informed that in the large cities such as Ancyra, the Phrygians and others probably constituted the great majority of the population, "while Gauls were found there only as a small aristocratic caste"; but in the rural districts the Gauls were more numerous. They were a "small conquering caste of barbarians" among a more numerous population.

"It is doubtful whether so much as FIVE PER CENT of the total population was of GALLIC origin, and it is practically certain that in the great cities, an even smaller proportion of the population was of Gallic descent" (ibid.).

These dispersed Israelitish peoples who were living in Galatia in New Testament times, constituted an aristocratic, ruling caste, and were in the minority. The main bulk of the Galatians (probably about 95%) were of Gentile descent!

> A highly developed religious system reigned over the country . . . Thus the government was a theocracy and the whole system, with its prophets, priests, religion, law, punishments, . . . presented a remarkable and real resemblance in external type to the old Jewish ceremonial and religious rule" (Hastings, Dictionary of the Bible, Vol. II, Art. Galatians).

The Keltic Gauls told Caesar that the Belgians were of "German" descent, but Dr. Beddoe shows that this was not true (The Races of Britain, p. 20). He says that those who came to Britain were not, in the strict sense, "Germans" (ibid, p. 25).

He also says that at the time of the Roman conquest: "No Germans, recognisable as such by speech as well as person had as yet entered Britain" (ibid., p. 29).

For a masterly discussion of the ethnology of the Gauls, Celts, Cymry, the Belgae and related peoples, study carefully Caesar's Conquest of Gaul, Part II, Sec. II—The Ethnology of Gaul, pp. 245-322, written by T. Rice Holmes.

Holmes quotes many historians and ethnologists on the subject of the racial background of these peoples. He points out that though there have always been brunet elements among the Celts, Cymry, Belgae, and the Gauls, yet most of these peoples have tended more toward blondism. Where these peoples have mixed with Mediterraneans and other dark-haired peoples, they have tended to introduce more brunet elements into their midst.

He then produces a number of statements from foremost ethnologists which tend to show that the typical Celtic head form was long-headed, though there were medium—or broad-headed elements among them.

Another thing which is clear from his numerous quotations and statements is that the ancient "Germans" definitely had more of a long-headed element among them than they possess today. The dolichocephalic elements of ancient Germany have crossed over the Rhine and have in most instances moved into Northern France, Belgium, the Low Countries or have gone to Scandinavia or to the British Isles. Holmes also mentions the matter that the ancient Germans were known as very tall and had a lot of redheads among them. This rufosity is almost totally lacking in Germany today, except among the Sephardic Jews; and since World War II, there are probably very few of these still remaining in Germany. Most of the redheads who had lived at one time in Germany have moved to the countries of Scandinavia, the British Isles, or to other parts of North-west Europe. Some of the North Germans are quite blond, however, and may still represent the true Teutonic and Celtic element which has never left Germany. The dominant type in Germany today is the round—or broad-headed Alpine.

GAULS AND GALATIANS

Dr. Beddoe also mentioned that the "Volcae Tectosages of Tolosa appear to have been the same people with the Tectosages of Galatia . . ." (ibid., p.28). Many historians show a definite connection between these Gaulish peoples of France and those of Galatia, and they also show that their languages were similar if not identical.

The Kelts, Gauls, Galatians (as well as the Gaels) are, racially speaking, closely related. They are, in fact, a segment of the Golah or Gaulah—the exiles of Israel!

WHO WERE THE GERMANI?

Before the racial affinities of the peoples of Europe can be untangled, there is one more name which must be looked into, and properly understood. That is the name "Germani" (the Germans).

While studying the origin and movements of the Celts, Gauls, Kymry, and the other tribes who have passed at one time or another through Central Europe, a certain amount of confusion at times arises regarding the differences between Scythians, Kelts, Gauls, and Cimmerian tribes on the one hand and the proper or true Germans on the other.

There can be no doubt that most of the peoples of present-day Germany (except in the North) and Austria, from an ethnological and historical point of view, have no close blood ties with the peoples of Scandinavia and the British Isles. There are many striking differences between the peoples of the Scandinavian countries, the British Isles, and the Lowland countries when contrasted with the peoples of Southern Germany, Austria and the Eastern and Southern Europeans.

It is necessary to show that the majority of the present-day Germans are quite different from the British and Scandinavian types. Here are some points to keep in mind:

(1) The Saxon and other tribes who invaded Britain had at one time or another lived in Germania, and were therefore prior to their invasion of England, known as Germans. (2) Some of the Kelts who formerly lived east of the Rhine, and who were known as Germans, later emigrated to England, Belgium, France, etc. (3) The Caledonians and others were called Germans. (4) The Goths and Teutons are often equated with the Germans, but many of them were not "German" if by that word we mean to imply the present-day Alpine type of German.

All history attests that the Keltic, Kymric or Scythian peoples who passed through Germany en route to Britain, Scandinavia, the Lowlands, and Northern France were, racially speaking, different from the Alpine and "Slavic" types which today mainly constitute the German people.

It would appear that some of the North Germans of the "Nordic" variety are fairly closely related to British and Scandinavian types.

Here are some interesting excerpts from an article entitled Are We Cousin to the German? by Sir Arthur Keith.

> In the standard Atlases and school geographies the Germans colour Great Britain, Holland, Denmark, Norway and Sweden with the same tint as their own empire, to indicate that all those lands are inhabited by branches of the great Teutonic family . . . It is an historical fact that the Anglo-Saxons came into lands lying on the western shores of the present German Empire. Those, however, who have studied the modern population of Britain, and Germany, have reached a very definite and very different conclusion, namely, that the Briton and German represent contrasted and opposite types of humanity (The Graphic, 4th Dec, 1915, p. 720).

In the same issue of The Graphic, Sir Arthur Keith illustrated prevalent British and German forms of skulls. He pointed out the marked difference between the typical British skulls when contrasted with that of the average German. Speaking of the typical British and German skull form, he says:

> The radical difference in the two forms leaps to the eye. In the majority of BRITON—English, Welsh, Scottish and Irish—the hinder part of the head, the occiput, projects predominately backwards behind the line of the neck; the British head is long in comparison with its width (ibid., p. 720).

Sir Arthur Keith says that "in the vast majority of Germans" the hinder part of the head is "flattened." He mentions, however, that this "peculiarity of the German skull" is not due to "artificial means."

> We know that the prominent occiput and flattened occiput are characters that breed true over thousands of years, and that they are characters which indicate a profound racial difference. Even in the sixteenth century, Vesalius,

who is universally regarded as the 'father of Anatomy,' regarded the flat occiput as a German characteristic . . . He came, rather unwillingly, to the conclusion that the vast majority of modern German people differed from the British, Dutch, Dane and Scandinavian in head form (ibid., p. 720)

It is important to keep those points in mind. There is no close affinity, judging from skeletal observations and measurements, between the "vast majority of the German people" who are different, according to Sir Arthur Keith, from the "British, Dutch, Dane and Scandinavian in head form."

The typical German head is quite round, says Keith in comparison to the British, Scandinavian, Dutch and Dane head form. The German occiput is not nearly as pronounced as that of the North-west Europeans just mentioned.

This is an important point to bear in mind, as we shall note later that the Scythians, the Sacae and many of the Kelts who formerly inhabited the steppes of South Russia, were in head-shape like the long-headed North-west Europeans. The Alpine and "Slavic" elements in Germany, Austria and in Eastern Europe are not the same in head form as were the predominantly long-headed Scythians, and Sacae.

It is undeniable, from an anthropologist's point of view, that British and Germans belong to opposite European types. The explanation is easy. With the exodus of the Franks to France and the Anglo-Saxons to Britain in the fifth, sixth, seventh, and eighth centuries of our era, Germany was almost denuded of her long-headed elements in her population . . . When the Franks and the Anglo-Saxons were moving into France and England the great area now covered by the German Empire had been invaded from the east—from the regions now occupied by Russians, Poles, and Czechs—by swarms of people with flat occiputs and round heads—men of the Hindenburg type. History relates that by the end of the sixth century this type had overrun all the area of modern Germany, except the lands along the western shores (ibid., p.720).

All history shows the general trend has been that N.W. European long-headed peoples have continually advanced westward from the area of the Caucasus, and have invariably been succeeded by the broad-headed Alpine types who were continually pressing them from the East. These "Nordics" have also been pressed northward by the Mediterraneans of South Europe; or to put it more accurately the Nordics have made many incursions into the Mediterranean lands, but have never effected any permanent settlements there. Another interesting fact worth noting is the aptitude of the dolichocephals (long-heads) for the sea, and the absence of this sea-faring proclivity among the brachycephals.

Yet there can be no doubt that certain aptitudes do belong to certain races and breed true from generation to generation. The flat occiput has never shown any aptitude for the sea. All the races which have commanded the sea—the Portuguese, Spaniards, Dutch, Norwegians and British—have long heads with prominent occiputs. It is remarkable that even at the present day the German navy recruits its crews from the western shores, where a long-headed element still manages to survive (ibid., p. 720)

Ripley says that the ancient peoples who commanded the seas—Phoenicians, Greeks, and others were also of the long-headed type (Races of Europe, p. 387).

The modern-day Ossetes, are racially speaking almost identical with present day Germans. Many of their customs, manners, their physical appearance and other things prove this beyond question. Many writers have held this opinion.

> . . . a small and decreasing minority of blond traits among the Ossetes, a tribe whose Aryan speech is related to that of the Armenians, and who while mainly brachycephalic [broad-headed] still retain some blond and dolichocephalic [long-headed] elements which apparently are fading fast (Grant, The Passing of the Great Race, p. 66)

Notice, the Ossetes, who are close relatives of the German people, are also primarily a brachycephalic or a broad-headed type of people, even though they include certain minor elements of long-headedness, just as does modern Germany.

Later, we shall notice that the Sarmatians were a broad-headed people, and they are the ancestors of many of the Germans and Slavs.

Notice, Grant shows that the true Alpine type of skull is almost totally absent in Britain.

"In the study of European populations the great and fundamental fact about the British Isles is the almost total absence there today of true Alpine round skulls" (ibid., p. 137).

What is the average cephalic index in England?

"The cephalic index in England is rather low, about 78 (ibid., p. 137).

THE ALPINE GERMANS

> In fact, from the time of "the 30 year's war" the purely Teutonic race in Germany has been largely replaced by the Alpine types in the south and by the Wendish and Polish types in the east. This change of race in Germany has gone so far that it has been computed that out of 70,000,000 inhabitants of the German Empire, only 9,000,000 are purely Teutonic in coloration, stature, and skull characters (Grant, The Passing of the Great Race, p. 185).

It is indisputable from both history and personal observation that the dominant type of German is today that of the "Alpine" variety.

There formerly lived in Germany certain Keltic and Scythic tribes who were not Alpines, but very few of these remained in Germany. Most of them settled in the coastlands of North-west Europe, or else in the British Isles. We shall see more corroborative proof of this later.

> The eastern half of Germany has a Slavic Alpine substratum which represents the descendants of the Wends, who first appear about the commencement of the Christian era and who by the sixth century had penetrated as far west as the Elbe, occupying the lands left vacant by the Teutonic tribes which had migrated southward (ibid., p. 72).

One of the reasons why many fail to differentiate between the true or proper Germans and the peoples who passed through "Germania" and who were consequently called "Germani," is that the ancient historians did not make a distinction between the so-called, and the real Germans.

THE KELTIC GERMANI

Notice that Tacitus failed to draw a clear line of demarcation between the true Germans, as we think of them today, and those who were Germans in name only.

Huxley and Haddon make the following interesting remarks regarding Tacitus' comments on the "Germani."

> Fourthly, he [Tacitus] makes no distinction between the inhabitants of Gaul and the tribes east of the Rhine. Both are for him "Germani" . . . Fifthly, the tribes that he describes were all or most of them driven across the Rhine by later westward movements of peoples to the east of them. Thus they cannot be the ancestors of the modern Germans (We Europeans, p. 34).

Fleure also says that "the dominant broad-headedness of the Alpine" race has been spread over most of modern Germany. He shows that the broad-headedness has permeated from the South toward the North of Germany. He mentions that this has occurred in ancient as well as in modern times (Fleure, The Peoples of Europe, p. 42).

Huxley and Haddon mention that, "In the Germans there is a very large Eurasiatic element which includes the Slavonic, and genes from the Mongoloid peoples have crept in via Russia" (We Europeans, p. 278).

Dr. Guest says that certain of the Germanic tribes were called Kelts (Origines Celticae, p. 27, 37), but we have, however, already seen that some Kelts had formerly lived east of the Rhine. They were very red haired and were totally different from the typical present-day Germans. Dr. Guest mentions that the Keltic Belgae were sprung from the "Germans" (ibid., p. 390). He further states:

It would appear, then, that as early as the third century B.C. there were certain races called Germani settled north of the Alps and in the upper district drained by the Saone . . . These Germani were undoubtedly Celts. In the first century after Christ there were also Germani in Spain, and there can be little doubt, that they were descended from the [Keltic] Cimbri who invaded the Peninsula in the second century B.C. (ibid., p.392).

Again we read of certain people called "Germani" who were of Cimbric descent. Dr. Guest was of the definite conviction "these Germani were undoubtedly Celts." There can be no question that the Cimbri were a Celtic people. This shows that there were certain peoples who were called Germani, (meaning war men), who were settled not only east of the Rhine, but even in Spain.

One can easily see this word "German" was anciently applied to many different peoples whose modern descendants are not (in most instances) closely related to the present day proper Germans.

Dr. Dinan, says there was a Celtic tribe who were called "Germara" (Monumenta Historica Celticae, p. 81).

Coon says, "The excessive brachycephalization which swept over central Europe in the Middle Ages, affecting especially southern Germany and Bohemia, followed the same pattern as the stature change" (The Races of Europe, Vol. I, p. 10). He again mentions the "South German Brachycephaly" (ibid., p. 538).

This broad-headed element crept into Germany both during and since the Middle Ages.

THE GERMANS CAME FROM THE CAUCASUS

"The Germans were a branch of the great Indo-Germanic race, who, along with the Celts, migrated into Europe from the CAUSASUS and the countries around the Black and Caspian Seas" (Smith, A Smaller Classical Dictionary, p. 231).

Notice carefully that the Germans were a branch of the different peoples who migrated "along with the Celts" into Europe from the Caucasus regions in the vicinity of the Black and Caspian Seas—the very area of Israel's captivity! Remember, Israel had been taken to ASSYRIA!

It is beyond the scope of this chapter to prove that the present-day Germanic peoples are at least in great part descended from the ancient peoples of Assyria. There is, however, much historical material which clearly proves that many of the present-day Germanic peoples were included in the great horde of people called by the name of "Sarmatians."

In regard of the Alpine broad-headedness which is today found in most of Germany, Professor Ripley says:

Northwestern Germany—Hanover, Schleswig-Holstein, Westphalia-is distinctly allied to the physical type of the Swedes, Norwegians, and Danes. All the remainder of the Empire—no, not even excluding Prussia, east of the Elbe—is less Teutonic in type, until finally in the essentially Alpine broadheaded populations of Baden, Wurttemberg, and Bavaria in the south, the Teutonic race passes from view (The Races of Europe, p. 214).

According to Ripley, the people of North-western Germany are related in physical type to the Scandinavian.

Let us notice another statement showing that the English are dolichocephalic, in sharp contrast to the typical broad-headedness of the German.

The most remarkable trait of the population of the British Isles is its head form; and especially the uniformity in this respect which is everywhere manifested. The prevailing type is that of the long and narrow cranium, accompanied by an oval rather than broad or round face (ibid., p. 303).

He then mentions that the average cephalic indexes in the British Isles lie between 77 and 79.

What is the meaning of the word "German?" According to Kephart, the word "German" means "warrior" (Races of Mankind, p. 380).

GAULS AND BELGIC TRIBES WERE CALLED "GERMANI"

Here is a very significant excerpt from The Encyclopedia Britannica:

Of the Gaulish tribes west of the Rhine, the most important was the Treveri . . . the Treveri claimed to be of German origin, and the same claim was made by a number of tribes in Belgium, the most powerful of which were the Nervii. The meaning of this claim is not quite clear, as there is some obscurity concerning the origin of the name Germani. It appears to be a Gaulish term, and there is NO EVIDENCE THAT IT WAS EVER USED BY THE GERMANS THEMSELVES. According to Tacitus it was first applied to the Tungri, whereas Caesar records that four Belgic tribes, namely the Condrusi, Eburones, Caeraesi, and Paemani, were collectively known as Germani. There is no doubt that these tribes were all linguistically Celtic, and it is now the prevailing opinion that they were not of German Origin ethnologically, but that the ground for their claim was that they had come from over the Rhine (Caesar De Bello Callico ii 4). It would therefore seem that the name Germani originally denoted certain Celtic tribes to the east of the Rhine (11th ed., Art. Germany, p. 830).

Notice the following points which were just mentioned. The origin of "GERMANI" is uncertain, but it is apparently a "Gaulish term." This name "Germani" was anciently not used by the Germans themselves. Julius Caesar records the name of four "Belgic tribes who were collectively known as Germani" in his time. Did you notice that the language of these tribes was Celtic. This article then shows that "it is now the prevailing opinion" that these Belgic tribes "were not of German origin ethnologically."

These and many other historical sources have proven that it is wrong to speak of the bulk of the present-day Germans as close relatives to the British, the Scandinavians and related peoples. The true Germans were not Celts.

This same article then explains that in Caesar's time the Menapii, a Gaulish tribe, lived east of the Rhine. It also says that a Celtic tribe, called Boii, was expelled from Bohemia (ibid., p. 830).

Augustus Caesar mentions a number of Gaulish tribes living east of the Rhine, "There is therefore great probability that a large part of Western Germany east of the Rhine had formerly been occupied by Celtic peoples" (ibid., p. 830). We are told that the Volcae in the south of France and the Tectosages of Galatia were off-shoots of this people (ibid., p. 830).

> The first Teutonic peoples whom the Romans are said to have encountered are the Cimbri and the Teutoni, probably from Denmark, who invaded Illyria, Gaul and Italy towards the end of the 2nd century B.C. When Caesar arrived in Gaul the westernmost part of what is now Germany was in the possession of Gaulish tribes. The Rhine practically formed the boundary between Gauls and Germans, though one Gaulish tribe, the Menapii, is said to have been living beyond the Rhine at its mouth. (ibid., p, 831).

Bear in mind that the Kelts and the Gauls were different in race from the present-day proper Germans.

Mallet informs us that the Germans and Gauls were two distinct people" (Northern Antiquities, p. 7).

> It is true, the Gauls and ancient Germans resembled each other in complexion, and perhaps in some other respects, as might be expected from their living under the same climate, and nearly in the same manner—yet that they differed sufficiently in their persons, appears from Tacitus, who says that the inhabitants of Caledonia resembled the Germans in features, whereas the Silures were rather like the Spaniards, as the inhabitants of South Britain bore a great resemblance to the Gauls (ibid., p. 9).

It is hoped that the numerous reference cited will give the reader a sufficient knowledge of the "Germani" to enable him to see that many peoples in North-west Europe are today spoken of as though they were of "German" or "Teutonic" descent who are quite different ethnologically from the true Germans who now inhabit Central Europe.

We have observed that the name "Germani" was never applied by the Germans to themselves, but was first used by Gaulish (Keltic) tribes. Also we have seen clearly pointed out that many different peoples once inhabited territories in "Germania" and were, therefore, called Germans, who are not proper Germans as we think of them today.

"THE PATRIARCHAL SQUARE-HEADS"

Robert Graves makes an interesting comment:

> Arianrhod's giving of arms to her son is common Celtic form; that women had this prerogative is mentioned by Tacitus in his work of the Germans—the Germany of his day being Celtic Germany, not yet invaded by the patriarchal square-heads whom we call Germans nowadays (The White Goddess, p. 318).

This statement that "Celtic Germany" in the time of Tacitus had not as yet been invaded by the "Patriarchal square-heads whom we call Germans nowadays" shows that Germany was once inhabited by a Celtic population, which has long ago been supplanted by the Alpine brachycephals.

Here is one final quotation on the subject of the "Germani" from Huxley and Haddon:

"Fifthly, the Keltic tribes that he (Tacitus) describes were all or most of them driven across the Rhine by later western movements of peoples to the east of them. Thus they cannot be the ancestors of the modern Germans" (We Europeans, p. 34).

They conclude:

> Hence their physique, despite their vast numbers, is identical: fierce blue eyes, red hair (rutilae comae), tall frames . . . Historical and archeological investigation, however, has failed to support Tacitus. It may be noted that red hair is rare among modern Germans, save among those of Jewish origin (ibid., p. 36).

One must continually bear in mind that many peoples (especially certain non-Germanic Kelts, Gauls, Belgae and Scythians) have been called Germans who are not proper or true Germans as this term is used today.

If one does not continually bear this in mind when studying the ancient histories mentioning the various "German" tribes, he will never be able to properly understand the racial connections between all of the various people who have, at one time or another been called "Germans."

EARLY SCANDINAVIAN HISTORY

We have considered the backgrounds of most of the peoples of North-west Europe. It has been pointed out that, generally speaking, all of these peoples were related to one another.

Here are some of the names which these bore when they arrived in Europe: (1) Cimmerians, Cymri, and Cimbri. (2) Kelts, Gauls, and Gaels. (3) Scythians, Teutons, and Goths. (4) Angles and Saxons. (5) Tuatha de Danaan, Danes, etc. (6) Other names such as Belgians, Fir-Bolgs, etc. have been considered.

It has been proven that many of the early Germans were of Celtic or Cimbric origin and were not therefore closely related to the proper Germans of today.

We have also seen clearly demonstrated that all of the afore-mentioned peoples are related, and are all from the great Scythian people or nation.

What is the origin of the peoples of Scandinavia? Did they also come from Scythia as the other North-west Europeans whom we have previously considered?

We shall but briefly consider Scandinavian history, but we shall examine it thoroughly enough to show that these Scandinavians were merely another branch of the Scythian peoples.

The following quotation supports the belief that Denmark, one of the countries of Scandinavia, was of Scythian origin:

> It is very probable, that the first Danes, were like all the other Teutonic nations a colony of Scythians, who spread themselves at different times over the countries which lay towards the west. The resemblance of names might induce us to believe that it was from among the Cimmerian Scythians (whom the ancients placed to the north of the Euxine Sea) that the first colonies were sent into Denmark; and that from this people they inherited the name of Cimbri, which they bore so long before they assumed that of Danes (Mallet, Northern Antiquities, p. 60).

All Scandinavian literature records the acts of a celebrated person by the name of ODIN. The traditions and chronicles of all the northern nations inform us that this extraordinary person formerly reigned in the north. He made great changes in the government, manners and religion of all of those northern countries.

THE GREAT ODIN

> His [Odin's] true name was sigge son of Frieulph; but he assumed that of Odin, who was the Supreme God among the Teutonic nations: either in order to pass among his followers for a man inspired by the Gods, or because he was chief priest, and presided over the worship paid to the deity (ibid., p. 79, 80).

From what country did Odin and his people come? Odin and his followers, the Aesir, were from a country which was situated between the Pontus Euxinus (Black Sea), and the Caspian Sea (ibid., pp. 79, 80). The principal city of this former country was Asgard. Odin united the youth of the neighboring nations and marched towards the north and west of Europe, subjugating all the people he found in his passage, and giving them to one or the other of his sons to govern. Many regal families of the north are said to be descended from these princes. Thus Hengist and Horsa and the other Anglo-Saxon chiefs, who conquered Britain in the fifth century, considered Odin, or Wodin as their illustrious ancestor. This word Odin signified, as seen above, the Supreme God of the Teutonic nations.

A number of points in the foregoing quotation need to be emphasized. Firstly, it was mentioned that Odin and his followers came from a territory between the Black and Caspian Seas. Remember, this is in the general vicinity to which the Ten-Tribed House of Israel had been deported. Secondly, notice that the Anglo-Saxon British princes, Horsa and Hengist, were descendants of Odin. In a later chapter, we shall see historical proof that the Anglo-Saxons were the descendants of Sceaf or Shem. Odin must have been a descendant of Shem likewise since he was the ancestor of so many of the Anglo-Saxon kings!

After having conquered many territories between the Black and the Baltic Seas, Odin directed his final energies in subduing all of Scandinavia, "After having disposed of so many countries, and confirmed and settled his new governments, Odin directed his course towards Scandinavia, passing through Cimbria, at present Holstein and Jutland" (ibid., p. 80).

He then subdued the rest of Denmark and Sweden. He extended his conquests over all the north, and governed all of this territory with absolute dominion. He enacted new laws, and introduced the customs of his own country, and established at Sigtuna (not far from Stockholm) a supreme council or tribunal, composed of twelve judges or pontiffs. All of the petty kings among whom Sweden was then divided were quick to acknowledge him as a sovereign and a god. He levied a poll-tax or impost upon every person through the whole country.

"The desire for extending farther his religion, his authority and his glory, caused him to undertake the conquest of Norway." (ibid., pp. 81, 82). He had great success in his campaigns against Norway and this kingdom quickly obeyed a son of Odin name Saeming. We are told that Odin was "the most persuasive" of men.

After subduing the whole of Scandinavia, Odin retired into Sweden where he assembled his friends and companions and gave himself a mortal wound which resulted in his death. This suicidal act was brought about by a lingering disease which had overtaken him. He had bravely hazarded his life on the battlefield countless times, and could not bare the thought of falling victim to disease.

What had fired Odin with this unquenchable ambition to conquer such a vast territory?

> Driven from his country by those enemies [the Romans] of universal liberty; his resentment, say they, was so much the more violent, as the Teutonic tribes esteemed it a sacred duty to avenge all injuries, especially those offered to their relations and country. (ibid., pp. 82, 83).

Odin's chief aim was to stir up the Northmen of Scandinavia so that Rome's injustices could be avenged.

It was these hardy northern barbarians (if we may call them that) who later did more than any other people to overrun the Roman Empire and lay it in the dust.

> The men of the North who settled and conquered part of Gaul and Britain, whose might the power of Rome could not destroy, and whose depredations it could not prevent, were not savages; the Romans did not dare attack these men at home with their fleet or with their armies. Nay, they even had allowed these northmen to settle peacefully in their provinces of Gaul and Britain (du Chaillu, The Viking Age, Vol. I. p. 3).

The above statement shows that even Rome knew that these Northmen were powerful enough to prevent her assault on their homeland. Were these men of the north savages or barbarians in the true sense of the word?

> Know, the people who were then spread over a great part of the present Russia, who overran Germania, who knew the art of writing, who led their conquering hosts to Spain, into the Mediterranean, to Italy, Sicily, Greece, the Black Sea, Palestine, Africa, and even across the broad Atlantic to America, who were undisputed masters of the sea for more than twelve centuries, were not barbarians (ibid).

Du Chaillu mentions that the facts show both Britain and Gaul were conquered by the Romans and later by the Northmen. It is also interesting to see that these Northmen had come from Southern Russia, had advanced to the Baltic, and finally to Scandinavia.

> The manly civilization the Northmen possessed was their own; from their records, corroborated by finds in Southern Russia, it seems to have advanced north from about the shores of the Black Sea . . . (ibid., p. 4).

We have noted earlier that many (if not most) of the Franks who settled in France were of Celtic, Cimbric or Scythian Origin. They were a totally different people from the Germanic Franks who remained east of the Rhine. The Anglo-Saxons were also a different type from the Old Saxons who remained in Saxony.

Many of the Northern tribes swarmed into England under such names as Angles, Saxons, Danes, Vikings, etc.

> A few years after the time fixed as that of their first supposed appearance we find these very Danes swarming everywhere with their fleets and warriors, not only in England, but in Gaul, in Brittany, up the Seine, the Garonne, the Rhine, the Elbe, on the coasts of Spain, and further eastward in the Mediterranean (ibid., p. 21).

The Swedes as well as the Danes were called Northmen, as were also the people of Norway: "The Sueones, or Swedes, reappear at the close of the eighth and commencement of the ninth centuries by the side of the Danes, and both call themselves Northmen" (ibid.).

We have earlier noted, according to Mallet, that the people of the North came from the regions of the Black and Caspian Seas—the general vicinity to which Israel was first deported. Now let us notice that such an origin is also corroborated by du Chaillu:

> The mythological literature of the North bears evidence of a belief prevalent among the people, that their ancestors migrated at a remote period from the shores of the Black Sea, "through South-western Russia to the Baltic. This belief seems to be supported by a variety of evidence" (du Chaillu, The Viking Age, Vol. I, pp. 25, 26).

Du Chaillu then mentions that archaeological data in the graves in the neighborhood of the Black Sea contain similar material to Frankish, Russian, English, and Arabic records, showing that the Viking Age must have lasted from about the second century to about the middle of the twelfth century A.D.

In The Viking Age, is also given an account of the life of Odin. He is called "the predecessor of the Norsemen" and is supposed to have come from the south or southeast of Europe, from the shores of the Black Sea. He, as we have already noted, extended his sovereignty over all of the North.

Some have asked if Odin was a real man, or a mythological figure, or was he a god?

Putting all the historical evidence together, there must have been a real person by the name of Odin, or according to some historical sources, he assumed this name Odin as a title to inspire fear, reverence, and loyalty in his subjects.

ODIN AND ADON

What is the origin of this word "Odin"?

"Adon is one of the three titles (Adon, Adonai, Adonim), all generally rendered Lord; but each has its own peculiar usage and association. They all denote headship in various aspects. They have to do with God as over-lord" (Bullinger, The Companion Bible, app. IV). Dr. Bullinger then proceeds to give a more lengthy explanation of these three words as found in the Hebrew.

One of the names of God in the Hebrew language is "Adon." This word is usually translated as "Lord" in the authorized version.

Since the people of Scandinavia are today known to be some of the descendants of the Lost Ten Tribes of Israel, need we be amazed if we find this name of God still being used by the cast-off people of God? Remember in the Hebrew language all of the words were written with the consonants only. The vowels were added or supplied by the reader. Thus we see that the basic sound of the word "Adon" and "Odin" is exactly the same. The vowels could be varied considerably and still not change the meaning or the basic sound of this word.

There must have existed, then, a real personage by the name of Odin, who assumed the name of Odin in order to secure the awe, respect, and obedience of his followers.

THE ORIGIN OF THE GOTHS

In this chapter on Scandinavia, it is fitting that we briefly consider the Goths. Who were the Goths, and what was their origin?

Many historians equate the Goths with the Getae. In a later chapter we shall see that the Getae (and their various branches) were of Scythian origin.

> Goths, a Germanic people whose original homeland may have been in Scandinavia. At the beginning of the Christian era, however, the Goths were living on the south shore of the Baltic just east of the Vistula River. Subsequently they moved southward to the Black Sea area where in the third century A.D. they held territory stretching from the mouth of the Danube to the Dnieper (Ency. Brit., 1960 ed, Vol. XIII, art. Goths).

In A.D. 272 the Emperor Aurelian surrendered to the Goths the whole of Dacia. It was about this same time that the Goths were divided into two divisions—the Ostrogoths or East Goths, and the Visigoths or West Goths. The Visigoths remained for some time north of the Danube, but under Alaric they invaded Italy and plundered Rome in A.D. 410. Not long afterward they settled permanently in Southwest Gaul, and founded a kingdom of which Tolosa was its capital. From this kingdom which they had established in South-west Gaul, they invaded Spain and founded a kingdom in that country which lasted for over two centuries, until it was overthrown by the Arabs.

The Ostrogoths settled in Moesia and Pannonia; but they later extended their dominions very nearly to the gates of Constantinople. Under their king, Theodoric the Great, they occupied the whole of Italy in A.D. 493. See A Smaller Classical Dictionary for a brief resume of the history of the Goths.

Turner says: "That the Getae were Goths cannot be doubted" (History of the Anglo-Saxons, Vol. I, p. 95).

The Goths were also called Scythians: "In the war which followed, the Goths, whom the historians would with characteristic pedantry, call Scythians, used boats to harry the coast not merely of the Euxine . . ." (Minns, Scythians and Greeks, p. 126).

Professor Coon asserts that the Goths were from Sweden. "The Goths claimed to have crossed the Baltic from Sweden (not from the island of Gotland) to the mouth of the Vistula. The Vandals and the Gepidae presumably had the same origin" (The Races of Europe, p. 205). Some of these Goths, according to Coon, established "an important kingdom on the north shore of the Black Sea."

GOTHIC RACIAL CHARACTERISTICS

What were the characteristics of the Goths?

> A series of Goths from the Chersonese north of the Black Sea, dated between 100 B.C. and 100 A.D. includes three male and eight female skeletons. All of these are long headed, and they belong to a large powerful Nordic type which reflects their Swedish origin . . ." (ibid., p. 206).

He then points out: "The same conclusion results when one examines the Visigothic skulls from northern Spain which date from the sixth century A.D." (ibid.).

Many historical sources can be produced showing that different peoples in the British Isles as well as in Scandinavia were called Teutons and Goths.

It would appear that many (if not most) of the Goths were not, racially speaking, true Germans as we think of them today, but were more "Nordic" in type than are most Germans. It is indisputable that the Goths were certainly not of the Alpine or "Slavic" type of the German stock.

It thus becomes clear that the Scandinavian peoples had their origin in the vicinity of the Black and Caspian Seas—the very place where we find the dispersed people of Israel living shortly after their final captivity of 721 B.C. They must have lived in this area for at least a few centuries before migrating into the countries of present-day Scandinavia.

We have previously noticed that the modern typical German is not of the same general racial type as the Scandinavian and British peoples, but there is great resemblance between these latter peoples (Keith, The Graphic, Dec. 1915, Are we Cousins to the Germans, p. 720).

Some of the North Germans are closely allied to the Danes, Dutch and other North-western Europeans. The exact racial affinity of the northern Germanic type to certain other Nordics of North-west Europe yet remains to be clearly demonstrated. But many North Germans have mixed to some extent with their neighbors, thus producing a people closely related to the racial type of Scandinavia, the British Isles, and the Low Countries.

Now that we have learned to differentiate between the original Keltio-Scythian "Germans" and the present day "Alpine" and "Slavic" Germans, we are better able to understand the racial connections of the different waves of peoples who have passed through (and temporarily inhabited) parts of Germany at one time or another!

With this knowledge kept firmly in mind we need never confuse the "Nordic" Northwestern type Europeans with the Latin, Alpine or Slavic types!

CHAPTER VI

THE SERPENT'S TRAIL

There is still one other name by which a portion of the Israelites were known after they left the Promised Land. This is a name which connects them directly with one of the tribes of Israel.

Bilhah, the handmaid of Rachel, one of Jacob's two wives, bare unto Jacob two sons, Dan and Naphtali (Gen. 35:25). The meaning of "Dan" in Hebrew is "Judge."

> Dan shall judge his people as one of the tribes of Israel. Dan shall be a serpent by the way, an adder in the path, that biteth the horse heels, so that his rider shall fall backward. I have waited for thy salvation, O Lord (Gen. 49:16-18).

Notice three points about these verses. First, Dan was to judge his people. This is definitely being fulfilled today. Many of the people of the tribe of Dan are scattered in the British Commonwealth, America and other nations, serving as policemen, as judges, and as priests—all in a capacity of judging!

Secondly, Dan was to be "a serpent by the way," i.e. just as a serpent leaves a trail or a path in the sand or dirt over which it crawls, so was Dan to leave his mark or name behind him wherever he went.

Thirdly, Dan would have to wait for his salvation (v.18). If you will check Revelation 7:5-8, you will notice that the only tribe of Israel which is not mentioned is that of Dan. At the time of the Second Coming of Christ, as the Messiah of Israel and the Saviour of the whole world, Dan will not, as a tribe, be reckoned among those who receive their salvation. He must wait for his salvation.

The people of Dan today are so steeped in "religious" paganism and superstition, and are so blinded that they are not, as a tribe, receiving their salvation at this time. Another important prophecy is found in Deuteronomy 33:22;

"And of Dan he said, 'Dan is a lion's whelp: He shall LEAP from Bashan!'"

What does it mean to leap from Bashan?

In Joshua 19:40-48, we read the account of Joshua dividing to the Danites their allotted portion among the tribes of Israel. The inheritance of the tribe of Dan lay on the Mediterranean coast (v. 41).

> And the coast of the children of Dan went too little for them: therefore the children of Dan went out to fight against Leshem and took it, and smote it with the edge of the sword, and possessed it, and dwelt therein, and called Leshem [Laish, Judges 18:29] DAN, after the name of their father (Josh. 19:47).

In the eighteenth chapter of Judges is another account of the expansion of the tribe of Dan.

"In those days there was no king in Israel: in those days the tribe of the Danites sought them an inheritance to dwell in; for unto that day all their inheritance had not fallen unto them among the tribes of Israel." (Judges 18:1). The rest of this chapter is an account of some scouts being sent out from the tribe of Dan to the far northern border of Israel, to a city called Laish (v.7). Later on, these Danites conquered Laish.

"And they called the name of the city (Laish) Dan, after the name of Dan their father, who was born unto Israel: howbeit the name of the city was Laish at the first" (Judges 18:29).

Have you noticed that we have now seen two accounts of the people of Dan changing the name of the city and naming it after their ancestral father, Dan? Remember, Dan was to be a serpent by the way—that is, he was to leave his name along the trail wherever he would go. History produces an abundance of evidence showing that these sons of Dan (Danites) have left their name on the rivers and coastlands all along their route from Palestine to North-west Europe.

Certain prophecies in the Bible show that Dan (as a serpent) was to leave a trail behind him, and it has been observed that the children of this tribe did, in fact, leave their mark in Palestine early in their history. These Danites began the habit of naming cities and rivers after the name of their father, Dan.

Now let us observe that the sons of Dan have continued to do this same thing ever since. Remember, we have noticed that the people of this tribe were a great seafaring people. "Why did Dan remain in ships?—the inspired prophetess Deborah had asked. Even at that early date, many of the Danites were sailing the Mediterranean, looking for treasure and adventure.

Have the children of Dan left their mark or trail on their route from the Promised Land to the country which they now inhabit?

There is ample evidence to prove that these adventuresome Danites had early exerted quite an influence in the regions of the Black Sea.

In order for one to get to the Black Sea by ship, he must first pass from the Mediterranean into the Aegean Sea; from the Aegean, he must pass through the DarDANelles in order to reach the Black Sea. If one were to walk counterclockwise from the east end of the Black Sea, he would pass by the mouth of the following rivers by the time he got completely around to the west side of the Black Sea: (1) Don, (2) Donets, (3) Dnieper, (4) Dniester, and (5) Danube Rivers.

If one will follow the DANube River in its westerly or north-westerly course, it will take him upstream into the heart of Europe. From here, if one leaves the Danube and takes a somewhat northerly direction when he gets to the point where the Danube flows through Vienna, Austria, he will come to DANzig, a city situated on the Baltic coast of North-central Poland. If one continues to follow the coast of the Baltic Sea, in a westward direction, he will soon come to DENmark (meaning Dan's mark). Following the coastline still further west-to-southwest from DENmark, one soon arrives at a city in Northern France call DUNkirk (meaning Dan's Church). From Dunkirk one can cross the English Channel to the British Isles where he will encounter many scores of cities, rivers and bays with the name of Dan, Den, Din, Don, or Dun somewhere included in them. All over the British Isles, one will find this name, showing that these Danites had traversed the British Isles at a very early date. In some instances this root word "Dan" may be used as a prefix, or as a suffix, or it may even occur in the middle of a word.

It is in Ireland, however, where one will notice the largest number of these words with some form of the word "Dan" in them. DUNgiven is the name of a town not far from Belfast, North Ireland.

There is also another very interesting thing about this name of Dan. It is found almost exclusively on rivers, and lakes or along the coastlines of Europe. This is again evidence that the people of Dan were, as the Bible indicates, a seafaring people. They have never been the mountaineering or Alpine type. They are always found near a river, lake or sea.

Bear in mind that there were no vowels written in the Hebrew language. The basic part of this word when the vowel is dropped is DN. In different European lagnuages one will find a different vowel inserted in the word "Dan" between the letters "d" and "n".

Some languages will use one vowel and some another when speaking or writing the word "Dan." Any of the vowels inserted in this word will not alter its basic sound.

These are just a very few of the many ways in which this name of DAN is found near the coastlands of numerous countries of Europe, where these adventuresome Danites have gone. In fact, as we noticed, one country in Europe is named after Dan i.e. Denmark (Dan's Mark). Truly, Dan has left his trail or mark wherever he has gone. The city of DUN Laoghaire is near Dublin.

Another important point in the 18th chapter of Judges is that of the vivid account of the IDOLATRY into which the people of Dan had already sunk, at this very early date in the history of Israel. In fact, this is the first recorded instance of any of the people of Israel sinking into idolatry, after the episode of the golden calf mentioned in Exodus 32:1-4.

Later we shall see that the modern descendants of Dan are among the most superstitious and idolatrous in all the world. They still reverence and bow before their images and idols of every description. They tremble at the thought of the leprechauns and the "wee folk."

DAN—A GREAT SEAFARING PEOPLE

The prophetess, Deborah, in reference to the then-recent struggle between Israel and the Canaanites, said of Dan, "Why did Dan remain in ships?" (Judges 5:17).

In other words, at the time when the Israelites were fighting for their freedom from under the oppression of the Canaanitish Sisera, undoubtedly the main body of the Danites was even then remaining in their ships, plying the waters of the Mediterranean with their Phoenician neighbors.

Both the Scriptures and early secular history make it very clear that the people of Dan were a great seafaring people. The city of Joppa, in Dan's inheritance, must have been a seaport of some importance. It was at Joppa that Jonah boarded a ship for Tarshish (or Spain) (Jonah 1:3).

If you will look at a map of the land of Palestine in the time of the Judges, you will notice that the tribe of Dan had a very small territory allotted to it along the Mediterranean Sea coast to the west and north-west of Jerusalem. Their territory only comprised about 500 square miles (Hurlbut, A Bible Atlas, p. 44). This allotment of land was not great enough for the people of Dan, so they had to push out northward and migrate to a new location.

We have already seen that a colony of Danites left their southern inheritance and went up to Laish, or Dan, at the extreme northern part of Palestine. This city was within the tribal inheritance of Naphtali, but the Naphtalites had not possessed the city of Laish, so Dan conquered and possessed it. If you consult a map of this period in Israelitish history, you will notice that Laish lay only twenty-five miles due east of the city of Tyre. Remember that the ancient city of Tyre was soon afterwards to become the most important maritime city in all the Mediterranean, or even the whole world!

Tyre has often been called the "New York" of the ancient world. So the people of Dan were very close to this great seafaring city.

At the time of the division of Israel into two nations (Israel and Judah), there must have been few Danites living in their original territory, because most of Dan's inheritance was included in the Southern Kingdom of Judah (Hurlbut, A Bible Atlas, p. 80). The people of the tribe of Dan, however, were never included among the people of the Kingdom of Judah.

According to secular history, some of these adventurous, seafaring Danites left Egypt even before the Exodus of the people of Israel, and migrated to Greece. They settled in the extreme southern part of Greece, and were later known as the Lacedemon (or Spartan) Greeks.

They were also known as Dorians or people from "Dor." Dor was a prominent city (in the tribe of Manasseh), on the Mediterranean coast (Hurlbut, A Bible Atlas, p. 45). It was from this city that many Israelites left the Promised Land in order to settle in the southern part of Greece as Dorians!

Diodorus Siculus (Circa 50 B.C.), who quoted Hecataeus of Abdera of the 6th century B.C., says that the most distinguished of the expelled foreigners (from Egypt) followed Cadmus and Danaus into Greece; but the greater number were supposed to have been led by Moses into the Promised Land (See Diodorus of Sicily, Book V). A number of other historians refer to this same incident.

The tribe of Dan is not mentioned in the genealogical list given in I Chronicles 5:6-8. If you will turn to the accounts of the captivity of Israel as found in II Kings, chapters 15 and 17, you will see that the name of Dan is not mentioned a single time among those peoples who were carried into the captivities of 741-721 B.C.

Dan and Naphtali had mixed with the Phoenicians of Tyre (Josephus, Ant., iii, 4; I Kings vii. 14; 2 Chron. 11, 14).

In fact, you will search in vain to find the Danites mentioned any more as a tribe in any of the Bible accounts of the people of Israel, from the time of the Judges to the Assyrian and Babylonian captivities.

What happened to Dan?

We have already seen a prophecy of the tribe of Dan which says "Dan shall leap from Bashan." The people of Dan migrated to the northern part of Palestine, and settled in the city of Laish, naming it after their father, Dan. This northern colony of Danites, living in the city of Dan, was located in the edge of the territory called Bashan. The Bible shows that these Danites were to leap from this territory—from Bashan.

What does it mean to "leap from Bashan"? The word leap means: "To spring or move suddenly as if by a jump" (Webster's New Collegiate Dictionary, p. 478).

A leap is a quick or sudden jump. It would appear, then, that this northern colony of Danites (perhaps because of the rumblings of the Assyrian armies about to invade Israel) emigrated hastily from their city of Dan.

Where did Dan go from here? The Bible does not specifically say. Did the Danites leave hastily, migrating by land into the area of the Black Sea where we find the name of Dan on many of the rivers in that area? Or does the word "leap" mean that they went by ships (perhaps from the city of Tyre), and fled by this means to the area of the Black Sea? Or, perhaps some of them went on directly to Ireland!

Later we shall have occasion to meet these roving tribesmen of Dan, under the appelation "Tuatha de Danaan."

THE LACEDEMONIAN GREEKS WERE DANITES

Herodotus, called "the father of history," who wrote in the fifth century B.C., also reveals the "Egyptian" origin of some of the Greeks. He says "If we ascend from Danae the daughter of Aerisus, we shall find that the ancestors of the Dorian princes were of Egyptian origin. Such is the Grecian account of the descent" (Herod., Bk. VI, I, iii).

Remember these "Greek" Dorians were Israelites who had once lived in Egypt before they lived in Palestine.

A number of historians refer to these Egyptian Danae. Herodotus says: "In what manner, being Egyptians; they became princes of the Dorians, having been mentioned by others, I need not relate; but I shall explain what they have omitted" (ibid., Bk.VI, iv).

All early histories of Ireland mention a people coming into Ireland called TUATHA DE DAN, which means "tribe of Dan."

Keating mentions that the Danaans were a people of immense learning and wealth. After a battle with the Assyrians, they left GREECE and some went to IRELAND. Others of them went to DENMARK and called it DAN-MARES, or Dan's country (History of Ireland, pp. 195-199).

From another source, The Annals of Ireland, we read:

> The Dan'ans were a highly civilised people, well skilled in architecture and other arts from their long residence in GREECE, and their intercourse with the Phoenicians. Their first appearance in Ireland was 1200 B.C., or 85 years after the great victory of DEBORAH.

Early Irish legends and traditions give much information showing that a colony of the tribe of Dan arrived in Ireland as early as the twelfth century B.C. They were known as the "Tuatha de Danaan." We shall discuss these people more fully in the chapter on early Scottish-Irish history.

Professor A.H. Sayce shows that a long-headed people from Palestine, whom he termed "Amorites," had migrated from the land of Canaan to the Peninsula of Spain and France and into the British Isles. It has already been clearly shown that some of the historians mistakenly call the Israelites "Amorites."

Josephus gives an account showing that at least some of the Lacedemonian Greeks were DANITES and were, therefore, related to the Jews.

At the time when Onias was High Priest in Jerusalem, Areus, the Lacedemonian king, sent an ambassage with a letter to the Jewish High Priest. Here is a copy of the letter as mentioned by Josephus.

Areus king of the Lacedemonians, to Onias, sendeth greeting: We have met with a certain writing, whereby we have discovered that both the Jews and the Lacedemonians are of one stock, and are derived from the kindred of Abraham. It is but just, therefore, that you, who are our brethren, should send to us about any of your concerns as you please. We will also do the same thing, and esteem your concerns as our own: and will look upon our concerns as in common with yours. Demoteles, who brings you this letter, will bring your answer back to us. This letter is foursquare; and the seal is an EAGLE, with a dragon in its claws" (Ant., Bk. XII, Chap. iv, par. 10 pp. 296, 297).

The tribal emblem or ensign of Dan contained the image of a snake (The Jewish Encyclopedia, Art. Flag, p. 405).

Fuller says that the emblem of Dan was an "adder biting horse heels." He also quotes the Jewish writer, Aben Ezra, a learned Jewish scholar of the time of Oliver Cromwell, as saying that the emblem of Dan was an "eagle with a dragon [serpent] in its claws" (Pisgah Sight of Palestine).

JEWISH HIGH PRIEST ACKNOWLEDGES KINSHIP
TO THE LACEDEMONIAN GREEKS

From these sources we learn that the tribal emblems used on the national ensign of Dan were those of the SERPENT and the EAGLE. We have seen from Josephus' Antiquities of the Jews, a letter written by the Lacedemonian Greeks, to the Jews in which these "Greeks" claimed to be the brethren of the Jews. They wrote an epistle to the Jewish High Priest relating their kinship to them. Their seal, which was affixed to the letter was that of "an eagle with a dragon [serpent] in its claws."

Excerpts from the reply to this epistle written by the Jewish High Priest to the Israelitish Greeks of South Greece is here given. As the Jewish ambassadors were returning from Rome they delivered this letter to the Spartan Greeks.

Jonathan the high priest of the Jewish nation . . . to the ephori and senate and the people of the Lacedemonians, send greeting:

When in former times an epistle was brought to Onias, who was then our high priest . . . concerning the KINDRED that was between US and YOU, a copy of which is here subjoined, we both joyfully received the epistle . . . because we were well satisfied about it from the sacred writings, yet did not we think fit, first to begin the claim of this relation to you, the glory which is now given us by you. It is a long time since this relation of ours to you hath been renewed, and when we, upon holy and festival days, offer sacrifices to God, we pray to Him for your preservation and victory . . . You will, therefore, do well yourselves to write to us, and send us an account of what you stand in need of from us, since we are in all things disposed to act according to your desires" (Ant., Bk. XIII, Chap. 5, Sec. 8, p. 318).

Josephus says that the Lacedemonians kindly received the ambassadors, and "made a decree for friendship and mutual assistance." They then dispatched the letter to their Lacedemonian kinsmen (Ant., Bk. XIII, Chap. 5, Sec. 8, p. 318).

Stephanus Byzantium shows that Alexander Polyhistor and Claudius Jölaus also affirm a direct kinship between the ancient Spartans and the Jews (Bryant, Ancient Mythology, vol. 5, pp.51,52,60).

The Jews of Christ's day knew some of the dispersed Israelites were among the Greeks. Notice the proper translation of John 7:35 as given in the Revised Standard Version of the Bible. "Does He intend to go to the dispersion (Gk. diaspara] among the Greeks and teach the Greeks?"

The Moffatt and other translations also properly translate this verse.

These historical references are sufficient to show that some of Danites were living in Southern Greece centuries before Christ.

From Greece many of these Israelites went to Ireland many centuries before Christ's time, and settled in that country. In a later chapter on Scottish-Irish history, we shall go into this subject more thoroughly.

Thus we have seen Dan's trail in Greece and throughout Europe. It was to Ireland (and Denmark), that these Danites called the "Tuatha de Danaan" finally migrated and settled, making it their home. It is in Denmark and Ireland that they finally established their permanent homeland; and it is in Eire that their name is the most widely diffused. The Dans and Daniels are common in Ireland and who has never heard The Londonderry Air, also called "Danny Boy"?

EARLY SCOTTISH-IRISH HISTORY

In previous chapters we have noticed many links connecting the people of England and Wales directly with the Holy Land. It has been clearly pointed out that the Anglo-Saxons are definitely descendants of Shem and are, therefore, Semitic (Shemitic). We have also seen according to the Anglo-Saxon Chronicle that some of the early immigrants to England were from Armenia—the very land to which Israel was taken in the captivities of 741 and 721 B.C.

Now let us examine early Scotch-Irish history to notice the many links directly connecting the people of Scotland and Ireland with the Promised Land, and consequently with the people of the Lost Ten-Tribed House of Israel in exile.

Ireland is reputed to possess genuine history several centuries more ancient than any other European nation possesses in its present spoken language. Having perused a number of Irish histories, it was finally decided that The History of Ireland by Moore would best convey the most important points of Irish history. Most Irish historians mention the same events and arrive at the same general conclusions as those expressed by Moore.

THE FIVE COLONIES

The five colonies who are said to have inhabited Ireland, are as follows:

The first colony known to have settled in Ireland was supposed to have been of the "race of Japhet." They are said to have gone to Ireland about the beginning of the fourth century after the Flood. The chief of this colony was named Partholan. After possessing Ireland for about 300 years (from circa 2069-1769 B.C.), all of the RACE OF PARTHOLAN were "swept away by a plague" (Moore, The History of Ireland, Vol. I, p.59).

"To this colony succeeded another [the 2nd colony] about the time, it is said, of the patriarch, Jacob, who were called, from the name of their leader, NEMEDIANS, and are said to have come from the shores of the Euxine, [Black] Sea" (ibid., p.63).

The derivation of this NEMEDIAN Scythian colony from the vicinity of the Black Sea agrees with the generally accepted European tradition which regards "the regions in the neighbourhood of the Caucasian Mountains . . . as the main source of the population of the West" (ibid., p.63).

This agrees completely with the scriptural account which shows that the Israelites were dispersed into the regions just south of the Caucasus Mountains; and all history is crystal clear in showing that all of the North-west European peoples came from this general area. This is one more proof that the peoples of North-western Europe are, in fact, different branches of dispersed Israel.

Fierce wars were waged between these Nemedians and some African sea-rovers called Fomorians. The African Fomorian mariners were joined by men and fresh supplies, and a battle ensued in which the Africans were victorious. The Nemedian colony (named after Nemedh, their leader) was dispersed and destroyed. They had dwelt in Ireland for about 217 years (1709-1492 B.C.). Because of oppression and enslavement under the fierce Formorians [sic. Fomorians], a colony of these Nemedians fled to Greece; but they later on returned to Ireland about 217 years after the first Nemedian Colony had first gone there. When they returned to Ireland, they bore a new name (FIR-BOLGS) which they had received while in Greece. Ireland was once more left to the mercy of the African foreign marauders and became a desolate wilderness for about 200 years.

These Fir-Bolgs were the third colony who settled Ireland—though they were descended from the Scythian Nemedian colony. They were the first people to establish regal authority over Ireland. Having divided Ireland into five parts or provinces, they established a Pentarchal form of government which continued, except for a few interruptions, until the beginning of the 15th century B.C.

THE TRIBE OF DAN

Ireland was ruled by the Fir-Bolgs for only 30 or 40 years.

> Their tenure of royalty, however, was but short: for, not more than thirty or forty years had this quintuple sovereignty remained in their hands, when they were dispossessed by the TUATHA-DE-DANAAN, a people famed for necromancy, who after sojourning for some time in Greece, where they had learned this mysterious art, proceeded from thence to Denmark and Norway (ibid., p. 60).

From those lands they went to Ireland and overpowered the "alarmed Belgians," meaning the Fir-Bolgs after which these Tuatha-de-Danaan became sole masters of the country.

The first contingent of the Tuatha-De-Danaan appear to have gone to Ireland about 1456 B.C.—during Israel's 40-year wanderings in the desert under Moses.

A second contingent of this tribe of Dan probably went to Ireland in the time of the Prophetess Deborah—circa 1213 B.C.

Who were these "Tuatha-de-Danaan"?

Let us first see what the definition of the word "TUATH" is. "TUATH (Tū.ah). Irish History . . . A 'tribe' or 'people' in Ireland" (A New English Dictionary on Historical Principles, Vol. X, Part I, def. Tuath, p.441).

Dr. Robert Gordon Latham, well-known nineteenth century ethnologist, definitely believed the Greek Danaans were the descendents of Dan. He says:

> Neither do I think that the eponymus [ancestral name] of the Argive Danai was other than that of the Israelite tribe of Dan; only we are so used to confine ourselves to the soil of Palestine in our consideration of the history of the Israelites (Ethnology of Europe, p. 137).

Dr. Latham then goes on to show that the people of Dan must have had close connections with the peoples of Southern Greece, and he concludes by saying: "Yet with Danai and the tribe of Dan this is the case, and no one connects them" (ibid.).

There can be no doubt that the people who were called by such names as Dan, Danai, and Danaans were all the same people. The histories of Ireland are replete with references to people of the tribe of Dan (Tuatha-de-Danaan) who had early come to Ireland from Greece.

Muller, commenting on some of the fragments of the Greek manuscripts of Hecateus of Abdera says:

Hecateus therefore, tells us that the Egyptians, formerly being troubled by calamities, [referring to the Ten Plagues at the time of the Israelitish Exodus] in order that the divine wrath might be averted, expelled all the aliens gathered together in Egypt. Of these, some, under their leaders DANUS and CADMUS, migrated into GREECE; others into other regions, THE GREATER PART INTO SYRIA [meaning Palestine]. THEIR LEADER IS SAID TO HAVE BEEN MOSES, a man renowned for wisdom and courage, founder and legislator of the state. Afterwards many Mosaic institutes followed. (Fragmenta Historicorum Graecorum, Vol. II, p. 385).

Both Hecateus of Abdera (3rd century B.C.) and Diodorus of Sicily mention that the people of DANAI, under their leader Danus, came from EGYPT, but Hecateus says that the greater part of the DANITES went into Syria or Palestine under the leadership of MOSES.

Notice the following interesting comments from Diodorus:

They say also that those who set forth with Danaus, likewise from Egypt, settled what is practically the oldest city of GREECE, Argos, and that the nations of the COLCHI in Pontus and that of the Jews, which lies between Arabia and Syria, were founded as colonies by certain emigrants from their country; and this is the reason why it is a long-established institution among these two people to circumcise their male children . . . the custom having been brought over from Egypt. (Diodorus of Sicily, Book I, Sec. xxviii, 1-5).

Putting all of these historical bits of information (and this is only a small portion of such information) together, it becomes quite clear that the people who settled Ireland by the name of "Tuatha-de-Danaan" were some of the descendants of the Israelitish tribe of Dan!

We have already observed that the Tuatha-de-Danaan were the FOURTH COLONY to settle in Ireland AFTER THE FLOOD. What happened to these Tuatha-de-Danaan?

THE MILESIAN SCOTS

In process of time, the Tuatha-de-Danaan were themselves dispossessed of their sway; a successful invasion from the coast of Spain having put an end to the Danaanian dynasty, and transferred the sceptre into the hands of that Milesian or SCOTIC race, which through so long a series of succeeding ages, supplied Ireland with her kings. This celebrated colony, though coming directly from Spain, was originally, we are told, of Scythic race (Moore, The History of Ireland, p. 60).

This Milesian or "Scotic race," arrived in Ireland in 1016 A.D. and remained the ruling people in Ireland for many hundreds of years. It was these Scythian Scots who finally settled the northern part of England, calling it Scotland.

Centuries later, descendants of this Scythic or Scottish people settled in Canada, naming the province in which they had settled "Novia Scotia."

This FIFTH COLONY to invade Ireland, called MILESIANS or SCOTS, had come from Scythia, as nearly all historians agree, and they definitely connected themselves with the people of Israel, the heroes of Israel, and the Holy Land!

Speaking of the Milesian Scots, Moore says:

> Tracing this chosen race in their migrations to different countries, and connecting them, by marriage or friendship, during their long sojourn in Egypt, with most of the heroes of Scripture history, our [Scotch-Irish] Bards conduct them at length, by a route not very intelligible, to Spain (ibid., p. 60).

There can be no doubt about the colony of the "Tuatha-de-Danaan" being Israelitish Danites, and the Milesian Scots were definitely also Israelites, but were of the tribe of Joseph.

We have just seen in the above quotation that the Scots connected their people with "most of the heroes of Scripture history," and we have also noticed that they had experienced a "long sojourn in Egypt." We know that this could only refer to people of the tribes of Israel, for it was only they who had resided a long time in Egypt, and who were also connected with "most of the heroes of Scripture history."

> I shall now proceed to the consideration of that latest and most important of all her settlements, the Scythic, or Scotic, from whence the whole of her people in the course of time received the name of Scots, and retained it exclusively to so late a period as the tenth century of our era (ibid. p. 69).

According to the preceding quotation, Ireland retained the name of "Scotia" until so late a period as the tenth century! If one will consult the older maps of Ireland, he will soon discover the truth of the above statement. It was at a later period that some of the Milesian Scots from Northern Ireland crossed the Irish Sea and established their rule in the northern part of England, naming their new country Scotland, meaning the land of the Scots.

Dr. Wylie mentions that when the early historians speak of Scotland, it is always "the Irish Dalriada" or the country of "Antrim" in North Ireland which they refer to.

> The name Scotia began to be of more general application, and to be given to the whole of Ireland. It was not until the tenth century that the name of Scotland was applied to the country on this side of the Channel, that is, to Scotland of today (History of the Scottish Nation, Vol. I, p. 298).

According to the oldest Irish chronicles, Abbot Tighernac, descendant of the Scotic king of Ulster, led a colony of Milesian Scots (Dalriada) from Antrim to the northern part of England. After a number of conflicts with the Picts, they were finally victorious, and gained complete control of the northern part of England, naming it after themselves, Scotland.

Moore further shows that these Milesian Scots traced themselves all the way back to some of the people of Israel. Speaking of their Scottish descent, he says:

> A scheme of descent which traces the ancestors of the Irish [referred to the Scotch-Irish] through a direct series of generations not merely to the first founders of Phoenician arts and enterprise, but even to chieftans connected by friendship with the prophet Moses himself (History of Ireland, p. 71).

Many historians look upon these historical accounts as fables, but there is ample scriptural and historical evidence to prove that this is not fable, but is fact of the most important significance!

> "It is indeed evident," says Moore, "that those persons to whom St. Patrick applies the name Scots, were all of the high and dominant class; whereas, when speaking of the great bulk of the people, he call them Hiberionaces, from the name Hiberione, which is always applied by him to the island itself (ibid., p. 72).

Dr. Wylie mentions that there were two different peoples dwelling in Ireland—Hiberni and Scoti. There was a marked distinction between the two. "The Scots are the military class; they are the nobles . . . The latter [the Hiberni] are spoken of as the commonality, the sons of the soil" (History of the Scottish Nation, Vol. I, p. 281).

The main difference between these people is that the Hiberni are descendants of Dan by Jacob and his concubine Bilhah. The people of Scoti are descendants of Joseph through Jacob and Rachel, Jacob's beloved wife. It was only the descendants of Joseph who were to be blessed with the birthright blessings (I Chr. 5:2).

"St. Patrick often uses Scoti and Reguli as equivalent terms. To the term Scottus he adds often the word Nobilis; whereas he has no other appellative for the native Irish but Hyberione, or Hyberni genae, the common people" (ibid., fn. p. 282).

Remember that such names as Iber, Eber, Heber, Ebernes, Hiberones, etc. are all words referring to the ancestor "Heber" from whom the Hebrews have all descended. The Scots, Irish, English and other branches of the so-called "Nordic" races are all descendants of Eber or Heber.

"In considering the Scots to have been a Scythian extraction, all parties are agreed" (ibid., p. 73).

Moore then mentions that the Bards sang of the Milesian Scots as having come from the East through Spain. He says:

> The Celto-Scythae, who founded a part of the mixed people of Spain, having come originally from the neighbourhood of the Euxine Sea [Black] and therefore combining in themselves all the peculiarities attributed to the Milesian colony, of being at once Scythic, Oriental, and direct from Spain (ibid., p. 73).

He then mentions that, of the actual settlement of a number of Spanish (meaning Celto-Scythian) tribes in the Emerald Isle (Ireland), there is no reason to doubt. Moore shows that the European Scythians had come from Persia.

"That the Scyths of Europe came from the northern parts of Persia, seems to be the opinion of most enquirers on the subject" (ibid., fn. p.73).

The above quotation tallies completely with the scriptural account which shows that Israel was taken into captivity to Assyria and Media which was in the vicinity of Persia.

It is also interesting to note that, according to the Bards, all of the colonies who settled in Ireland (excepting the earliest colony which was destroyed with a plague) were all of the same race. They were, in fact, all descendants of Israel!

> The Bardic historians themselves, who represent the Scoti to have been of Scythic descent and to have from thence derived their distinctive appellation . . . and to confirm still further the origin of the Scots from that quarter, it is added by the Bards that they were of the same race with the three colonies that had preceded them; namely, the Nemedians, the Tuatha-de-Danaans, and the Firbolgs or Belgae (ibid., p. 74).

It is also interesting to note that, according to Dr. Wylie, the Scots, Caledonians, Belgae (Firbolgs), Gauls, PICTS and Cimric or Celtic settlers of the British Isles were all of the same race (The History of the Scottish Nation, Vol. I. pp. 264, 265).

THE PROBLEM OF THE PICTS

Before we continue our study of Scottish-Irish history, let us briefly examine the enigma of the Picts.

The problem of the Picts has baffled many historians. There is hardly any subject which is shrouded in more mystery (Moore, The History of Ireland, Vol. I, p. 85). Also there is virtually no subject on which there is more disagreement by the so-called authorities. A number of the histories imply that some of the Picts were Celts; others, judging from their social customs, must have contained a racial element with close affinities to some of the North American Indians.

Here are facts which have caused some to equate the original Picts with certain American Indian tribes: (1) the practice of matriarchy, (2) the art of canoes made from skins, and (3) the fact that their huts or tents resembled the tepees of the American Indians, might lead one to agree with those proponents of the "Indian theory" of origin for at least some of the Picts.

There is, however, abundant material to show that at least a great part of the later "Picts" must have been of "Celtic" descent.

On one occasion the Milesian Scots gave their daughters to the Picts for wives. This is a strong indication that these Picts must not have been an Indian type.

In a work entitled History of the Scottish Nation, by Wylie, page 306, we are told St. Columba (an Irish missionary—7th century A.D.) went from Ireland to Scotland where "He obtained an interview with the Pictish king, Bruidi, son of Malcolm, at his Dun or castle, on the banks of the Ness, near where the river issues from its parent Loch." After this interview Bruidi declared himself a convert to Christianity.

Here we note the Pictish king living in a castle! The American Indians never lived in castles! Neither did the Indian-type "Picts," who inhabited Northern England at one time, ever dwell in proper house or castles.

ANCIENT IRISH HISTORY

Dr. Guest points out very clearly that the people in Ireland called "Scoti" were distince from that great body of the Irish people, who were name Hiberiones.

He then quotes Nennius, on the primitive populations of Ireland.

> If any here would know at that time Hirbernia [Ireland] was uninhabited and waste, this was the information the learned among the Scots gave me . . . when the sons of Israel passed through the Red Sea the Egyptians followed them and were drowned as is read in the Law. But there was among the Egyptians a nobleman from Scythia with a great retinue, who had been before driven from his kingdom, and was there when the Egyptians were drowned, and who did not go out to persue the people of God. But they who survived took counsel and expelled him, less he should overspread their country, as their princes were drowned in the Red Sea (Origines Celticae, Vol. II, p. 24).

Nennius then shows that these Scythians who witnessed the drowning of Pharaoh and his army in the Red Sea, left Egypt and sailed through the Mediterranean to the Columns of Hercules (Straits of Gibraltar) and went to Spain where they dwelt many years. After increasing greatly in numbers "they came to Hibernia, a thousand and two years after the Egyptians were drowned in the Red Sea."

The Britons came to Britain in the third age of the world, and the Scots got possession of Hibernia in the fourth (ibid., pp. 22-26).

Did you notice that Nennius mentioned the "sons of Israel" and their passing "through the Red Sea?" He also mentioned "A nobleman from Scythia with a great retinue" who, he says, had been driven from his kingdom, and was there when the Egyptians were drowned at the Red Sea (at the Exodus), but that he did not go out to pursue the people of God. Also, the people of this nobleman later came through the Mediterranean to Spain. Afterwards they left Spain and came to Ireland a thousand and two years after the Egyptians were drowned in the Red Sea.

This is undoubtedly a somewhat garbled account of the Israelites, who were the progenitors of the Scots and the Irish.

In the library of the Royal Irish Academy is a poem on "the kings of the race of Eibhair" (Heber—the ancestor of Abraham). Here is the introduction to this poem:

> The Use of Armes and Escouchions is anciently observed by the Irishry, in imitation of ye Children of Israell, who began to use them in Egypt (at which time the Ancestor of all the Irishry, called Gaoidhil, or Gathelus, there lived), which Armes, The Israelites at their passing through ye Redd Seas, under the conduct of Moyses, did carry in their severall Banners. They were in all Twelve Tribes, and each Tribe had a cetain number of men under his own command with Distinct Banners and Armes.

From a work entitled "Leabhar Gabhala," or the Book of the Conquest of Ireland is the following account: "Now Nel lived southward in Egypt, in Capachirunt [Pi-hahiroth] Exodus xiv. 2, on the shores of the Red Sea, which is called the Mare Rubrum. That was the time when the Children of Israel escaped from the Egyptian bondage wherein they were with Pharaoh" (O'Cleirigh, Leabhar Gabhala, p. 127).

A considerable amount of material is given describing the conversation and the relationship of this nobleman, named Nel, with Moses and Aaron. Then follows an account of the land of Scythia being mentioned a number of times.

We are told of "THIRTY SHIPS" with three score in each ship (ibid., p. 137). The Caspian Sea is also mentioned in this history on numerous occasions. This account also speaks of the "Graecian Scythia" and relates a number of instances of contacts between the Scythian people and the Egyptians. The Scythian nobleman, Golamh, later is given Scotia, the daughter of Pharaoh, in marriage.

From here they or their descendants traveled through the Mediterranean Sea to Spain and finally arrived in Ireland. They had to subdue the people of the tribe of Dan on their arrival.

> The Tuatha de Danaan did not suffer them to come to land there, for they had not held a parley with them . . . They encircled Ireland three times, till Thursday, so far as the day of the week, on the day before the Calendes of May, the 17th day of the moon: Anno Mundi 3500 (ibid., p. 122).

In the Annals of Clonmacnoise we read of the patriarch Abraham, and also mention is made ". . . of the Raigne of Semiramis then monarche of the world in Assiria." This account also mentions "Nibroth [Nimrod] Sonn of Chus, [Cush] who was son of Cham [Ham], who was sonne of Noeh."

We next read of some "Fffirvolge" (Fir-Bolgs) who were in Ireland, but who were continually molested and harassed by Carthaginian African Sea rovers and who, because of this, finally went back to Greece. Later these same people returned to Ireland where they finally settled.

Upon them [Fir-bolgs] came in the people called Twathy De Danaan out of Greece too. Being a Braunch of the same stock that ffirvolge [Fir-Bolgs] were of and were kinsmen. Dureinge the time of ffirvolge which was 37 yeares, there Raigned in Assiria 3 monarchs . . . Twany de Danaan after they had spent much tyme abroad in learneinge nigromancy, Magicke, and other Diobolicall artes wherein they were exceedingly well skilled, and in these Dayes accounted the cheefest in the world in that profession, Landed in the west part of Connaught. ffirvolge hearinge of theire comeing made towards them, and meeting them in a greate plaine calle Moytoyrey in Connaught, fought with them, where ffirvolge was overthrone and one Hundred thousand of them slaine with there said King Eochy McEirche, which was the greatest slaughter that was hard of in Ireland in one meeting (Annals of Clonmacnoise From the Creation to A.D. 1408,1627 ed.).

Detailed accounts are then given of the history of the Israelites, and mention is made of the "Twathy De Danaan" (Tribe of Dan) and of the "Egiptians" and of the "Raigne of Dauid King of Israel and Judea" and of "Pharao" and also of "Solomon," King of Jerusalem.

The nation or kingdom of "Assiria" and of the "Assirians" are mentioned repeatedly as well as the "Twathy de Danaan." It is interesting to note that the historians who wrote or compiled this history continually sought to harmonize the events in the history of Ireland with those of Egypt, but more especially with Assiria.

Since a colony of Danites had lived in the extreme northern part of the land of Israel, they must have been well acquainted with the Assyrians and their monarchs, especially since the frontier of Israel had been extended on occasions all the way to the Euphrates which would have bordered on the land of the Assyrians. At this period, a segment of the people of Israel must have been next door neighbours of the Assyrians. This would undoubtedly account for the many references to the Assyrians and their monarchs in the ancient chronicles of Ireland.

We notice similar accounts of the Irish history in a work entitled The History of Ireland from the Earliest Period to The English Invasion, by Geoffrey Keating.

In this work we read of the confounding of the languages in the time of Nimrod. Keating also mentions a Scythian nobleman called "Niul" who went to Egypt with his family, and who was dwelling in Egypt at the time of the Exodus of the children of Israel.

We are informed by Keating that Niul (Nel) showed kindness to Moses and Aaron and the children of Israel, for which he incurred the enmity of Pharaoh.

Pharaoh Intur and the Egyptians, in time, remembered their old grudge to the descendents of Niul and the family of Gaedal, namely, their resentment for the friendship the latter had formed with the children of Israel. They, then, made war upon the GAELS, who were thereby compelled to exile themselves from Egypt (Keating, History of Ireland From The Earliest Period to The English Invasion, pp. 153-156).

With this account Thomas Walsingam agrees, in the book called Hypodeigma, where he states that

> When the Egyptians had been drowned in the Red Sea, those of their countrymen who survived, drove out a certain chieftain of the Scythian nation, who lived among them, that he might not assume sovereignty over them. Banished with his tribe, he came to Spain where he resided many years, and where his posterity grew numerous, and that thence he came at last to Ireland (ibid.).

These are only a very few of the many references in ancient Irish history to the people of Israel. Irish history is replete with statements showing a direct connection between Ireland and the Holy Land.

JEREMIAH—OLLAMH FODHLA

Among the famous persons who have illuminated the pages of Irish history, the Royal Sage, Ollamh Fodhla (pronounced Ollav Folla) stands out preeminently as "a being of historical substance and truth" (Moore, The History of Ireland, Vol. I, p. 86). He was the "celebrated personage" who was known as a great legislator in Ireland.

There are different conjectures as to when this Sage ruled in Ireland. Moore quotes the author of Dissertations (Sect. 4) as showing that this Royal Sage held sway in Ireland about 600 B.C. There are, of course, other conjectures as to when this Royal personage lived in Ireland; but according to scriptural history and prophecy, we know it must have been about 600 B.C. or shortly thereafter when this Royal Sage exercised his powerful influence in Ireland.

Let us consider the background leading up to the arrival of this Royal Personage in Ireland.

JUDAH—THE REGAL TRIBE

Speaking of Judah and his descendant, Genesis 49:10 says: "The Sceptre [the king's royal staff of authority] shall not depart from Judah nor a lawgiver from between his feet, until Shiloh come; and unto him shall the gathering of the people be." This prophecy shows very clearly that the sceptre would not depart from the tribe of Judah until the coming of Shiloh (Christ), and the establishment of Messianic rule over all the earth.

It is well to remember that regal authority was vested in the tribe of Judah, through the great material birthright blessings were to devolve upon the tribe of Joseph. "For Judah prevailed above his brethren, and of him came the chief ruler; but the birthright was Joseph's" (I Chr. 5:2)

God solemnly promised David that He would establish forever the throne of his seed after his death! As long as human beings were being begotten, David's throne was to be ruling somewhere on this earth (II Sam. 5:13, 29).

"Once have I sworn by my holiness that I will not lie unto David. His seed shall endure for ever, and HIS THRONE as the sun before me" (vv. 34, 36).

In Jeremiah 33:17, God solemnly declares: "For thus saith the Lord, DAVID SHALL NEVER WANT [lack] A MAN to sit upon the throne of the house of Israel." Most people don't believe God meant what He said regarding David always having a son ruling somewhere on this earth! They think that when the Jewish throne was overthrown in Jerusalem circa 585 B.C., that this brought an end to the throne of David. But "God cannot lie" (Titus 1:2). "The scripture cannot be broken" (Jn. 10:35).

In Jeremiah 1:10, we read: "See, I have this day set thee (Jeremiah) over the nations and over the kingdoms, to root out, and to pull down, and to destroy, and to throw down, to build, and to plant."

What was Jeremiah to pull down and throw down, and what was he to build and to plant?

God, through the prophet Jeremiah, had predicted that the Babylonish King Nebuchadnezzar, would invade the land of Judah and destroy the Jewish kingdom. For this prophecy Jeremiah was looked upon as a traitor, and was imprisoned (Jer. 38:1-10).

But later, as Jeremiah had prophesied, Nebuchadnezzar did march against Judah, and destroyed the city of Jerusalem and the Jewish kingdom. This occurred in the eleventh year of the reign of King Zedekiah circa 585 B.C. All of Zedekiah's sons (royal seed) were slain before his very eyes; then his own eyes were put out; afterward he was carried to Babylon, where he died in bonds (II Ki. 25; II Chr. 26; Jer. 39 and Jer. 52).

God had used Nebuchadnezzar to punish the Jewish people for their sins and to bring about this punishment upon His people. Jeremiah was released from his imprisonment by the Babylonians (Jer. 40:1-5). In fact, he obtained such favour in the sight of the captain of the guard that "the captain of the guard gave him victuals and a reward, and let him go" (v. 5).

JEWISH PRINCESSES IN EGYPT

Without attempting to give all of the scriptures showing all the movements of Jeremiah, let us next turn to Jeremiah chapter 43, verses 1 through 7 to pick up the main thread of this story.

In the first few verses of this chapter, we see Jeremiah and his scribe, Baruch, had a controversy with the chief leaders of the remnant of the Jews regarding whether or not they ought to flee to Egypt for protection.

> But Johanan the son of Kareah, and all the captains of the forces, took all the remnant of Judah, that returned from all nations, wither they had been driven, to dwell in the land of Judah; even men, and women, and children, and the king's daughters . . . and Jeremiah the prophet, and Baruch the son of Neriah. So that

they came into the land of Egypt: For they obeyed not the voice of the Lord: thus came they even to Tahpanhes (vv. 5-7).

Notice, Jeremiah and his scribe Baruch and "the king's daughters" all "came into the land of Egypt . . . even to Tahpanhes."

This same city is referred to as a garrison of the Egyptians (Jer. 2:16).

In a work entitled Egypt and Israel, by Sir. W.M. Flinders Petrie, we find archaeological confirmation of the visit of Jeremiah and the royal daughters to Tahpanhes. In reference to a prophecy uttered in Ezekiel 30:14-18, Sir Flinders Petrie says:

> These references show that Tahpanhes was an important garrison, and as the Jews fled there it must have been close to the frontier. It is thus clear that it was the Greek Daphnae, the modern Tell Defneh, which is on the road to Palestine . . . Of this an echo comes across the long ages; the fortress mound is known as the Qasr Bint el Yehudi, the palace of the Jew's daughter. It is named Qasr, as a palace, not Qala, a fortress. It is not named Tell Bint el Yehudi, as it would be if it were called so after it were a ruinous heap. Qasr is a name which shows its descent from the time of habitation and habitation for nobility and not merely for troops. So through the long ages of Greek and Roman and Arab there has come down the memory of the royal residence for the king's daughters from the wreck of Jerusalem (Petrie, Egypt and Israel, pp. 85, 86).

Thus we have indisputable archaelogical proof verifying the biblical account that Jeremiah and the "king's daughters" did go down to Tahpanhes" (Gk. Daphnae), being carried there by Johanan and all the captains of the forces of the remnant of Judah who were fleeing from the wrath of the Chaldeans.

What happened to Jeremiah and the king's daughters? Remember, Jeremiah was also commissioned to build and to plant. But what was he to build and to plant? Was he not to build and plant that which he had also torn down—the throne of David?

We know that Jeremiah, his scribe Baruch, and some of these fugitive Jews later left Egypt and went to the far west, to an island called Ireland, where they settled, living out the remainder of their lives in the "Emerald Isle."

Isaiah 37:31, 32 gives another link which explains this mystery.

> "And the remnant that is escaped of the house of Judah shall again take root downward, and bear fruit upward; for out of Jerusalem shall go forth a remnant, and they that escape out of Mount Zion: the zeal of the Lord of Hosts shall do this."

This clearly shows that the royal seed of Judah would again be established on a throne.

Now read Ezekiel 21:18-27.

> And thou, profane wicked prince of Israel, whose day is come, when iniquity shall have an end, thus saith the Lord God: remove the diadem, and take off the crown: this shall not be the same: exalt him that is low, and abase him that is high. I will overturn, overturn, overturn it: and it shall be no more [overturned] until He come whose right it is; and I will give it Him (vv. 25-27).

Verse 25 referred to the profane and wicked king, Zedekiah, who was going to be humbled and abased. The diadem or crown was to be taken from his head, and put on the head of one who had been of low rank. There is nothing in the Bible or in history to show that the Davidic crown passed to any one other than to the sovereigns ruling in Ireland!

The throne was first overturned at Jerusalem. The crown of the Jewish kings was thrown to the ground. (1) From here this crown was transferred to Ireland where its possessors ruled for many centuries. (2) From Ireland it was transferred to Scotland where the Scottish sovereigns all wore this crown. (3) From Scotland it was transferred to London, England (the third overturning); and it shall be overturned no more until the Second Coming of Christ—until Shiloh come.

The expression "I will overturn, overturn, overturn it: and it shall be no more" cannot possibly mean that the throne would cease after the third overturning, because we have seen a number of scriptures in which God solemnly promised David that he would have a decendant sitting upon this throne throughout every generation as long as the sun, the moon and the stars continued to exist!

Neither can this mean, as some would have us believe, that this throne (after being thrice overturned) would forever thereafter remain in London, England. The Bible shows that it would not be overturned any more after arriving in London, until the Second Coming of Christ, when it will once more be overturned and taken back to Jerusalem never again to be overturned. Here in Jerusalem, Shiloh shall sit (Jer.3:17), ruling for 1,000 years (Rev.20:4-6).

Now notice Ezekiel 17:1-24. This riddle or parable pertains to God's throwing down the Jewish nation and the Jewish throne in Jerusalem (the high tree). It also depicts the exalting of the "low tree" (the dry tree) which God had determined to make to flourish.

> Thus saith the Lord God: I will also take of the highest branch of the high cedar, and will set it; I will crop off from the top of his young twigs a TENDER ONE, and will plant it upon a high mountain and eminent (v. 22).

There can be no doubt that the "tender one" refers to a daughter from the high twig (the royal family) of the Davidic line who had been ruling in Judah. "In the mountain of the height of ISRAEL will I plant it." God showed that in Israel, it would become a mighty tree, and would bear much fruit. This is exactly what happened when the Jewish throne was overturned. The king's daughters were taken by Jeremiah from the land of Palestine to Egypt; and from there to Ireland. Their descendants have ruled over the British Isles, in the mountains (nations) of

Britain and her Commonwealth ever since. Queen Elisabeth II possesses a chart showing here decent all the way back to King David and through him on back to Adam!

We have already seen, according to Moore, that one of the dates when the Royal Sage, Ollamh Fodhla, came to Ireland was given as about 600 B.C. From the biblical account we know that this prophet or Royal Sage was none other than Jeremiah himself!

"Some of the most useful institutions of Ollamh Fodhla are said to have but a short time survived himself" (Moore, The History of Ireland, Vol. I, p. 87).

> Among the important offices transmitted hereditarily in Ireland were those of heralds, practictioners in physic, bards, and musicians. To the professors of these arts Ollamh Fodhla assigned lands for their use; and also instituted a school of general instruction at Tara, which became afterwards celebrated under the name of the Mur-ollam-ham, or College of the Learned (ibid., p.88).

The ancient histories of Ireland also show that when this Royal Sage came to Ireland, he was accompanied by a scribe called Baruch or Brec.

This Royal Sage brought a Royal Princess from the East. A marriage between this Royal Eastern Princess and Prince Herimon of Ulster (Northern Ireland) was effected and soon thereafter Herimon became king.

JEREMIAH IN IRELAND

Even to this very day a very strong tradition prevails in Ireland showing that many centuries ago a prophet by the name of Jeremiah had come to the "Sacred Isle."

The writer, while touring Ireland a few years ago, was passing through a town called Enniskillen. The local inhabitants informed him that the burial place of the prophet Jeremiah was supposed to be nearby. Thereupon the writer and a friend with whom he was travelling hired a guide to take them to "Jeremiah's Tomb." The traditional TOMB OF JEREMIAH is located on Devenish Isle, Lough Erne, North Ireland!

Some may discount this as mere tradition, but remember that tradition often contains kernels of truth buried beneath some chaff.

We know, especially from the Bible (as well as from history) that Jeremiah did journey to Northern Ireland bringing the royal seed—the daughters of King Zedekiah—with him.

One of these daughters, Tea Tephi, married Prince Herimon, a descendant of Zarah, a son of Judah. Princess Tea Tephi was a descendant of Pharez, whose descendants had been reigning in Jerusalem, Palestine. This marriage united the Pharez and the Zarah line, and the "breach" (Pharez means "breach") was at last mended.

But how do we know that the descendants of Zarah were in North Ireland?

THE RED HAND OF ULSTER

From time immemorial the people of Northern Ireland (Ulster) have used the "RED HAND" as an emblem on their heraldry. This "red hand" goes back to the time of Zarah's birth, when a RED or SCARLET THREAD was tied around his HAND, signifying Zarah's right to a regal position (Gen. 38:28, 29). His brother, Pharez, was born first, causing a breach.

Some of the "Scotic" people of North Ireland were descendants of the Zarah line of Judah!

"The St. George's Cross with the ANCIENT regional emblem, the BLOOD-RED RIGHT HAND of Ulster, at its center surmounted by the Royal Crown, forms the flag of Northern Ireland. A shield bearing the similar emblem and surrounded by a wreath at the center of the Union forms the flag of the Governor of Ireland" (Evans, The Observer's Book of Flags, p. 28).

On page 27 of this book is illustrated the flag of Northern Ireland. The flag has a white background with a red cross. In the centre is a SIX POINTED STAR, and in the center of this white star is "the BLOOD-RED RIGHT HAND OF ULSTER." Above the six-pointed "star of David" is the Royal crown. This six-point star, called "the star of David," does not appear to be of Davidic origin but ante-dates King David by many centuries. Whether or not this six-pointed star is of pagan origin, the fact remains that the Jews have used this star from time immemorial. Why does Ulster use this star if it is not connected with Judah through the Zarah line?

On page 194 of this same book is a display of a number of the flags of Yacht clubs. The "Royal Ulster" flag consists of a purple flag with a Union Jack in the upper left hand corner, but in the lower right hand corner of the flag, there is a white shield, on which is superimposed the Red Right Hand of Ulster. Above the shield and hand is the Royal crown.

It is also interesting to observe that the people of Ulster (the Milesian Scots) not only ruled all of Ireland and imposed their name upon the island until so late a date as the tenth century A.D., but later many of these Scythian Scots crossed the Irish Sea and settled in the northern part of the island of England, which they named "Scotia." Scotia was later called "Scotland" (land of the Scots).

From a book entitled The Scottish Tartans, illustrated by William Semple, we are informed that there are about ten or twelve of the clans of Scotland, whose coats of arms to this very day still include the "blood-red Right Hand of Ulster." On page 103 of this book he mentions the Matheson clan (called Mac-mhathan or Mac-mhagan in Gaelic), which has on its coat of arms a white shield with three of the blood-red Right Hands of Ulster.

Thus we can easily see the influence of the Zarah line of Judah in Ulster. This does not mean that all of the people of Ulster are descendants of the Zarah branch of Judah. Most of the Northern Irish are undoubtedly descendants of Joseph. But those Israelitish sons of Joseph arrived in Ireland under the name of "Scythian" (Skuthes or Scots, etc.).

We have already noted that those Milesian Scots from Scythia gave their name both to Ireland and to Scotland. Ireland retained the name of Scotia even until the tenth century A.D.

SCOTTISH-IRISH SETTLERS—"FROM ISRAEL"

In one of the oldest histories in the English language we are informed that Britain was formerly called the "White Island" or "Albion" and that it was situated in the Western Ocean between Ireland and Gaul. Britain, according to this ancient history, was inhabited by five different nations—Britons, Saxons, Romans, Picts, and SCOTS (Roberts, The Brut or The Chronicles of the Kings of Briton).

In The Brut, we are informed of Gwrganr, son of Beli, King of Britain, who went to Denmark to persuade the king of Denmark (by force of arms if necessary) to resume payment of tribute to him. Notice how clearly the following quotes reveal the ISRAELITISH ORIGIN OF THE SCOTCH-IRISH!

> On his return [meaning Gwrgant's return to England] as he was passing through the Orkney Isles, he came up with thirty ships, which were full of men and women; and finding them there, he seized their chief, whose name was Barthlome. Thereupon this chief prayed for protection, telling him that they "were called Barclenses," had been driven from Spain, and were roving on the seas to find a place of settlement; and that he therefore entreated Gwrgant to grant them permission to abide in some part of the island [of England] as they had been at sea for a year and a half. Gwrgant [King of England] having thus learned whence they were, and what was their purpose, directed them with his goodwill to go to Ireland, which at that time lay waste and uninhabited. Thither therefore they went, and there they settled, and peopled the country; and their descendants are to this day in Ireland (ibid., p. 60).

A very interest footnote referring to this Israelitish Chief, "BARTHLOME" says:

> "He [Barthlome the chief of the 30 ships] had his name from a river of Spain called Eirinnal, on the banks of which they had lived. This chief related to the king the whole of their adventures, from the time they had been driven from Israel (Palestine) their original country, and the manner and circumstances in which their ancestors dwelt in a retired part of Spain, near the Eirnia, from whence the Spaniards drove them to sea to seek another abode" (ibid., fn., p. 60).

Notice here were thirty shiploads of people, who according to their chief, Barthlome (a good Hebrew name) had come from ISRAEL, their original country, and had first gone to Spain. After having been driven from Spain, they came to the Orkney Islands, and were there directed by Gwrgant, the King of England, to go on to Ireland, where they permanently settled!

This is one more vital link of historical proof, connecting some of the ancient people of Ireland (who, in other accounts are called "Milesian Scots") directly with their original homeland of Israel in Palestine!

Some people would treat this very old historical reference to the early British settlers of these islands as mere fable; but a number of prophecies reveal that many of the Israelites would settle in the isles in North-west Europe.

SIGNIFICANCE OF THE DECLARATION OF ARBROATH

Perhaps the most prized historical document in possession of the Scottish nation is their historic "Declaration of Arbroath," otherwise called "The Scottish Declaration of Independence" (written in 1320 A.D.). This document is proudly displayed at the Register House, Edinburgh, Scotland.

In the years preceding 1320 A.D. there had been continual wars between England and Scotland. Under Robert Bruce, king of the Scots, the English were on many occasions defeated in battle.

> By 1313 only the castle of Stirling remained in the hands of the English. Edward II set out (1314) to relieve the castle; Lancaster and the baronichal party refused to support the expedition. At Bannockburn (1314) Edward was overwhelmingly defeated, and Scottish independence won (Langer, An Ency. of World History, p.264).

But wars continued between England and Scotland. Edward II finally appealed to the Pope at Rome, the international arbiter during the Middle Ages, to support him against Robert Bruce, King of Scotland. Edward asked the Pope to persuade Robert the Bruce to acknowledge the sovereignty of the King of England.

The Pontiff sent a letter with special representatives from the "Holy See" to persuade Robert Bruce to acknowledge the overlordship of Edward II, king of England. Following are some excerpts from the reply of Robert Bruce and his barons to the Pope:

> We know and gather from ancient Acts and the Records, that in every famous nation, this of Scotland hath been celebrated with many praises. This nation, having come from Scythia the Greater, through the Tuscan Sea and the Hercules Pillars, and having for many ages taken its residence in Spain in the midst of most fierce people, could never be brought in subjection by any people how barbarous soever; and having removed from these parts, above 1200 years after the coming of the Israelites out of Egypt, did by many victories and much toil obtain these parts in the West which they still possess, having expelled the British and entirely rooted out the Picts, notwithstanding the frequent assaults and invasions they met with from the Norwegians, Danes and English. (Scottish Declaration of Independence).

The foregoing excerpts from the Declaration of Arbroath were taken from a translation printed by Gordon Wilson, Edinburgh, second edition, February 1951. Another similar translation of this historic document may be found in Scots Magazine, April 1934, pp. 16-18.

There are a number of important points worth noting in regard to this document. First, this document was addressed to Pope John XXII, and signed by the Scottish barons and ecclesiastics of Robert Bruce in Parliament at Arbroath Abbey, April 1320.

Secondly, the Declaration of Arbroath shows conclusively that the Scots came from Scythia through Spain and finally to Scotland. Their arrival in Scotland, according to this Declaration, was 291 B.C. or 1,200 years after the Exodus of the children of Israel from Egypt. The Exodus occurred, according to Archbishop Usher's Chronology, circa 1491 B.C. Subtract 1,200 years from that date, and it will bring you to about 291 B.C. when the Scots, according to their own records, must have first gone to Scotland. They had, however, lived in Ireland for some time before going to Scotland.

Thirdly, notice the Scots mention directly the Exodus of the people of Israel. Why did they mention this Exodus unless they were part of the people of Israel who had taken part in this Exodus? They mentioned the Exodus because it was a memorable occasion in their national history.

We have already seen that these Milesian Scots who first went to Ireland definitely claimed that their "chieftans (were) connected by friendship with the prophet Moses himself" (Moore, History of Ireland, Vol. I, p. 71).

Who were the only chieftans connected by friendship with the prophet Moses? This can only refer to the Princes or chieftans of the tribes of Israel with whom Moses continually dealt in the long trek from Egypt to the wilderness of Sinai! Yes, Moses had dealt with these self-willed and stiff-necked Scots, who were at the time of the Exodus included under the banner of Joseph.

We noticed that these Milesian Scots were not only connected with the prophet Moses, but they were connected "by marriage or friendship . . . with most of the heroes of Scripture history."

> From thence [the plain of Shenaar] tracing this chosen race in their migrations to different countries, and connecting them, by marriage or friendship, during their long sojourn in Egypt, with most of the heroes of Scripture history (Moore, History of Ireland, Vol. I, p. 61).

These "heroes" of Scripture can only refer to such leaders as Moses, Joshua, Gideon, Samson, David, and others. These "Milesian Scots" knew their past history had been directly connected with the Bible heroes already mentioned.

Were these Milesian Scots descendants from Japheth, as many misguided historians would have us believe?

I confess that but for the universal tradition which assigns our descent to Japheth, I should have been rather inclined to attribute to the British Celts a Semitic origin (Lysons, Our British Ancestors, p. 18).

Remember the Milesian Scots were "Scythians" and also bear in mind that the Celts were merely a branch of the Scythian people.

ORIGIN OF THE TARTAN

In the reign of Achy, who succeeded Tighernmas in Ireland, a law was passed regulating the number of colours by which the garments of the different classes of society were to be distinguished. Plebeians and soldiers were to have but ONE colour in their dress; military officers of an inferior rank, TWO; commanders of battalions, THREE; the keepers of houses of hospitality, FOUR; the nobility and military knights, FIVE; and the Bards and Ollamhs, who were distinguished for learning, SIX; being but one colour less than the number (seven) worn by the reigning princes!

> These regulations are curious; not only as showing the high station alloted to learning and talent, among the qualifications, for distinction, but as presenting a coincidence rather remarkable with that custom of patriarchal times which made a garment of many colours the appropriate dress of kings' daughters and princes . . . From the party-coloured garments worn by the ancient Scots, or Irish, is derived the national fashion of the plaid, still prevailing among their descendants in Scotland (Moore, History of Ireland, pp. 85, 86).

There existed also among the Celts of Gaul a fancy for garments with all varieties of colour. Their braccae, or breeches were so name because of their plaided pattern; the Celtic word 'brac' denoting anything speckled or "party-coloured."

The historian, Tacitus, describes the Gaulish dress as including breeches and a plaid mantle (ibid., fn. p. 85).

Thus JACOB made a coat of many colours for his son, JOSEPH (Gen.37:3) and Tamar, one of David's daughters, wore a garment of diverse colours as was customary for kings' daughters that were virgins (II Sam. 13:18).

It is interesting to note that, to this very day, the Scots have a "Jacobite Tartan" which may be worn by anyone not having a clan tartan of his own (Bain, The Clans and Tartans of Scotland, pp. 286, 287).

It is not by coincidence that the tartan is still a garment of pride among some of the descendants of Joseph—the present-day Scots!

THE ORIGIN OF THE SAXONS

There is another name mentioned on the Behistun Rock Inscriptions—the name Saka (in the Persian language), or according to Professor Rawlinson, Sacae, (in the Susian language Sakka). Is this name "Saka" connected with the people of Israel? It certainly is!

We are informed by the Bible that the descendants of Israel were known as Israelites. The suffix "ite" means "son of." The descendants of the twelve sons of Jacob were likewise called after the names of the twelve Patriarchal Fathers. The sons of Levi were called Levites, the descendants of Benjamin were called Benjaminites and the children of Dan were called Danites, and so on.

THE SONS OF ISAAC

Were the descendants of Isaac never called after his name? "And God said unto Abraham, 'Let it not be grievous in thy sight because of the lad [Ishmael—Abraham's first-born son], and because of thy bondwoman; in all that Sarah has said unto thee, hearken unto her voice, because in ISAAC shall thy seed be called" (Gen. 21:12).

Notice also that this same statement is repeated twice in the New Testament. See Romans 9:7 and Hebrews 11:18. Why did God solemnly declare in three different places in the Bible that Abraham's seed would be called after the name of Isaac, if he did not mean exactly what He said? Where (and how) in history were the progeny of Abraham and Isaac ever called after the name of ISAAC?

The names "Saxon," "Saksun," "Sakaisuna," and "sons of Sacae" all definitely refer to the "sons of Isaac."

THE "I" HAS BEEN DROPPED

It is quite common in some languages to drop the initial syllable from a word. Dr. Schrader points out that the Assyrians dropped the "i" when they spoke of an Israelite. "Ahab is called by Shalmanessar II A-HA-AB-BU SIR-'-LAI i.e. 'Ahab of Israel' in an inscription discovered on the banks of the Tigris . . ." (The Cuneiform Inscriptions of the Old Testament, Vol.I pp.137,138).

This is undoubtedly what has happened in regard to the Isaac-sons (Saxon). The "i" has been dropped and the basic part of the word "sak" or "sac" has been retained. "Son" simply means son of. So the word "Saxons" means "sons of (I)SAC" or "sons of Isaac." Later, we shall see quotations from reliable historical sources proving that "Saxon" derives from "sons of Sac" or "sons of Sak" meaning "sons of Isaac."

In the days of the Judges, the Ephraimites could not sound the "h" in the word "Shibboleth."

During a struggle between Israelitish factions, the inability of the Ephraimites to pronounce the "h" cost many of them their lives. Speaking of fugitive Ephraimites we read: "Then said they unto him, Say now Shibboleth: and he said Sibboleth: for he could not frame to pronounce it right. Then they took him, and slew him at the passages of Jordan: and there fell at that time of the Ephraimites forty and two thousand" (Judges 12:6).

Many Hebrew-speaking Jews have difficulty pronouncing their "h's" to this day. Why do we all say "Semitic" instead of "Shemitic"? Is it not because the "h" has been dropped in this word?

It is quite common among many of the people of the British Isles even today, to drop an initial letter in some words. This is especially true of the letter "h", which is often dropped by many English-speaking people who live in Great Britain.

"Where did I 'ang me 'at?"—a friend of mine once asked. And our plumber told me one day, that it was "'air" which had stopped up our drain. He had to repeat himself several times before it was realised that he meant "hair" instead of "air".

THE ANGLO-SAXONS DESCENDANTS OF SHEM

Before we pursue further the derivation of the word "Sacae", we will consider historical evidence proving that the Anglo-Saxon peoples have descended from Shem.

We have already noted that Lysons made this confession:

> I confess that but for the universal tradition which assigns our [the British] descent to Japhet, I should have been rather inclined to attribute to the British Celts a Semitic origin, both on account of the relics of worship which we find in Britain, and also on account of the language . . ." (Our British Ancestors, p. 18).

Lysons then shows that there are literally thousands of words in the English language which come from the Hebrew language (ibid., p. 21 ff.). He says:

> Thus I propose to show in the course of these pages when we come to the relics of British worship remaining in the country, and retaining with little variation or corruption their aboriginal names, the remarkable similarity between those names and the HEBREW and CHALDEE languages" (ibid., p.21).

He then points out that many of the "old British families" have Hebrew names. "Now, whatever may be the historical value of the Welsh poems, it is undoubted that Talies in his Angar Cyfyndawd, says that his lore had been 'DECLARED IN HEBREW, Hebraig . . .'" (ibid., p. 22).

On page 93 of this same work, Lysons says:

Yet this we gather from the names attaching to the British monuments still remaining among us, when divested of modern corruptions, that there is a strong affinity between these British names and that language of which HEBREW is either the original or one of its earliest off-shoots; and that therefore HEBREW, CHALDEE or some other very near cognate, must have been the language of the first inhabitants in this island" (ibid., p. 93).

Lysons then proceeds to show the similarity between many ancient British and Hebrew words, and between the corrupted religion of the Palestinian Israelites and that of the ancient British people. Lysons finally makes this startling statement:

We cannot avoid the conclusion that our British ancestors were devoted to that kind of worship which they brought with them from the East, whence they came at a very early period, even close upon the Patriarchal times of Holy Writ (ibid., pp. 93, 94).

It has already been clearly pointed out that the early British ancestors said they came from Armenia in the area of the Caucasus Mountains; and we know that many of them arrived in the British Isles centuries before Christ's birth.

Robert Owen also substantiates this view by the following statement:

Most Welsh scholars have employed their time on the production of grammars and dictionaries. The Hebrew learning of Dr. John Davies of Mallwyd seems to have influenced his countrymen to accept the Puritan atavism of referring Welsh to the language of Moses as its fountain (The Kymry, pref. v., vi.).

For any who still might have any lingering doubts regarding the similarity between the Hebrew and the early British languages which were used by its ancient peoples, one need only study the present-day Welsh language. There are many strong similarities between modern Welsh and Hebrew. Even one who is unskilled in the science of languages cannot fail to detect a close similarity between the spoken Hebrew language when contrasted with modern Welsh. Many Welsh words are almost devoid of any vowels whatsoever, just as the ancient Hebrew language was written without any vowels.

A number of books have been written besides the ones mentioned here which show the close affinity between the languages as spoken by some of the early British peoples and the Hebrew language.

As an example of some modern Welsh names with few written vowels, here is part of the address of a friend of mine. The name is fictitious, however. Nathan Evans, Tyddyn Valley, Llanddoget, Llanrwst, Denbighshire. Notice that the anglicized words have far more vowels written in them than do such words as "Llanrwst."

We have already observed that it has been commonly taught that the British have descended from Japheth. Nothing could be farther from the truth!

Here is proof that the British have descended from Shem, and are therefore Semitic (Shemitic).

> Alfred, king of the Anglo-Saxons, was born in the year of our Lord's incarnation eight hundred and forty-nine . . . King Alfred was the son of Geata . . . This Geata was the son of . . . Heremod . . . the son of Sem (Church Historians of England, Annals of Exploits of Alfred Great, Vol. II, pp. 443-44).

We have noticed that Alfred the Great, king of the Anglo-Saxons was a descendant of "Sem." This same quotation continues as folows: "Heremod . . . the son of Sem, the son of Noe, the son of Lamech, the son of Methusalem, the son of Enoch, the son of Malaleel, the son of Cainan, the son of Enos, the son of Seth, the son of Adam" (ibid.).

Alfred the Great, who was himself a Saxon (son of Isaac), traced his genealogy right back to "Sem" (or Shem) and on back to Adam.

> So the Anglo-Saxons may well have had records of the ancestry of their kings, beginning with Sceaf . . . and calling Sceaf the son of Noe, born in the ark, or even identifying him with the patriarch Shem (Haigh, The Conquest of Britain by the Saxons, Chapter III, p. 115).

Haigh makes the grave mistake that many others do. Many simply cannot believe the plain records of the ancient peoples who came to the British Isles! They just can't possibly believe that these peoples could really have been descendents of Shem. We shall notice the same tendency for critics of early Scotch-Irish history. They think the early history (which they call folklore) of these peoples cannot be true when it connects such peoples directly with the lands and peoples mentioned in the Bible.

We shall see in a later chapter that the Scythians, who were the ancestors of the Anglo-Saxons, spoke a language that had a strong similarity with Hebrew. Should this fact amaze us? It should not cause any alarm, especially when one sees that these Scythian peoples came from the regions of the Caucasus Mountains not long after they were taken as captives to that general area by the Assyrian kings in 741, 721 B.C.

Time does not permit us to give the innumerable similarities between the early British words and the Hebrew; but consider the words "British" (Heb. covenant man), and "Britain" (Heb. covenant land). All of the early British languages had many points in common with the Hebrew language.

WHO WERE THE SACAE?

The Bible had prophesied, as we have already observed, "In ISAAC shall thy seed be called" (Gen. 21:12).

Have you ever known of any people being called after Isaac?

It might be well to point out here that the Persians spoke of all the people of Scythia as the Sacae or Sakka, because the Sacae were a branch of the Scythian people who dwelt nearest to them. Modern research confirms conclusively that the Sacae were a very important branch of the people who were called by the name of Scythians.

A very reliable historical account of the Anglo-Saxons, by Sharon Turner, gives a number of salient points regarding the Anglo-Saxons. It is so important that it is here given verbatim:

> The Saxons were a . . . Scythian tribe; and of the various Scythian nations which have been recorded, the Sakai, or Sacae, are the people from whom the descent of the Saxons may be inferred with the least violation of probability. Sakai-suna or the sons of Sakai, abbreviated into Saksun, which is the same sound as Saxon, seems a reasonable etymology of the word Saxon. The Sakai, who in Latin are called Sacae, were an important branch of the Scythian nation. They were so celebrated, that the Persians called all the Scythians by the name of Sacae; and Pliny, who mentions this, speaks of them as among the most distinguished people of Scythia (Pliny, lib. vi. c.19). Strabo places them eastward of the Caspian . . . (The History of The Anglo-Saxons, Vol. I, p.87).

Note that Turner shows the Sacae were an important branch of the Scythian nation. They lived to the east of the Caspian Sea. According to Turner, these Scyths (Sacae) seized the most fertile part of Armenia! Also observe that this was the same general area (Armenia) to which Israel had been deported.

> This important fact of a part of ARMENIA having been named Sakasina, is mentioned by Strabo in another place (Strabo, p.124), and seems to give a geographical locality to our primeval ancestors, and to account for the Persian words that occur in the Saxon language; as they must have come into Armenia from the northern regions of Persia (ibid., p. 87).

Turner says that "our primeval [Saxon] ancestors" went into Armenia from northern Persia. This again shows the general vicinity of Israel's dispersion.

This quote from Turner is so significant that it must be given in toto:

> That some of the divisions of this people were really called SAKA-SUNA, is obvious from Pliny; for he says that the SAKAI, who settled in Armenia, were named SACASSANI (Pliny. lib. vi. c.11); which is but SAKA-SUNA spelt by a person unacquainted with the meaning of the combined words. And the name SACASENA (Strabo. lib. Xi. pp. 776, 778), which they gave to the part of Armenia they occupied, is nearly the same sound as SAXONIA. It is also important to remark, that Ptolemy mentions a Scythian people sprung from the Sakai, by the name of SAXONES. If the Sakai who reached Armenia were called Saca-sani, they may have traversed Europe with the same appellation; which being pronounced by the Romans from them, and then reduced to writing from their pronunciation, may have been spelt with the x instead of the ks, and thus

SAXONS would not be a greater variation from SACASSANI or SAKSUNA than we find between French, Francois, Franci, and their Greek name, Phraggi; or between Spain, Espagne, Hispania (ibid., p.88).

Turner is undoubtedly correct in saying that the "ks" was changed to an "x." These variations of the word Sacae (or Saka) are not any greater, says Turner, than the variations of names for such modern nations as France and Spain (ibid. pp.87, 88, 95).

He then says that Ptolemy placed another people, the Sasones, north of the Sacae. These have been selected as our ancestors . . . Sasones, Sacaesons, Saxones (ibid., fn., p. 95).

Turner then mentions that some of these marauding Sakai or Saca-sana were, in all probability, gradually propelled to the west coast of Europe, on which they were found by Ptolemy, and from which they made incursions into the Roman Empire, in the third century A.D. A people known as the Saxoi, lived on the Black Sea, according to Stephanus (Stephanus de urb. et Pop. p. 657).

"We may," says Turner, "consider these, also, as a nation of the same parentage." These Sakai wandered far and wide from Asia to the German Ocean. He also points out the traditional descent of Odin as preserved by Snorre in the Edda and his history which represents the Saxon and Scandinavian chieftans as having migrated from a city, east of the Tanais, called Asgard, located in a country called Asaland, meaning the city and the land of the Asae or Asians (Snorre Ynlinga Saga, c. 2. and 5).

Thus, we see that Turner equated the Sacae with Odin and his people, the Asae, from Asgard, north of the Black Sea—the very area where we find many of the Israelites located shortly after their exile (ibid., pp. 88, 89).

> But that of the most learned German seems most probable and worthy to be embraced, which makes the Saxons descend from the Sacae, the most considerable people of Asia, and to be so called quasi Sacasones, q.d. sons of the Sacae, and to have gradually overspread Europe from Scythia or Sarmatia Asiatica, with the Getae, Suevi, Daci and others. Nor is their opinion ill-founded, which brings the Saxons out of Asia, in which the human race had both its rise and increase . . . (Camden, Britannia, Vol. I, p. 151).

Camden seems to completely agree with Turner in identifying such peoples as: Saxons, Sacae, Sacasones, ("sons of the Sacae"), Saci, q.d. Sassones, Sacasena. Note that they came "from Scythia." He says that "these people kept almost as near to one another in Europe" as they had before in Asia.

> The Sacae, who are Scythians, had on their heads caps, which came to a point and stood erect: they wore loose trousers, and carried bows peculiar to their country . . . These, though they are Amyrgian Scythians, they call Sacae, for the Persians call all the Scythians Sacae (Herod., Polymnia, Bo. VII, par. 64).

From Herodotus' statements, we can see that the Sacae were actually a Scythian tribe. Herodotus called them "Amyrgian Scythians."

According to the Encyclopedia Britannica, the Angli or Angles were merely a branch of the Saxons. The Anglo-Saxons invaded England in the 4th, 5th and 6th centuries A.D. (Ency. Brit. 11th ed., Vol. XXIV, Art. Saxons, pp. 264, 265).

We shall later have occasion to refer to the Sacae or Saxons as we study the Scythian and other tribes.

Here is a final quotation that clearly shows that "Saxon" is derived from "sons of Sacae." Milton says that the Saxons were a heathen and a barbarous nation, famous for their robberies and cruelties done to all their neighbours, both by land and sea.

> They [the Saxons] were a people thought by good writers to be descendants of the Sacae, a kind of Scythians in the north of Asia, thence called Sacasons, or sons of Sacae, who with a flood of other northern nations came into Europe, Toward the declining of the Roman Empire (History of England, 1835 ed., Bk. III, pp. 406, 407).

Notice how many different historians equate the Scythians with the Sacae; and also note how many show that the "Sacasons" (or Saxons) were "sons of Sacae" ((I)saac)!

The Saxons are descendants of Isaac. "In Isaac shall thy seed be called" (Gen. 21:12). It is primarily through the Saxons that this prophecy has been (and is still being) fulfilled!

CHAPTER VII

THE SCYTHIANS

We have seen that the name Cimmerian or Gimiri, as mentioned on the Behistun Rock Inscriptions, referred to the people of the House of Omri, Khumri, or Ghomri.

But what is the origin of the word "Scythia," as mentioned in the Persian and Susian languages on the Behistun Rock Incriptions? Is this name connected in any way with the dispersed "Lost Ten Tribes of Israel"?

The word "Scythian" is used only once in the Bible. "There is neither Greek nor Jew, circumcision nor uncircumcision, Barbarian, Scythian, bond nor free: but Christ is all, and in all" (Col. 3:11).

The Scythians were looked upon as barbarians in the eyes of the Greeks and the Romans. They did not have their culture, but they had a highly developed culture of their own. They were not ignorant savages like the aborigines of Africa or Australia, or like the natives of the Americas.

True, they were nomads who roamed far and wide over the vast Euro-Asiatic steppes of South Russia in tents and in covered wagons. But they were not barbarians in the strict sense. This does not imply that they were "angels." They committed many barbarities; but did not the so-called civilised Romans, Greeks, Assyrians, Egyptians, Babylonians and Medo-Persians do as bad or worse?

Let us notice Strong's definition of this word "Scythian."

"Scythian. (Scuthes=Gk.) A Scythene or Scythian i.e. (by implication) a savage" (The Exhaustive Concordance of the Bible).

"Scythian" is thought by some to mean "the tribes," but hardly anyone will really venture to dogmatically say what the derivation of this word is.

MOST OF THE SCYTHS WERE ISRAELITES

Who were these Scythians, or Scyths, as they were often called? And how did the name "Scythian" originate?

139

This was one of the names that the Ten-Tribed House of Israel bore in their captivity. The most likely derivation of this word is as follows:

This word "SCYTHIAN" appears to be derived from the Hebrew word "SUCCOTH." We shall later see that the language of the Scythians (Scythiac) was very similar to the Hebrew. Strong's Exhaustive Concordance defines this word as follows. "Cukkouth, sook-kahthr'; or Cukkoth, sook-kohth'; . . . booths; Succoth, the name of a place in Egypt and of three in Palestine" (Strong's Exhaustive Concordance, Hebrew and Chaldee Dictionary, p.82).

The Hebrew language was written only in consonants. The vowels had to be supplied by the reader. If one takes out the vowels from the Hebrew word "Succoth" the basic part of the word is "Scth." In Strong's Exhaustive Concordance it is spelled phonetically both with a "c" and also with an "s." Remember the "c" and the "s" often have the same sound, as in our English words, "cell" and "sell." Both English words are pronounced exactly alike.

There were three Succoths in Palestine, and one in Egypt. There is every reason to believe that the Israelitish Hebrews who migrated to Egypt, founded the city by the name Succoth near the border of Egypt and Israel. If you will locate the Egyptian Succoth on a map, you will see that it lies immediately west of the Suez Canal in the vicinity of Goshen.

Abraham, and also Jacob and his twelve sons, all sojourned at one time in the land of Egypt, very near this town called Succoth. In Genesis 33:17 we read that Jacob made booths for his cattle. The word translated as "booths" is from the same Hebrew root which we have been considering.

Keep in mind that if one takes the vowels out of Succoth, the consonants remaining will spell Scth, or Skth.

As an example, let us take one of God's names. How was the name "Jehovah" pronounced in Hebrew? Not one single Hebrew scholar can answer this question. This Hebrew name YHWH or JHVH was probably pronounced as YEHWEH. No one can say for sure how this word was originally pronounced because, as already mentioned, only the consonants were written. The present vowel points which one finds in the Hebrew manuscripts were added much later.

THE ISRAELITES WERE TENT (SUCCOTH) DWELLERS

"Ye shall dwell in booths seven days; all that are Israelites born shall dwell in booths: That your generations may know that I made the children of Israel to dwell in booths, when I brought them out of the land of Egypt" (Lev. 23:42,43). This was to be observed by Israel "forever" (v.41).

The Hebrew word used in verses 42 and 43, translated as "booths" is from the Hebrew SCTH or SKTH.

The Greek word for "Scythian" is "Scuthes," and is pronounced much like the Hebrew word for "booth."

The Scythians were undoubtedly booth dwellers or Succoth-dwellers originally, though at a later period in their history, many of them lived in covered wagons.

After the Israelites were deported from their homeland in Palestine, unto the region of Media and Assyria, they were an unsettled people. They undoubtedly wandered about in tents or booths, and were called "Scythians," meaning booth or tent dwellers. Some historians think "Scythian" means "the tribes".

We have already observed that God said the people of Israel would be punished for their sins and would become "wanderers among the nations." They were to be "scattered among the countries," "sifted among the nations." These references indicate that they were to dwell in tents or booths for many years; for people who are moving or wandering about do not live in fixed abodes. They must resort to tents, or portable abodes, even as do the Gypsies.

For many hundreds of years the dispersed Israelites wandered from the region of the Caucacus Mountains (to which they had been deported from Palestine) through the lands of Central and South Asia, and finally made their way to North-western Europe. In some instances, we see them traversing or even retracing their steps under various names. But they were always on the move—that is, until they reached their present homes in North-western Europe.

These new territories in North-west Europe were to become their new "Promised Lands." After occupying these choice, fertile lands they were to be blessed with the overflowing promises which God had made thousands of years earlier to the faithful patriarchs of the people of Israel.

We have already read in Deuteronomy 32:8 that God Almighty had foreordained the inheritance of all nations, and that He set the bounds of the peoples of the world—the Gentile nations—according to the number of the children of Israel (Deut. 32:8).

Later on, we shall see from a number of historical sources that such names as "Scot," "Scotch," and "Scythian" are all derived from the Greek name "Skuthes"—all of which appear to be derived from the Hebrew "Succoth" meaning "booth."

Thus the people of Scotland have to this day retained one of the early names which the people of Israel bore in their captivity.

THE TERRITORIAL EXTENT OF SCYTHIA

It is only after much painstaking research that one can accurately determine the limits of the territories which were once inhabited by the Scythians.

The Scythians (Gk. Skuthai, Latin Scythae, Persian Saka) were the first nomads of which we have any knowledge.

Heredotus assigned to them the country between the Don and Dniester, but their tombs show that they once held the region on the Kuban River, east of the Sea of Azov, and that they penetrated far to the west. A Scythian burial was found . . . just outside of Berlin (Chamber's Ency., Vol. XII, Art. Scythians).

We are further informed that traces of the Scythians have been found in Poland, in all parts of Hungaria and Transylvania, and some in Rumania. A number of very rich tombs have been exhumed in Bulgaria (ibid.).

According to Herodotus, the Scythians had come from "out of Asia" and from "across the Araxes" (Minns, Scythians and Greeks, p. 44). This further shows that the Scythians had formerly lived south of the ARAXES which lies in Armenia, just south of the Caucasus Mountains. Modern Armenia is divided among the Soviet Union, Turkey and Iran.

"We find the Cimmerians, Gimirrai, first N. of Urartu (Ararat) . . . so that the identity with the Greek Kimmerios and Scuthes is almost complete" (Minns, Scythians and Greeks, p. 42).

The above statement is further proof of what has been mentioned earlier—that the SCYTHIANS and CIMMERIANS were all basically the same people. The Cimmerians were, in fact, merely a branch of the Scythians. Also note that these Cimmerians or Gimirrai were first noticed north of Urartu or Mount Ararat.

This is further confirmation of the fact that these Gimirrai or Cimmerians were the people of Bit Ghomri (House of Omri), who were taken captive into the regions south of the Caucasus Mountains, in the vicinity of Mount Ararat in the eighth century B.C.

The foremost authority regarding this subject of the Scythians is unquestionably Professor E.H. Minns. In his monumental work, Scythians and Greeks, he analyzes the Scythian subject very thoroughly.

Among the various rivers which were located in Scythia were the Danube, Don, Dnestr and the Dnepr (ibid., p.27). The exact limits of Scythia are not easily discernible, but some of the Scythians had, at a fairly early period, penetrated as far east as China!

We have tried to show that information from China and the west tally completely as far as the conquest of Bactria, owing to the great trek, is concerned. Konow supposes, following Rapson's opinion, that the cause of the invasion into India must be sought for in the action taken by the Sakas [Scythians] in Seistan, when, after the reign of Mithradates II, they made themselves independent of the much weaker Parthia (Van Lohuizen-de Leeuw, The Scythian Period, Chap. VII, p.324).

We are then informed by Van Lohuizen-de Leeuw that the Scythians, Sakas, and the Yueh-Chi were allied in their fight against Artabanus I, whom they killed in battle. Another mention is made of the Scythians in the East, fighting against Mithradates II who had succeded Artabanus I. Mithradates II was successful in his fight against the Scythians in the East (ibid. pp. 324, 325).

Phrates II (138-127) defeated Antiochus VII in Media (129), and as a result the Seleucides were permanently excluded from the lands east of the Euphrates; but he died in battle fighting the Tochari (the Scythians or Sacae of the Greeks), a tribe driven forth from Central Asia by the Yue-Chi (Langer, An Ency. of World History), 1956 ed., p. 83).

Notice the name, Yue-chi.

Langer, Minns and others show that the Scythians had penetrated as far east as the vicinity of China. This is also indicated by Minns in his work, Scythia and Greeks, on the back cover map.

Thucydides (Thus. II. 96, 97), for instance, must mean all the people of Scythia together when he says that uncivilised though the Scythians were, no single nation of Europe or Asia could stand against them in war, if but they were all of one mind (ibid., pp. 35, 36).

There can be no doubt that up to the coming of the Goths and the Huns, the Steppes around the Black Sea were "chiefly inhabited by an IRANIAN population."

The Encyclopedia Britannica shows that Scythia (Gk. Skuthia) was originally the country of the Scythae, and it included all of the territory from the Carpathians to the Don River (11th ed., Vol. XXIV, Art. Scythia).

This article mentions that throughout classical literature the word "Scythia" generally meant all the regions to the north and north-east of the Black Sea, and a Scythian was any barbarian who came from those parts.

We are informed of a group of "rebel Scyths" who broke away from the main body of the Scythians and migrated to the north-west of Lake Balkash, settling in an area called Sacae. Scythian burial grounds and tombs are found not only on Hungarian soil, but also in Rumania and Bulgaria. Some of these SCYTHIANS were undoubtedly adventurers, and others were, according to historical sources, driven relentlessly by the Sarmatians advancing from the east (Rice, The Scythians, p.55).

Rice mentions that the name Scythia is reserved by a group of authorities in the U.S.S.R. for the tribes which once ruled over all of the territories stretching from the Don in the east to the Carpathian Mountains, near the Danube in the west.

Collier's Encyclopedia says that Scythia included Southern Russian between the Caucasus and the Danube, but in Roman times this territory was called Sarmatia (Vol. XVII, Art. Scythia).

According to this article, the Scythians, who ruled from the Don River to the Carpathian Mountains, remained in power until they were defeated by the Sarmatians in the first and second centuries B.C.

The Scyths ruled Media for twenty-eight years, and were then massacred or expelled, according to Herodotus. "Most writers think that the SCYTHIANS who troubled Asia were SACAE from the east of the CASPIAN . . ." (Ency. Brit., 11th ed., Vol. XXIV, Art. Scythia, p. 527).

Here is a significant statement from the Encyclopedia Britannica:

> About the same time, similar peoples harrassed the northern frontier of Iran, where they were called Saka (Sacae), and in later times Saka and Scyths, whether they were originally the same or not, were regarded as synonymous. It is difficult always to judge whether given information applies to the Sacae or the Scyths (ibid., p. 528).

It is interesting to see how many authentic historical statements there are which equate the Scythians and the Sacae.

SCYTHOPOLIS IN PALESTINE

The Dictionary of the Bible, by James Hastings, mentions that the nomadic Scythians lived "between the Danube and the Don"—instead of the Carpathian Mountains and the Don, as some affirm. But the Carpathian Mountains are very near the Danube River, so this is roughly the same territory. We are futher informed by this source that in the time of the elder Pliny the name Scythia was rather vaguely applied to the remote regions of South-east Europe and Central Asia. See Map XI.

> Herodotus mentions (I.103-105) that a horde of Scythians invaded Media, and become masters of Asia, and intended to attack Egypt. Psammetichus, the king of Egypt met them in Palestine when he was besieging Azotus, and prevailed on them by bribes to retreat . . . Thuc. (II. 96) connects the SCYTHIANS with the GETAE, their neighbours with whom they afterward coalesced (ibid., pp. 369, 370).

Did you notice that the SCYTHS are equated also with the GETAE, who were later known as GOTHS?

After the Scythians were bought off by the Egyptian Pharoah, they returned to Asia.

It was during this general period that the name of Scythopolis was given to a town west of the Jordan River and south of the Sea of Galilee in Palestine. This name shows the influence of the Scythians even in Palestine.

By piecing together all of the above information regarding Scythia, one can see how vast an area it covered. At one time Scythia stretched from India and China in the East to the Danube River and the Carpathian Mountains in the West.

SCYTHS—SECOND GREAT BRANCH
TO ENTER EUROPE

In the foregoing chapters, we have studied the racial backgrounds of the Cimmerians (Cymry) Gauls, Celts and related tribes. We have observed that all of the aforementioned peoples were merely different branches of the same basic race. Also, it has been pointed out that the Cimmerians were, after all, merely an offshoot of the great Scythian nation; and we have further noticed that the main body of the Cimmerian peoples coalesced with the Scyths. The name "Celto-Scyths" is an indication of how much these tribes had mixed.

On one occasion it was pointed out that the Cimmerians and Scythians had met each other on the battlefield, but this does not imply that they were not closely related.

Sharon Turner shows that most of the nations of modern Europe have descended from the Scythian peoples (History of the Anglo-Saxons, Vol. I, p. 3).

It is important to note that it is sometimes difficult to draw a clear line of demarcation between the Scythian and Cimmerian peoples. The reason for this is quite easy to understand when one considers that the Cimmerian branch was (as we have already proven historically) merely an offshoot of the great Scythian nation.

One need only peruse the histories of such countries as America, England, France and Germany to note the many internal struggles which have been waged within these nations even in modern times.

The American, French, British and German civil wars are examples of the struggles that have often been waged between closely related peoples.

SCYTHIAN ORIGINS

Now let us answer the following questions: What was the origin of the Scythians? Who were they? From where did they come? When are they first noticed in history? What is their importance as a people? What part have their descendants played in modern times? What social and religious customs did they have? These and other questions shall be answered in our discussion of the Scythians and the part they played in ancient times.

Though much has been written on the subject of the Scythians, most people know very little about this prolific and widely scattered people. The reason for this is quite natural. The Scythians lived beyond the pale of the civilized world, and therefore were not known except as they came into contact with the more "civilized" peoples such as the Greeks and the Romans, and it was their enemies who were their historians.

The Scythians lived, as we shall later observe, to the north of the historic peoples—the Romans, Greeks, Babylonians, Assyrians, and Persians—and are not widely known except through contact with them.

We shall presently note that no nation could withstand these Scythian peoples when they were united—which was seldom, if ever.

It has already been brought to our attention that, according to the BEHISTUN ROCK INSCRIPTIONS, this name "SCYTHIAN" is one of the first names which ISRAEL bore in exile. God had determined to bury the identity of these exiles whom he had expelled from the Promised Land, so that they would lose their identity until the latter days, when their identity was to be revealed to them.

In this section on the Scythians, the foremost authorities will be consulted and, in order to thoroughly understand the Scythian background and their connection with Israel, we shall examine this subject through the eyes of many different historians who have diligently studied Scythian history.

First, we shall consider this subject through a classic work written by Sharon Turner. He had an unusually penetrating way of analyzing the ethnological entanglements of the peoples of Europe.

Turner shows that Europe has been peopled by three great streams of population from the east, which have followed each other at intervals so distinct as to possess languages clearly separable from each other. These "three streams of population" were: (1) Cimmerian or Celtic, (2) Scythian or Gothic, and (3) Sarmatian or Slavic. He points out that the earliest people who came to Europe were of the Cimmerian, Cymric or Celtic race. The second people to migrate into Europe were the Scythian, Gothic or German peoples. It would appear that Turner did not mean that the Scythian peoples were synonymous with the true Germans of today.

We have already noticed that the first branch of people who came to Europe were the Cimmerians or Celts. They settled primarily in the north or western parts of Europe—mostly on the coastlands and islands of that continent. But the Scythian or Gothic peoples occupied the great body of the European continent (Turner, History of the Anglo-Saxons, Vol. I, p. 24).

> The early occupation of Europe by the Kimmerian and Keltic races has been already displayed. The next stream of barbaric tribes, whose progress formed the second great influx of population into Europe, were the Scythian, German, and Gothic tribes. They also entered it out of Asia (ibid., p. 81).

> Herodotus, beside the main Scythia, which he places in Europe, mentions also an Eastern or Asiatic Scythia, beyond the Caspian and the Iaxertes . . . The Anglo-Saxons, Lowland Scotch, Normans, Danes, Norwegians, Swedes, Germans, Dutch, Belgians, Lombards, and Franks, have all sprung from this great fountain of the human race, which we have distinguished by the terms SCYTHIAN, German or Gothic (ibid., pp. 81-83).

What did the Scythians call themselves? "Their general appellation among themselves was SCOLOTI, but the Greeks call them SCYTHIANS, SCUTHOI or Nomades" (ibid. p. 84).

"The emigrating Scythians," says Turner, "crossed the ARAXES, passed out of Asia, and invading the Kimmerians, suddenly appeared in Europe IN THE SEVENTH CENTURY BEFORE THE CHRISTIAN ERA" (History of the Anglo-Saxons, p. 85).

The Araxes was just south of the Caucasus Mountains! This was the very region to which the tribes of Israel were deported some in 741 and some in 721 B.C.—in the 8th century B.C.

Yes, the Scythians left the Caucasus in the 7th century B.C. or about one hundred years after the first tribes of Israel were taken into captivity by the Assyrians.

Turner mentions that these Scythian tribes have become better known to us in recent times "under the name of GETAE or GOTHS, the most celebrated of their branches" (ibid., p. 86). We have discussed the Goths in more detail in an earlier chapter.

The Saxons were, according to Turner, a Gothic or Scythian tribe, and he further equates them with the SAKAI or SACAE who were the same people as the "SAKAI-SUNA," which he explains to mean "the sons of the SAKAI" (ibid., p. 87).

Turner shows that the THIRD GROUP of closely related peoples to arrive en masse in Europe were the SARMATIANS.

SARMATIANS—THIRD BRANCH TO ENTER EUROPE

Who were the Sarmatians? Where did they come from? Were they a Scythian tribe, or were they always clearly distinguished from the Scythians? Were they the ancestors of the Slavic peoples as many have believed, or were they the progenitors of the Germans as others have held?

Since the Sarmatians were from the earliest times the neighbors of the Scythians, and especially because some have mistakenly confused the Scythians and Sarmatians, it is needful to briefly examine this subject.

SARMATIAN ORIGINS

"The THIRD great branch of people to come into Europe were the SARMATIAN or SLAVONIAN peoples who were bordering on the Scythian (or Gothic) tribes, as these Scythians spread over the great body of the continent of Europe" (Turner, History of the Anglo-Saxons, Vol. I, p. 4).

These Sarmatian or Slavonic tribes have, according to Turner, settled in the eastern parts of Europe—Poland, Bohemia, Russia, etc.

There is a great abundance of material to prove beyond question that the Sarmatians (Sauromate) are the ancestors of the present-day Slavs (and some Germans) inhabiting the countries just mentioned, plus such South-east European nations as Czechoslovakia, Rumania, Hungary, and others. All of these Slavic peoples, according to reliable historical sources, came from the Carpathian Mountains which was the central point of their diffusion.

Included in the Sarmatian tribes were undoubtedly many of the German peoples—especially the "Slavic" elements to the east, and some of the Alpine peoples of Central and Southern Germany, and Austria.

We shall notice later that the most discriminating historians always differentiate between the Sarmatians and the Scythians, though these people have always been in close proximity to one another! There are no other peoples mentioned in history from whom the millions of Slavic peoples could have descended, other than the great Sarmatian horde. This is the view which is commonly held and is undoubtedly correct.

We shall not, however, consider the Sarmatians to any great extent, except as they are associated with the Scythians.

Later, we shall see that the overwhelming majority of the Scythians were dolichocephalic (long-headed). The Sarmatians were brachycephals (round-headed): "A series of eighteen Sarmatian crania from the Volga . . . has a cranial index of 80.3" (Coon, The Races of Europe, p. 200).

"Most of the modern Slavs are rather short-headed" (Ency. Brit., 11th ed., Vol. XXV, Art. Slavs, p. 229).

In an earlier chapter we have seen that many of the present-day Germans are "Slavic" by descent, and are therefore of Sarmatian descent. Their social customs and their other habits would also lead one to belive this.

Let us notice two or three authors who clearly distinguish the Scythians from the Sarmatians.

Professor Rostovtseff distinguished the Sarmatians, who were definitely Iranian, from their predecessors, the Scyths (Iranians and Greeks in South Russia, 1922 ed., pp. 60, 122f).

"He [Hippocrates] draws a very clear line between them [the Sauromatae] and the rest of the Scyths" (Minns, Scythians and Greeks, p. 45).

History shows that a great horde known as the Sarmatians or Sauromatae were, in Roman times, inhabiting the land which had formerly been inhabited by the far-flung Scythian peoples.

"With the disappearance of the Scythae as an ethnic and political entity, the name of Scythia gives place in its original seat to that of Sarmatia" (Ency. Brit., 11th ed., Vol. XXIV, Art. Scythia).

The reason why the Sarmatians were able to dispossess the Scythians was that most of the Scythians had already migrated to Europe, leaving a vacuum in their lands, with only a few of their people still in possession of these Scythian territories in the steppes of South Russia.

The Encyclopedia Britannica mentions that many have thought the Slavs were descended from the Sarmatians (11th ed., Vol. XXV, Art. Slavs, pp. 228-230).

Madison Grant identifies the Sarmatians with the modern Slavs (The Passing of the Great Race, pp. 143, 245, 269, 272). Also see Mallet's Northern Antiquities, p. 15.

Speaking of the Wends, Czechs, Slovaks, Poles, Serbs and other Slavs, Grant says: "The Centre of radiation of all these Slavic-speaking Alpines was located in the Carpathians . . . These early Slavs were probably the Sarmatians of the Greek and Roman writers" (ibid., p. 143).

"From this centre," says Grant, "in the neighborhood of the Carpathians and in Galicia eastward to the head of the Dnieper River, the Wends and Sarmatians expanded in all directions. They were the ancestors of those Alpines who are to-day Slavic-speaking. From this obscure beginning came the bulk of the Russians and the South Slavs" (ibid., p. 272).

Kephart is also of the same general opinion. He shows that the Poles, Ukrainians and others are descendants of the Sarmatians (Races of Mankind, p. 506).

The nations who entered Europe after the Gothic or Scythian tribes, were the Slavonian or Sarmatian. These peoples have occupied Russia, Eastern Prussia, Poland, Bohemia, and Moravia.

> "The Poles became the most distinguished of the Slavonian nations in the sixteenth and seventeenth centuries, but the Russian branch has since attained a pre-eminence, which, for power, influence, and extent of empire, transcends now, beyond all competition, every other people of Sarmatian descent" (Turner, History of the Anglo-Saxons, Vol. I pp. 90, 91).

The Encyclopedia Americana mentions that "The authors who have best described these Scythian peoples distinguish the SCYTHIANS proper or Scolotes, as they call themselves, the immediate neighbours on the north of the ancient Greeks, from the Sarmates . . ." (Vol. XXIV, Art. Scythians, p.471).

This is further confirmation of the view which has consistently been expressed—that the Sarmatians properly speaking, were always distinguished from their Scythian neighbors!

THE SCYTHIAN MASSAGETAE

One branch of the Scythians was known as: Getae, Massagetae and Thyssagetae.

The Massagetae, who lived east of the Caspian Sea and north of the Oxus River, were involved in a struggle for pastoral lands with the Scythians. This assault by the Massagetae caused the Scythians to attack the Cimmerians. The mounted Scythians were superior to the Cimmerians who fought on foot. The Cimmerians were routed and found themselves forced to retreat through the Dariel Pass.

"That the Getae were Goths cannot be doubted" (Turner, History of the Anglo-Saxons, Vol. I, p. 95).

Speaking of the Massagetae, Herodotus says:

> Now, this nation [the Massagetae] is said to be both powerful and valiant, dwelling towards the east and the rising sun beyond the river Araxes, over against the Issedonians; there are some who say that this nation is Scythian (Herod., Clio I, par. 201).

> The Caucasus, then, bounds the western side of this sea, which is called Caspian, and on the east . . . is an extensive plain . . . inhabited by the Massagetae, against whom Cyrus resolved to make war (ibid., par. 204).

The above statements show that the Massagetae were a Scythian tribe who lived to the east of the Caspian Sea! Some of the Israelites had been deported to Media near the southern shores of the Caspian Sea. They must have migrated around to the eastern side of the Caspian soon after their captivity!

Herodotus informs us of a very interesting encounter between the Persians, under the leadership of Cyrus the Great, and this Scythian tribe which was known by the name of Massagetae. At the time of this encounter, the king of the Massagetae was dead and his widowed queen Tomyris was ruling over the Massagetae.

Cyrus had decided to invade the country of the Massagetae, and was constructing a bridge across a river in preparation for this struggle. Queen Tomyris informed him that if he were determined to fight with her people, he could save himself the trouble of building this bridge. She thereupon informed him that she and her people would withdraw a three-days' journey from the river and allow his army to get across safely before giving battle; or if Cyrus preferred, he and his people could withdraw into their own territory for the distance of a three-days' journey, and allow her and her army to safely cross the river before attacking them.

After counsel and much deliberation, Cyrus decided to let Queen Tomyris and her people to withdraw into their territory for a three-days' journey, with the idea of giving battle with the Massagetae in their own territory, thinking this would be to his advantage.

He had a premonition that disaster was going to overtake him; but still he persisted in his conquests. Cyrus decided to resort to stratagem in order to defeat these Scythians. He slew many animals and prepared a big feast and provided wine in abundance. After preparing this huge feast, he left the weaker part of his army behind at the place where he had prepared this feast. The main body of the Persian army then retired from the place where the banquet was spread. Shortly thereafter a third division of the army of the Massagetae attacked and defeated the small and weak division of the Persian army which Cyrus had left behind. The victors promptly began celebrating what they thought to have been a great victory. They glutted themselves with an abundance of food and wine. Shortly thereafter, most of them fell into a stupor.

While they were in this stuporous condition, the Persian army attacked and defeated this division of the Massagetae. But fortunately for the Massagetae, only one-third of their army was involved in this encounter. Not only had the Persians defeated this third division of the army of the Massagetae, but they also captured one of the Queen's sons.

The Queen of the Massagetae demanded of Cyrus that her son be set free. If the Persians didn't free him, her declared intentions were: "I will glut you with blood." Cyrus finally set her son free, but as a result of the disgrace which had befallen him, this son took his own life.

Tomyris was determined to revenge her son's death. A battle followed in which the Massagetae were victorious and the greater part of the Persian army was hewed to pieces. Cyrus was slain in this battle.

> "But Tomyris, having filled a skin with human blood sought for the body of Cyrus among the slain of the Persians, and having found it, thrust the head into the skin, and insulting the dead body, said: 'Thou hast indeed ruined me though alive and victorious in battle, since thou hast taken my son by stratagem; but I will now glut thee with blood, as I threatened'" (Herodotus, Clio I, para. 205-214).

Herodotus also says: "The Massagetae resemble the Scythians in their dress and mode of living" (ibid., Clio I, par. 215). They were one of the branches of the Scythian people! Two other important branches of the Scythians, as we have already seen, were the Cimmerian (or Cymric) branch in the west, and the Sacae who lived near the Massagetae to the east of the Caspian Sea.

DARIUS INVADES EUROPEAN SCYTHIA

The Western or European Scythians had an interesting encounter with the Persians. About 515 B.C. Darius the Great, who had determined to conquer and utterly destroy Greece, knew that his first step would have to be the cutting off of the vital supplies and timber imports of Greece, especially from the Balkans and her consignment of grain from Scythia.

With an army of seven hundred thousand (see "Epitome of History" by Ploetz, p. 28), he launched a campaign in Europe, crossing the Bosphorus over a bridge built especially for him by a clever Greek engineer named Mandrocles of Samos. He then marched into Thrace and on to the Danube, which he also crossed by means of a bridge of boats, drawn across the river at a place a little below the present day Galatz. Before marching on to attack the Scythians, he left a detachment of Ionians with instructions to guard this bridge for sixty days pending his return, failing which they were to retire across it, destroying it behind them. He then proceeded to attack the Scythians.

But the Scythians, realizing they could not overcome the Persians in a pitched battle, appealed to their neighboring tribes for help; and having been refused, they decided to rely on their own cunning, to preserve themselves. The Scythians adopted the "scorched earth" policy. They divided their army into three groups, as was customary, each commanded respectively by one of the three Royal Scyths. They agreed that whichever of the three was pursued by Darius, would retreat to the interior part of Scythia, breaking up water supplies and destroying the food and fodder of the land.

Darius immediately took the offensive. The Scyths promptly retreated before him. The sixty days which he had set as a time limit for conquering the Scyths, were fast slipping away, his men were becoming weary, his supplies were running short—yet the Scyths continued to retreat, scorching the earth behind them.

Their determination not to give battle exasperated Darius. He at last determined that he would force the issue, and challenged their king, Idanthyrsus, in the following words:

> "Thou strange man," shouted his messenger, "why dost thou keep on flying before me, when there are two things thou mightest do so easily? If thou deemest thyself able to resist my arms, cease thy wanderings and come, let us engage in battle. Or if thou art conscious that my strength is greater than thine—even so thou shouldest cease to run away—thou has but to bring thy lord earth and water, and to come at once to a conference." (Elsworth Huntingdon, The Pulse of Asia).

However, the undaunted Scythian king, proudly informed Darius that he didn't flee from him out of fear, but only because he wished to follow a peaceful way of life. He told Darius that his Scythian people did not cultivate lands or possess towns which (through fear of loss or ravaging) might induce them to join battle.

He then dared Darius to molest their father's tombs, saying that such sacrilege would provoke them to fight with heated revenge. Otherwise they would not fight with the Persians until they pleased (ibid.).

At this Darius was greatly disheartened. He realized further pursuit was useless, and decided to retreat. The Scythians harassed and reduced his troops as he withdrew, but Darius felt greatly relieved, only to get the greater part of his army back safely across the Danube. He and his army had escaped a disastrous experience, and this kept him from ever again invading northern Europe.

On one occasion when the Persian infantry was ready to engage the Scythian cavalry in a minor skirmish, up jumped a hare, and off galloped the yelling Scythians howling after the hare, chasing it at full speed on their horses, leaving the startled Persians covered with their dust—thereby revealing their arrogance and contempt towards the Persians.

Smith mentions the custom of the Scythians of living in a kind of covered wagons which were constructed as lofty houses of wicker-work, on well-wheeled chariots.

> They kept large troops of horses, and were most expert in cavalry exercises and archery; and hence, as the Persian king Därī'us found, when he invaded their

country (B.C. 507), it was almost impossible for an invading army to act against them (A Smaller Classical Dictionary, 1910 ed., Art. Scythia, p. 475).

He then mentions that the Scythians simply retreated, taking their wagon-homes with them before their enemies; and as they did this they kept harassing the enemy with their light cavalry; and left famine and exposure in their wake.

Philip II of Macedon and his son, Alexander the Great, who defeated the Medo-Persians, both had to engage the Scythians on different occasions, in order to keep them from encroaching upon their territory.

SCYTHIAN CUSTOMS

Rice informs us that the Scythians were a prosperous people, obtaining much of their wealth from their trade—especially with Greece. The Scythians exported grain, furs, hides, meat, honey, salt, fish and also many of her slaves to Greece.

Some of the Scyths followed patriarchal rule as did the people of Israel (The Scythians, p. 51).

The Royal Scyths were relatively few in number, but they were fearless fighters and such capable rulers, that they had little difficulty in governing a vast territory and controlling with ease the population consisting of their own husbandmen and the agriculturalists whom they had found established in the region and who outnumbered them greatly.

We are further informed that some of the Scythians were agriculturalists and raised wheat for export; others were pastoral Nomads. The Royal Scyths were from among the Nomadic Scyths. The Nomadic Scyths lived on a diet of milk products, which included fermented mare's milk (Collier's Ency., Vol. XVIII, Art. Scythia).

It is interesting to note that the Scythians had no use for pigs, either in sacrifice or in any other way (ibid., p. 49).

We have proved the Scythians to be the same as the Sacae and the Gimiri, and we have shown that these people were the same as the people of the House of Omri or "Beth Omri" and that the people of the House of Omri were the Ten-Tribed Northern Kingdom of Israel.

There is nothing to show that the Ten-Tribed House of Israel ever made any use whatsoever of swine while in the land of Palestine. In fact swine were held in great contempt and the pig was used as a form of contempt. The God of Israel strictly forbade them to eat swine (Lev. 11; Deu. 14). We know that many of the modern-day descendants of the ancient Scythian or Sacae people do eat the pig, and use it generally; but this practice has been formed only after many generations of turning aside from the principles and the teachings which God had given them under Moses.

We have shown conclusively that the Celts, the Gauls, the Galatians, the Kimbri, the Ombri, and such peoples were all closely related—descendants from a common ancestor; and that they were all different branches of the Cimmerian nation, the Cimmerians being a Scythian people.

The Scythians practised polygamy; but so did the pre-captivity Israelites!

The Scyths were fond of a sort of "Haggis" reminding us of the fondness of their descendants, the modern-day Scots, for this same dish (Rice, The Scythians, p. 63).

SCYTHIANS EXPERTS IN WARFARE

The Scythians owed much of their prowess in battle and in hunting to the superb skill with which they handled their mounts.

> All the horses' trappings which have so far been found, regardless of whether they come from the east or the west of the plain, reveal the great importance which the Scythians attached to the turnout of their mounts. Can the inhabitants of England have inherited this outlook together with the decorative elements which effected "Celtic" art? (ibid., p. 74).

Rice implies that the English have inherited their fondness for horses from their Scythian ancestors. Historical evidence proves the majority of the people of England have descended from Scythian tribes.

There are two other points of interest mentioned by Rice. (1) Some of the Scythian tables were "of a startling Victorian character" (The Scythians, p. 137). (2) There is a striking similarity between Scandinavian, Viking, Celtic and Saxon art when compared to Scythian art (ibid., pp. 186, 187).

It was customary for the Scyths to have rather elaborate burials—especially for their chiefs. After an ordinary person died, his body was carried about for forty days in a wagon among the tribal camps and then buried.

> "For a king, the funeral cortege was more elaborate. On burial the body was placed in a square pit. After some of his concubines, attendants, and horses had been strangled and laid beside the Royal courts, a great mound was built over the grave. A year later fifty youths and fifty fine horses were strangled, stuffed and mounted in a circle around the tomb" (Collier's Ency., 1959 ed., Vol. XVII, pp. 433-34).

THE FROZEN TOMBS OF SIBERIA

The Russian archeologist Rudenko, carried out some interesting excavations on the frozen tombs at Pazyrik in western Siberia. These frozen tombs were certainly unique. They had been plundered centuries earlier. The tomb-robbers had worked down deep enough to reach soil perpetually frozen, but they had not encountered any water. When the tomb robbers disturbed the filling of the shaft, the moisture from the upper soil seeped down into the timber-lined chamber and slowly filled it to the brim. This water later froze, out of reach of the summer's sun, and everything which the robbers had left was preserved in COLD STORAGE until Rudenko opened these frozen tombs! He was delighted to see the good condition in which the objects were found.

> When he came upon the ice, through which he could faintly glimpse objects lying on the chamber floor, normal methods of excavation had to be abandoned; Rudenko simply poured boiling water on the ice, pumped it all out, and the contents of the tomb lay there exposed! (Wooley, History Unearthed, 1958, ed., p. 159).

In one tomb Rudenko found a huge burial chamber which contained the skeletons of about seven to sixteen horses which had been pole-axed. The tomb contained a number of heavy wooden carts, pots, and many other objects. The treasures of gold and silver had been taken by the robbers, but the ice had preserved many objects in deep-freeze condition.

These hermetically-sealed tombs had preserved some of man's most perishable possessions including carpets, embroideries, hangings of applique felt; and there were two coffins containing the remains of the king and his wife or favourite concubine. The bodies had been embalmed after a fashion. There were many interesting objects found in some of these tombs including in some instances treasures.

In the account of the invasion of Scythia by Darius, we have noticed how much the Scythians prized the tombs of their dead. There is nothing which would incense them as much as to have someone disturb the resting place of their fathers.

Darius presumably feared the unabated wrath of the Sythians enough that he dared not provoke the Scythians by desecrating the tombs of their forefathers.

We shall now examine further historical proof verifying that the majority of these Scyths who lived in South Russia (especially in the Crimea) were exiled Israelites.

ISRAEL'S CRIMEAN GRAVESTONES

Here is a very interesting quotation taken from an article entitled Synchronous History, Volume III (1874), written by J.W. Bosanquet:

> "The old gravestones in the Crimea", writes Neubauer, "which are now recognized as genuine by all men of learning, attest that there were Jewish [Israelitish] communities in the Crimea as early as the year A.D. 6, and that the Jews there held themselves to be descended from the TEN TRIBES."

> I Jehuda Ben Mose ha-Nagolon of the East country . . . of the tribe of Naphtali . . . who went into the exile with the exiles, who were driven away with Hosea, the king of Israel, together with the tribes of Simeon and Dan, and some of the generations of the other tribes of Israel, which (all) were led into exile by the enemy Shalmanezer . . . the cities of the exiled tribes of Reuben, Gad, and the half of Manasseh, which Pilneser drove into exile and settled there . . . (ibid.).

The author of the above quote, like almost everyone, thought these exiles of the "Lost Ten Tribes" of Israel were "Jews." But the people of Ten-Tribed Israel were never called "Jews" in the Hebrew Scriptures!

Notice that the person whose name was found on this Crimean Epigraph was of the tribe of NAPHTALI, who was taken into captivity with the captives in the time of Hosea, king of Israel, with the tribes of SIMEON, DAN, REUBEN, GAD, and the half tribe of MANASSEH. This is another proof that the exiles of Israel (those of the so-called Lost Ten Tribes) passed through the area of the Crimea, in the vicinity of the Black Sea!

The exiles of the Lost Ten Tribes of Israel wandered for centuries in the steppes of Southern Russia under such names as Cimmerians and Scythians.

Myers says that the long-headed stocks of the British Isles and of Scandinavia seem to be an early offshoot of the "Tumulus people" of South Russia, who are the ancestors of these Nordics. This is further confirmation of the facts that have been reiterated in this thesis.

> In the British Isles, there are more or less pure descendants of . . . old long-headed stocks. In Scandinavia and the whole north-western area of the Continent. They are the tall, massive, long-headed folk who had apparently been developing there . . . They seem to be an early offshoot of the "Tumulus people" [meaning Scythians] of Southern Russia, and are the ancestors of the present "Nordic" blondes (Myers, Cambridge Ancient History, Vol. I, p. 98).

RACIAL CHARACTERISTICS OF THE SCYTHIANS

We shall now carefully examine historical, archaeological, and portrait evidence to see what the physical characteristics of the Scythians were like. Before we have finished our investigation, we will notice complete unanimity among all of these fields of study.

"The general opinion has been that the Scyths were Iranian [white European types]" (Ency. Brit., 11th ed., Vol. XXIV, Art. Scythia).

Because of the nomadic life which most of the Scyths led, some have erroneously believed the Scythians were of Mongolian origin.

This opinion is, however, no longer held. The little we know of their language, customs and religion leads rather to the conclusion that they were IRANEANS. About the 2nd century B.C. the Scythians were conquered [driven further west] by the Sarmates . . . Thereafter they disappear from history (ibid., p. 471).

Notice that the Scythians disappear from history about the 2nd century B.C. Some claim they survived until the early centuries of the Christian era. Since the Apostle Paul mentioned them (Col. 3:11) we know they were still in existence in the 1st century A.D. It would appear, however, that most of the Scyths had migrated or were driven into Europe in the centuries immediately after the birth of Christ.

We are informed by the Encyclopedia Britannica that the Scythian power began to decline in the early centuries A.D., so that by the middle of the 4th century the Sarmatae, the eastern neighbors of the Scyths, had crossed the Don River.

As the Scyths are pressed by Sarmatians to their east, they, in turn, exert pressure on the peoples of the Danube, and finally emerge in North-western Europe under various tribal names. After this time the name of "Scythia" is purely geographical. The lands which they had formerly occupied were completely taken over by the Sarmatians.

SCYTHIAN RACE ANALYSIS BY MINNS

It is difficult to see how some who have studies Minn's classic work on the Scythians, can make him say something which is contrary to his plain statements. Some have asserted that Minns attributed a Mongoloid origin to the Scythians. Let us see what Minns really did say regarding this subject: "On the other hand Scheifner absolutely annihilated K. Neumann's attempt to derive any Scythian words from Mongolian" (Scythians and Greeks, p. 40).

The Scythians' mode of life consisted of the men riding on horseback and the women in wagons. Minns also mentions the habit of the Scythians of tattooing or branding various parts of their bodies.

This slackness they counteract by a custom of branding themselves on various parts of their body (Cf. J.G. Frazer, The Golden Bough, III. p. 217). Further he says that the cold makes their colouring purros, which seems to mean a reddish brown, the colour that fair people get from being much in the open. It cannot be any kind of yellow (Minns, Scythians and Greeks, p. 45).

The above statements show that Minns definitely believed the Scythians were not Mongolians, but were a "fair people" having "reddish brown" colouring due to tanning. Yet some who have studied Minn's classic work on the Scythians have claimed that he believed the Scythians to be of Mongoloid descent!

There was undoubtedly some Mongoloid influence among certain of the Scythians because of intermarriage. Herodotus informs us of marriages between Scythian kings and various foreign women.

> So too some of the skulls illustrated by Count Bobrinskoj in Smela slightly suggest Mongolian forms, others are purely European (Sm. II., pl. XXVII.-XXX). To this same conclusion came Professor Anatole Bogdanoy (Congres International d'Archeologie Prehistorique et d'Anthropologie, II Session A Moscou, T.I., Moscow, 1892, p.5), who says that in Scythic tombs the skulls are mostly long though occasionally Mongoloid, and notes a general tendency towards brachycephaly during the Scythic period. For, strangely enough, although Slavs and Finns are now short-headed, they seem to have become so only during the last few centuries (Minns, Scythians and Greeks, p. 47).

Minns was very explicit in the foregoing statement. He showed that the Scythic skulls were "mostly long, though OCCASIONALLY MONGOLOID," according to Professor Anatole. Minns nowhere says he disagrees with him on this point; Minns' silence must mean that he is in agreement with Professor Anatole on this point!

Scythians had penetrated into Hungary and other Slavonic countries at a fairly early period, but these Scythians were not Slavs or Mongols.

There can be no reasonable doubt that the overwhelming majority of the Scythians were a long-headed people (whose descendants are only found today in North-western Europe and territories settled by them). There must have been occasional Mongolians among them. We have just read in the quotation preceding that the Slavs and Finns are short-headed. It is not at all difficult for one to see how the present Slavs are in the main a short-headed people though the skeletal remains in the ancient graves of these Slavic territories show a long-headed people formerly resided there.

The answer to this enigma is quite simply explained. The following picture emerges when all of the histories on this subject are properly pieced together.

At one time most of Western, Northern and Central Europe, as well as Western and Southern Asia as far east as the Don (in some instances, as far east as China), were inhabited chiefly by dolichocephalic (long-headed), Scythian people.

Many historians show clearly that some of the Scythians came into Europe as peaceful colonists and settlers, filtering into Europe year after year, and season after season, with their flocks and herds from the south steppes of Russia, to the lands in the regions of the Danube and the Baltic. Others were undoubtedly impelled or catapulted into Europe by pressure brought upon them by invading tribes (such as the Sarmatians) to their east.

These eastern round-headed Sarmatian neighbors swarmed into the lands which the long-headed Scythians had formerly inhabited and were buried. Thus, it is only because one racial type succeeded another to these lands, that one can find a satisfactory explanation for the broad-headed skulls prevailing in the latter cemeteries and among the modern populations of these Germanic and Slavic lands.

The ancient historians do not tell us much about the type of clothes worn by the Scythians, but they mention that they wore belts, baggy trousers and pointed caps.

Professor Minns mentions some representations on Greek vases which depict Northern nomads. He says that one of these nomad archers was called "Kimerios" and that he was equipped in the representations with a bowcase.

"Kimerios, about whose name there can be no doubt, is similarly equipped but has a bowcase instead of a quiver. In the case of another painting of barbarians attempts have been made to identify them as Cimmerians" (Scythians and Greeks, p. 53).

There is every reason to believe that this person called "Kimerios" was a Scythian or a Cimmerian by race. The tall, pointed caps worn by these Scythian nomads, as depicted by the Greeks, show that they were the same people as the Sacae or Saka.

The Persians called all of the Scythians by the name of Sacae or Saka as we have already observed.

There can be absolutely no doubt whatsoever, according to many reliable historical sources, that the ancient Sacae were the ancestors of the ANGLO-SAXONS.

The Israelites, while living in Palestine, were famous archers (I Chr. 5:18; 12:1-2). So were the Scytians well known for their archery. Their descendants in Europe—especially those who came to the British Isles—were often very expert in the use of the bow. Surely every one is familiar with the story of Robin Hood and his followers, who were expert archers and wore pointed caps also.

"The Asiatic nomads had very high-pointed head-gear, according to Herodotus and the Bisutun [same as Behistun] bas relief of Sakunka Saka" (ibid., p. 57).

> On the bas relief of the Bisutun we have a Saka labelled as such in the inscription of Darius: unfortunately being a prisoner he is without his weapons and his national dress. The only thing distinctive about him is his very tall cyrbasia [tall pointed cap] upon his head. He is fully bearded (ibid., p. 60).

Herodotus says that the Sacae had tall, pointed caps (Herodotus VII, 60 through 66). Minns mentions "a Blonde race" which he equated with the Scythians.

SIMILAR EVIDENCE BY RICE

Speaking of the pastoral nomads in the Ukraine districts of South Russia, Rice says these Scythian nomads were "fair-haired men of a long-headed type" (The Scythians, p. 23).

We are informed that "what [anthropological material] is available seems to support the Indo-European attribution" (ibid., p. 37). "An examination of the male skulls and mummified heads found at Pazirik confirms this view" (ibid., p. 39).

> Indeed, there is nothing surprising in the occasional presence of people of Mongol blood among the tribes inhabiting the eastern section of the Asiatic steppe, for there was probably intermarriage between them and the locals, just as the Royal Scyths at times intermarried with Greeks or Thracians from neighbouring regions in the west (ibid., pp. 40, 41).

A close examination of all of the male skulls and the mummified heads found at Pazirik confirms such a view.

Notice that Rice shows there was "the occasional presence" of Mongol blood among the tribes inhabiting the eastern section. This statement should cause no great alarm if one remembers that the people on the eastern border of Scythia were Mongolians. One would naturally expect a little racial mixing between the Scyths and the Mongols.

Later we shall show cranial statistics proving that the people who lived in Scythia—South Russia especially—at this time were not the same people as the broad-headed "Alpine" or "Slavic" people who dwell there today. All archaeological remains prove that the people who formerly inhabited this region in the Scythian age were definitely different from the present-day inhabitants of that country. They were predominantly a long-headed people.

Note carefully the following statements which show that some of the Scyths lived near China.

> The ancient Greeks applied the names Scyth, Saka, or Caha indiscriminately to all the nomads of the Eurasian steppe, without distinguishing between those inhabiting lands within reach of China and those living close to the Carpathians . . . there seems reason to think that at any rate the MAJORITY were linked by some sort of racial tie. A definite affinity [a blood relationship] is indeed suggested by the nature of their art, which shows well-nigh identical features over so wide an area (ibid., p. 42).

We are told that not only did the Scyths wear peaked hoods, but they also had suspenders attached to their belts to hold their soft, high boots. The only other people known to wear the same type of clothes were the "tall, red-haired, blue-eyed people" from Turkestan whose faces were "pronouncedly European, thus giving support to the theory that the Scythians were of Indo-European stock. The statues of the women show high hats somewhat similar in shape to those worn by Welsh women of the eighteenth century" (Rice, The Scythians, pp. 68, 69).

> Rudenko has succeeded in establishing that the majority of the skulls found at Pazirik and at such allied burials as Shibe, Tuekt, Kurai and Katanda were European in type. This bears out Jettmar's view that, at any rate until the fifth or fourth century B.C., the inhabitants of western Siberia were a fair-haired people

of European origin, and that it was after that date that an influx of Mongoloids resulted in a very mixed type of population . . . Most scholars are, however, convinced that no racial links exist between the Slavs and the Scythians, and Ripley draws attention to the fact that in the central Russian burials of the stone age, as many as three-quarters of the skulls were dolichocephalic, [long-headed] from the ninth to the thirteenth century only half belonged to this group, and after that date only forty per cent remained, the rest of the population being brachycephalic [broad-headed] (ibid., p. 77).

Speaking of a Scythian tomb, Rice says: "The woman lying at the chief's side, however, had the soft hair and the dolichocephalic [long-headed] skull of an Indo-European (The Scythians, p.122).

Speaking of the Scythians, Child says: "Many people hold that these Scyths were IRANIANS" (The Aryans, 1926 ec., p. 38). He then shows that there is archaeological evidence to prove that the Scyths had made incursions into Bulgaria, Hungary, and Eastern Germany from the east.

We have now seen various statements from numerous historians showing that the Scythians were North-west European in type. They, as we have observed, had "occasional" brachycephalic (broad-headed) elements among them.

COON'S ANALYSIS OF SCYTHIAN CRANIA

Coon is the "last word" regarding craniological data of the Scythians. Speaking of the Scyths, he says: "About 700 B.C. the Scyths were first noticed in the lands to the north of the Black Sea" (The Races of Europe, p. 196). This was about 50 years after Israel's First Captivity in 741 B.C! He then shows that the Scythians, including their eastern branches, the Massagetae and the Saka (Sacae) people, "formed the continual cultural zone from the CARPATHIANS to CHINA" (ibid., p. 196).

He mentions that some believe the Scythians to have been Mongoloid, while others believed that they were Iranian or North-west European in type. He says: "Another school holds that they were European in physical type, and spoke Iranian, while their cultural breeding ground lay somewhere to the east of the CASPIAN" (ibid., p. 196).

The Scythians were decidedly North-western European according to Coon:

> There can be little doubt, even before examining skeletal evidence that the Scythians and Sarmatians were basically, if not entirely, white men, and in no sense Mongoloid. The only definite description of them which we have from classical literature is that of Hippocrates, who called them white-skinned and obese (ibid., p. 198).

He then shows that the Scythians produced a very distinctive style of realistic art. Their representations include a number of Scythian portraits in very realistic and life-like poses.

They show a well-defined type of heavily bearded, long-headed men with prominent, often convex, noses. The brow ridges are moderately heavy, the eyes deep set. These faces are strikingly reminiscent of types common among northwest Europeans today, in strong contrast to those shown in the art of the Sumerians, Babylonians, and Hittites, which are definitely Near Eastern. The face, therefore, is definitely Nordic (ibid., p. 199).

We are next informed of the research of Donici's collection of seventy-seven Scythian crania from Kurgans of Bessarabia, which was one of the Scythian's favorite pasture lands during the height of their domination of the South Russian steppes. "The fifty-seven male crania of this series" (according to Coon) "are not homogeneous but fall into two types, a long-headed and a round-headed, with the former [long-headed] greatly in the majority" (ibid., p. 199).

The means of these Scythian skulls show them to be low mesocephals [medium to long-headed] of moderate cranial dimensions, but with a low vault height. The cranial means are, in fact, almost identical with those of the Keltic series from France and the British Isles (ibid., p. 199).

This would mean that they would be dolichocephals (long-headed) in the general classification which so many use—i.e. 80 and under representing the dolichocephals. According to Coon, the mean or average cephalic indexes would fall in the low (medium-headed) range, and this undoubtedly included some mongoloid brachycephals.

"When the brachycephalic element is eliminated, these Scythian skulls are narrow faced, and narrow nosed, and fit more nearly into a central European Nordic category. Other series of Scythian crania from Southern Russia and the CAUCASUS show the same general characteristics, but are in most instances purely dolichocephalic, which leads one to understand that the brachycephalic element in the Rumanian skulls may have been at least partly of local origin" (ibid., pp.199, 200).

This shows that some Scythians were long-headed, while some had heads of medium breadth.

He continues, "Other collections of Scythian crania vary in their mean cranial indices from 72 to 77. Those from the Kiev government, a Scythian center, have a mean of 73" (ibid., p. 200).

In sharp contrast to this long-headed type for the overwhelming majority of the Scythians, Coon mentions that "A series of 18 Sarmatian crania from the Volga, although otherwise the same as the other, has a cranial index of 80.3" (ibid.).

Again, this is in complete agreement with what has already been observed. The Sarmatians are the ancestors of the Slavic peoples, and of the Alpine and "Slavic" type Germanic peoples of Germany, Austria, etc. We have repeatedly seen that discriminating historians all draw a clear line of demarcation between the true or proper Scythians and the Sarmatians.

Coon then mentions that some of the skeletal data for some of the ancient Germans shows them to be a "purely long-headed element in the Keltic blend . . . They closely resemble the Keltic crania of Gaul and of the British Isles, and those of the Scythians" (ibid., p. 203).

This further proves what has been previously shown—that many of the Keltic, Cymric and Scythian tribes who formerly lived in "Germania" and were called "Germani" actually were not true Germans as we know the Germans of today. They were Keltic peoples who migrated through Germany and into Northern France and the British Isles.

Speaking of the Slavs who "penetrated Russia," we read:

> The skulls of these invaders belong to a generalized Nordic form, with a cranial index of 75 to 76, and an intermediate vault height. The Ukranian skulls from the eighth to the ninth centuries A.D. do not greatly diverge from this general standard, but the early Slavic [Nordic] crania from the Moscow region in Russia dated from the eleventh to twelfth centuries A.D., are, in fact, almost purely dolichocephalic, with a mean cranial index of 73.5 (ibid., p. 219).

And on page 220 we read:

> On the whole, the Slavic racial type, as exemplified by skeletal series from Poland, Germany, Bohemia, Austria, and Russia, were reasonably uniform . . . The Slavs, like all the other Indo-European-speaking peoples whom we have been able to trace, were originally Nordic, and there is no suggestion in their early remains, in the region studied, of the numerically predominant brachycephalic [broad-headedness] racial increments which today are considered typically Slavic (ibid., p. 220).

Most of the "Slavs" retained their original dolichocephalic (long-head) cranial form until about the thirteenth or the fifteenth century. At that time, those who inhabited Central Europe and Russia grew progressively broad-headed, at a rapid but consistant rate.

"Well-documented series from Bohemia and the Moscow government show how this change progressed from century to century, so that normal means of 73 to 75 rose as high as 83 by the nineteenth" (ibid., p. 220). Few Slavs were spared this change to brachycephaly which was parallel to that which affected the South Germans and other peoples of Central and Eastern Europe. Although it occurred in the full light of medieval and modern history, no one has, as of yet, offered a fully satisfactory explanation (ibid., p. 220).

Here then, without doubt, is the explanation of this baffling question. The overwhelming majority of cranial measurements from the ancient mounds of the countries just mentioned (Western Russia, Poland, Bohemia, Austria, and most of Germany) were mainly the dolichocephalic or long-headed type. They were of Keltic and Scythian descent, but have mostly all moved out of those lands and into Britain, Scandinavia, and Northern France.

All history is crystal clear in showing that the general movement of the peoples of Europe and Asia was in a westward direction. The Asiatics (broad-headed people) kept pushing the Nordic long-headed element further and further west before them. The ancient Scythians (who were mostly long-headed) and their off-shoots—Cimmerians, Kelts, Gauls, and others—were in many instances purely dolichocephals (long heads), and in other cases had heads of medium breadth. These Nordics contually migrated peacefully or were driven by force of arms before their enemies from the general territory of Central Asia and Eastern Europe further and further west.

It is easy to see that the long-headed Iranian or Nordic element, which at one time inhabited Europe, from the Carpathian Mountains in the west to the river Don in the east, were driven continually westward. The vacuum which they left behind was filled with the Asiatic Alpine or broad-heads. The peoples today living in these lands are generally spoken of as "Slavs" or "Alpines."

The author of this work concluded that the "ancestral Slavs of Poland were Nordic, within the range of the Indo-European group".

But the simple truth is that the Nordics, at one time, lived in Poland, Austria, in parts of Germany, the Balkans, Northern Italy and Spain, as well as in all of North-western Europe. The Eastern and Southern European Kelts were later all pushed into North-western Europe, where they are today found—in the British Isles, Scandinavia, and Northern France. The same is true of Bohemia. According to Coon, the Bohemians were "very close to an older Keltic mean. They formed, without question, a mixed group and included in their number a minority of round-headed forms . . . The skulls of these invaders belong to a generalized Nordic form" (ibid., p. 219).

He then mentions that the skulls of the Anglo-Saxons (of Scythic descent) who invaded England in the 4th and 5th centuries were almost identical with the skulls of some of the early Germans from Hanover; they were also very similar with the Spanish Visigothic skulls. The old Frisians from Northern Holland were identical in every respect with these long-headed Nordic, Swedish types (ibid., p. 207).

> A number of individual cemeteries which date from the earliest period of Saxon invasion, give us a lively picture of the manner in which the first Saxon raiders and settlers operated . . . All of the adult males 30 years of age or older represent a single type, the classical Saxon, and are all long headed (ibid., p. 210).

From these statements, it is easy to see that the Anglo-Saxons (who were all of Scythic descent) were mainly a long-headed people.

We shall have occasion later to investigate the subject of the Goths, but it should be understood that nearly all of the cephalic indexes of the Goths, regardless of where they are measured, show that they were primarily a long-headed people. Coon makes this very plain (ibid., pp. 205, 206).

When all the foregoing evidence is carefully weighed, the only conclusion one can come to is this—the Scythians and cognate peoples who formerly inhabited the steppes of South Russia from China to the Danube River were primarily long-headed people. What is the significance of this inescapable conclusion?

When one considers that the peoples who now inhabit the territory from the Danube to China are mainly a round-headed or broad-headed type, then he can see that something has happened to cause this change from dolichocephaly to brachycephaly. Furthermore, when one learns that the cephalic index (the general head form) does not change, as we have proven earlier, except by intermarriage or deformity, then one is forced to the inevitable conclusion that these Slavic or Alpine type peoples who now inhabit these steppe lands are a totally different people.

Also, when one sees such an avalanche of historical and archaeological evidence proving that the long-headed type of peoples who formerly inhabited the vast stretches of Scythia are only found today among North-west European peoples (and their colonial offspring)—then one is compelled to the conclusion that there, and only there, are these people found in any appreciable number today!

We have previously seen proven from the Behistun Rock Inscriptions that the exiles of Israel were called by three different names (Gimiri, Sacae and Scythians) yet they all refer to the same people. It has been clearly demonstrated that these people are the same as the Cimmerians and as the Ghomri, or the people of Omri, who was a well-known king of the Northern Kingdom of Israel.

It should now be clearly established in our minds that the Cimmerians, Celts, Gauls, Sacae (Saxons), and the Massagetae were all branches or offshoots of the great Scythian nation.

What LANGUAGE did the Scythians speak? This will give us a further insight into the origin of these peoples.

The most exhaustive and authoritative dictionary in the English language is unquestionably A New English Dictionary on Historical Principles, edited by Sir James Murray LL.D. Here is the definition of the Scythian language as found in this dictionary:

"Scythiac . . . There is a strong similarity between the Hebrew and the Scythiac languages" (Vol. VIII, def. Scythiac).

This is quite understandable since we know that the majority of the Scythians were the exiles from the land of Israel; and there can be no doubt that the language which they spoke while in the Promised Land, and at the time of their captivity, was Hebrew!

The Scythians were not an ancient people, but they themselves declared that they were "the newest of races" (Minns, Scythians and Greeks, p. 43). Many nations existed before the nation of Israel was conceived (Deut. 7:7). This shows that these Scytho-Israelitish exiles knew that the historic nations of Egypt, Assyria, Greece, and many others were in existence before Israel was born.

According to Herodotus the Scythian nation had existed only 1,000 years to the time of Darius. This shows they had their national beginning at the same general time Israel left Egypt in about 1491 B.C.

Before concluding the subject of the Scythians, it should be stressed that not all of the Scythians were of Israelitish extraction. It has been definitely proved, however, that most of them were wandering exiles of the Lost Ten Tribes of Israel.

Even at the time of the Exodus there was a "mixed multitude" (meaning non-Israelites) who accompanied Israel to the Promised Land (Ex. 12:38, Num. 11:4).

Israel was given many laws whereby the people were informed clearly that they could permit Gentiles to settle among them.

We have seen that the Scythians were a numerous and mighty nation. What happened to this by-gone people?

Proffesor Minns shows that it took the successive hordes of Sarmatians, Huns, Avars, Khazars, Pechenags, Polvtses and Tartars and other tribes many centuries to sweep the Iranian or SCYTHIAN folk completely off the plains over which they had wandered; the Scythians finally succumbed to this fate only because they were living in open country upon a "highway of nations."

"About the 2nd century B.C. the Scythians were conquered by the Sarmates . . . thereafter they disappear from history" (Ency. Brit., Vol. XXIV, Art. Scythians, p. 47).

"By the fourth century A.D. they [the Scythians] had been completely forgotten by the civilized world of the day" (Rice, The Scythians, p. 23).

From many historical sources cited we can see that these Scythic peoples filtered into Europe from the seventh century B.C. to our era. By the second century B.C. so few were remaining in Scythia that the Sarmatians easily over-powered the remaining few. The name "Scythia" is swallowed up thereafter in the many tribal names which these Scythic people had assumed by the time of their final settlement in North-west Europe.

We have also seen that the Kymry, Celts, Gauls, Saxons, Goths, Keltic, "Germans," and similar peoples all traced their racial origins back to the Scythian nation or tribes! These Scythian peoples were all closely related and are definitely equated by history with the people of the House (dynasty) of Omri—the House of Israel!

CONCLUSION

What is the key that unlocks the true ORIGINS and affinities of the peoples of North-west Europe?

That key is the knowledge that the overwhelming majority of the Anglo-Saxon-Keltic peoples are descendants of the dispersed exiles of the LOST TEN TRIBES of Israel. This knowledge is revealed through: (1) Scriptures, (2) secular history and (3) archaeology.

We have examined many proofs which exploded the THEORY OF EVOLUTION showing it is not a safe guide for determining the origin and racial affinities of mankind!

We observed that all of the races of mankind have descended from Shem, Ham, and Japheth—just as the Bible had said thousands of years ago! These three patriarchal ancestors were the progenitors of the White, Yellow and Dark races—otherwise called Caucasoids, Mongoloids and Negroids.

All of the DARK races have descended from Ham; the YELLOW from Japheth; and the WHITE peoples have come primarily from SHEM. However, a number of the descendants of Japheth have fairly light skins, but most of them have a yellowish or olive tint to their skins. Even many of the Latin descendants of Japheth have olive-coloured skins.

Furthermore, the various sub-races are merely crosses between two or more of the three afore-mentioned primary "races."

The people of Israel were of the Semitic (Shemitic) branch of the human family, through Abraham, Isaac and Jacob.

Reliable calculations show that there must have been about three million Israelites at the time of the Exodus from Egypt and about the same number when they occupied the Holy Land forty years later (Circa 1429 B.C.).

When David numbered Israel (three centuries before Israel's captivity) there were 1,570,000 able-bodied "men-at-arms" (Moffatt trans.) in Israel and Judah—excluding the tribes of Levi and Benjamin (I Chr. 21:5, 6).

There must have been at least FIVE MILLIONS of Israelites dwelling in the Northern Kingdom at the time of the captivities of Israel in 741 and 721 B.C. and there must have been about two millions in the Kingdom of Judah at that time.

What happened to those teeming millions of Israelites?

167

Various opinions were quoted which expressed, more-or-less, the general misconception regarding these lost tribes. Most people think the Ten Tribes have be "irretrievably lost" among the nations. They assume they became so mixed and amalgamated among the Gentile nations that they have just been swallowed up or absorbed by them.

We have seen that the very Word of God is at stake on this very point. If these peoples of the dispersed Ten Tribes have vanished from the earth, then God's Word has been broken! Many prophecies speak of a future restoration of Israel when both the House of Israel and the House of Judah will once again become one nation, united in their Promised Land (Ezek. 37:15-28).

The TEN TRIBES of Israel were taken into captivity to MEDIA and ASSYRIA. They were deported to the lands lying south of the CAUCASUS MOUNTAINS, near the BLACK and CASPIAN SEAS.

We have observed that the foremost historians (although they do not necessarily accept the scriptural accounts) agree that the peoples inhabiting SCANDINAVIA, the BRITISH ISLES, the LOW COUNTRIES, NORTHERN FRANCE, SWITZERLAND and other northwestern European countries came from the vicinity of the CAUCASUS MOUNTAINS!

The value of the CEPHALIC INDEX (which has no connection with phrenology), was demonstrated to be ONE of the best ways of determining racial affinities—from skeletal remains. The C.I. has nothing to do with the size of the head, or with the cranial capacity, but is merely a term used to express the width of the head when expressed as a percentage of its length.

Skulls do not lie (except for deformations), and do not change in a particular race except by intermarriage with another race having a different skull type. It is primarily through the use of the C.I. that we are able to know the racial type of such peoples as the SCYTHIANS, KELTS and GAULS.

We noticed the two main types of Jews—the Ashkenazim and the Sephardim. We saw that the Jews contain many long-headed elements as well as round-headed ones.

We also examined the Scriptures to see what the original Israelites were like, and what their racial characteristics were.

An examination of the Scriptures revealed the original Israelites were not necessarily like the typical Jew of today. Many of the Israelites were more like the Sephardic Jew, that is, they were more Nordic or North-west European in their features.

There was a considerable amount of blondism among them.

Our investigation further revealed that the modern ARABS are more HAMITIC than Semitic. They are not, therefore, typical of the Semitic peoples.

Moreover, the importance of the name of OMRI, King of Israel, was shown from the Assyrian inscriptions and other archaeological data. This name is the main connecting link between pre-captivity and dispersed Israel! We know that Omri's name was pronounced as GHOMRI, according to the older way of pronouncing the Hebrew. Furthermore, this name is the same as Gimiri.

On the Behistun Rock Inscriptions, the 19th province over which Darius ruled was called by the following names: (1) Saka (Sakka) or Sacae, (2) Scythia, (3) Gimiri and Cimmerians—all referring basically to the same people!

We examined the name SACAE (or Sakka) and noticed that it derives from ISAAC—the initial letter "i" having been dropped. The SACAE who lived EAST OF THE CASPIAN SEA were, as we have seen, a branch of the SCYTHIAN people.

Scythians (Gr. Skuthes) appears to be derived from the Hebrew "SCTH," "SKTH" or "SUCCOTH," meaning "booth" or "tent."

The names GAUL, Gael and Galatians all derive from the Hebrew "GAULON" or "GOLAH," meaning the exiles or dispersed ones.

We have proven that the KELTS, the KIMMERIANS, the GAULS, the GALATIANS, CYMRY (or Kymry) were all closely related peoples, and had all sprung from the SCYTHIAN NATION!

As we traced the descendants of the Lost Ten Tribes, we saw that the name "Dan" stands out more than any other—referring to the Israelitish ancestor of one of the tribes of Israel. The name "Dan" was early left on geographical locations in Palestine, and we noticed this same custom prevailed among the latter descendants of Dan, who left their patriarchal name on rivers, towns and territories all over Europe. Many of these Danites arrived in Ireland under the name of "Tuatha de Danaan" (Tribe of Dan).

The Milesian Scots, who had come from Scythia via Spain, were the fifth and last of the colonies which settled in Ireland.

We examined a number of statements from ancient Irish histories showing that the MILESIAN SCOTS definitely connected themselves with most of the HEROES OF THE BIBLE, and with the prophet Moses! We noticed that the ancestors of the Scots were in Egypt at the time of the EXODUS, but were not in sympathy with the Egyptians. These Milesian Scots were driven out of Egypt. These ancient Scottish and Irish legends are garbled accounts of true historical incidents!

On one occasion we observed that thirty ship-loads of Israelites direct from the land of ISRAEL settled in Ireland!

We noticed that the prophet Jeremiah visited Ireland (circa 600 B.C.), where his tomb remains to this very day!

We also examined the history of the SCANDINAVIANS and noticed they and the GOTHS were offshoots of the SCYTHIANS, and therefore closely related to the rest of the Northwest European Nordics.

There are great resemblances between the Scythiac and Hebrew languages, as well as between the Welsh and Hebrew.

It was observed that the languages of the early inhabitants of Britain were either Hebrew or closely related to it. These early British languages had their roots in the Hebrew. We know that the Israelites were soon submerged in Scythia after their captivity. They must have begun to change (or in some instances lay aside) the Hebrew language of their fathers not long after their captivity in 741-721 B.C.

What is the significance of all these facts and what bearing will this knowledge have upon your life?

Bear these two points in mind: (1) The Anglo-Saxon-Celtic peoples (who sprang from the Scythian "nation"), are the descendants of the "Lost Ten Tribes" of Israel! (2) It is vitally important for modern Israel to KNOW HER IDENTITY, for Almighty God shows He will permit these peoples to be OPPRESSED and AFFLICTED (in the Great Tribulation) as no people have ever suffered before (Jer. 30:7; Dan. 12:1; Matt. 24:21)!

These prophesies certainly will come to pass in the near future!

It is important for the present-day people of Israel to know their identity so that they can throw themselves upon God's mercy, in order that they may be protected from the terrible calamities soon to befall the Anglo-Saxon-Celtic peoples who inhabit North-west Europe and those countries settled by them—America, Canada, Australia, New Zealand and the Republic of South Africa (Lu. 21:36).

The GREAT TRIBULATION is also called the time of "JACOB'S TROUBLE," but God will rescue him from his sore travail, and finally the people of Israel will again be gathered unto their own lands to have another chance to serve and obey their God, thereby setting an example before all of the Gentile nations.

After Israel turns from her perverseness she will be blessed as no people have ever been blessed. God then promises as no people have ever been blessed. God then promises that He will cause the remnant of Jacob to "take root." "ISRAEL shall BLOSSOM and bud, and fill the face of the world with fruit" (Isa. 27:6). Also Jeremiah was inspired to prophesy of the peace, prosperity, joy and overflowing blessings which Israel shall ultimately attain unto (Jer. 31)!

APPENDIX I

Israelites. The name Israel does not occur in the inscriptions as a general term for the Israelites. Nor does it, as a rule, appear as the name for the Northern kingdom. Instead of this the name that is usually employed is mat Bit-Humri, i.e. land of the House Omri . . . compare above Bit-Amman "House of Ammon" or mat Humri "land of Omri" in the inscription of Ramannirar . . . The name Israel occurs only once on the inscriptions, where it means the kingdom of Israel, viz. on the monolith of Salmanassar II in which Ahab of Israel is spoken of as (mat) Sir'lai i.e. "he of Israel . . ." (Schrader, The Cuneiform Inscriptions of the Old Testament, Vol. I, pp. 137, 138).

We know now that Israel came in contact with Assyria at a much earlier period, and that the former was in fact tributary to Assyria as far back as in the ninth century. For example, not only does king Rammannirar of Assyria (who according to the Assyrian Canon of Rulers reigned from 812 to 783 B.C.) mention in a list of kingdoms that were tributary to him the "land Omri" (mat Humri) along with Sidon, Tyre, Edom and Philistia . . . not only do we find in the cuneiform inscriptions a generation earlier that "Jehu, son of Omri" offered tribute to Salmanasser II (2 Kings IX:2); but we also learn from the inscription of Asur-nasir-habal (885-860) that as early as in the first half of the 9th century the whole of Phoenicia was overrun by the Assyrians and made tributary (ibid., p. 144).

Israel . . . The usual term for the kingdom of Israel in the Assyrian inscriptions is not this, as we have already observed. The ordinary designation was rather mat Bit-Humri or mat Humri "land of the house of Omri" or "land of Omri," or merely "land Omri" (ibid., p. 177).

Juda occurs as the name of the Southern of the twin Israelite kingdoms many times in the inscriptions after the time of Tiglath-Pileser II, under the form Jahuda, written (mat, ir) Ja-u-du-(di). First of all we meet with the gentile name Ja-u-da-ai "Judaean" in the inscription of Tiglath-Pileser . . . in which Ja-u-ha-zi i.e. Joachaz=Ahaz is mentioned as a tributary vassal, as well as in the other inscription . . . where there is a record of Az-ri-ja-u Ja-u-da-ai i.e. "Azariah" (Uzziah) of Juda." In the same inscription line 4 we read the name of the country itself mat Ja-u-di. Sargon, who so often refers to mat Bit-Humri "Land of Omri," only mentions Juda in one passage, viz in the Nimrud-inscriptions . . . in the words . . ."(Sargon) who subdued the land of Juda whose situation (is) a remote one." Juda is mentioned frequently in the records of Sanherib; first in the Nebbi-Junus inscription at Constantinople line 15, where we read . . . "the wide district of the land of Juda—its prince Hizkia (Hezekiah) I reduced him to subjection . . ." Juda is repeatedly named in the annalistic inscription of Sanherib, where Hizkia is several times designated Jahudai "Judean" . . . Moreover Asarhaddon mentions as his vassal . . . "Manasseh, king of Juda." the same who is called Mi-in-si-i in the inscription of Asurbanipal . . . (ibid, pp. 177, 178).

Omri, king of Israel. His name appears on the inscriptions in the form Hu-um-ri-i and also Hu-um-ri-a . . . We first meet with it on the Nimrud-obelisk of the elder Salmanassar, in the small inscriptions which stand separate . . . in the phrase ma-da-tu sa Ja-u-a abal Hu-um-ri-i "tribute of Jehu, the son of Omri." On the same obelisk we find a reference to the kings of Damskus Hadad-'idri (Hadadezer) and Hazael . . . Hence there can be no doubt that by Jehu, son of Omri, the Jehu of the Old Testament is meant who succeeded the rulers of the House of Omri . . . The dynasty of Omri must on the whole have enjoyed a great reputation abroad. In this way we understand why the Assyrians designated Israel simpy as mat Bit-Humri "land of the house Omri," or more briefly mat Humri "land Omri" . . . It should be observed in this connection that according to 1 Kings XVI. 24 Omri built the capital of the kingdom, Samaria (ibid., pp. 179-81).

I now propose to cite all the passages in the cuneiform inscriptions in which reference is made to "land of the house Omri" i.e. Northern Israel. Of course I omit the parallel passages in the inscriptions of Sargon. The most ancient extract is from the Nimrud-obelisk as well as the stele of Salmanassar II (see above). Then follows the mention of the mat Humri in king Rammannirar's list of tributary states. The sequence is: Surru (Tyrus), Sidunnu (Sidon), mat-Humri (Samaria), Udumu (Edom), Palastav (Philistia). Tiglath-Pileser II mentions Northern Israel in a fragment of his annals . . . in close connections with Gaza and the other Philistine or rather, Kanaanite towns . . . Next come Sargon who refers to the land of the house Omri, first of all in the cylinder-inscription . . . in which we read Mu-ri-ib mat Bit-Hu-um-ri-a rap-si "Combatants (subjugators) of the land Omri, the extended"; next in the bull-inscription . . . sa-pi-in ir Sa-mi-ri-na ka-la mat Bit-Hu-um-ri-a, "destroyer of Samaria, the entirety of the land Omri," Pave des portes . . . ka-sid ir Sa-mir-i-na gi-mir mat Bit-Hu-um-ri-a "conquerors of the city Samaria and the whole of the land Omri." After the time of Sargon the "kingdom Omri" is never again mentioned. It was through Sargon that it was brought to a definite end (ibid., pp. 180-81).

Samaria, capital of the Northern kingdom, founded by Omri, is frequenty mentioned under this name of Sargon's inscriptions, where it appears in the forms Sa-mir-i-na . . . Sa-mi-ri-na . . . and lastly Sa-mi-ur-na . . . We also meet the form Sa-mi-ri-na in an inscription of Tiglath-Pileser II . . . in which there is mention of a king Mi-ni-hi-im-mi ir Sa-mi-ri-na-ai "Menahem of Samaria" in connection with Ra-sun-nu "Rezin" of Damaskus. Similarly in Layard 66, 18, where of a "king" of Samaria (sarru-su-nu) it is said that he ir Sa-mi-ri-na i-di-nu-us-su u-mas-sir "alone left the city Samaria." . . . From the passage first-cited, occurring in the inscriptions of Tiglath-Pileser, it is evident that, at least in later times, the rulers of the territory situated North of Judah were simply named after the city Samaria. For even as late as the times of Asurbanipal (who reigned in Assyria after 668) we find a viceroy of Samirina (Sa-mir-i-na) mentioned as an eponymus . . . (ibid., p. 181).

Thus we have no occasion to question the statement of the Bible and of the inscriptions, that with the conquest of Samaria by Salmanassar the independence of the state come [sic. came] to an end. And this is only confirmed by the intelligence that Samaria formed an alliance with Hamath, Arpad, Zemar and Damskus, and rose under the rule of and against Sargon, in the second year (720 B.C.) of that monarch's reign . . . (ibid., p. 182).

Ahab is called by Salmanassar II A-ha-ab-bu Sir-'-lai i.e. "Ahab of Israel" in an inscription discovered on the banks of the Tigris . . . (ibid., p. 182, 183).

Observe that here Ahab, the Sir'lite, and Hadadezer-Benhadad II (see below) of Damskus appear in conjunction; also that this same monarch (Salmanassar II) in the inscription subsequently drawn up, on the Nimrud-obelisk, mentions Jehu the son of Omri as well as Hazael of Damaskus. Hence there is no room for doubt that the Biblical Ahab of Israel is meant by this "Ahab the Sir'lite." On the other hand, the circumstance that Ahab appears in alliance with Damaskus is completely in accord with the Scriptural account. From the latter we learn that Ahab, after the battle of Aphek, concluded an alliance with Benhadad, which mainly involved the restoration to Israel of the cities which had been lost, and the session of "allys" in Damascus to the Israelites (I Kings XX. 34 Foll.Wellhausen) (ibid., p. 189).

Jehu is mentioned twice in the inscriptions; both times in those of Salmanassar II (806-25). The first passage occurs in the king's obelisk among the separate inscriptions, above a figure, which represents a prince or deputy kneeling before the Great King, the former being followed by men bringing tribute. The passage runs thus . . . "tribute of Jehu, son of Omri: bars of silver, bars of gold, a golden bowl, a golden ladle, golden goblets, golden pitchers, bars of lead, a staff for the hand of the king, shafts of spears: that I received" (ibid., p. 199).

Hazael of Damaskus trusted in the multitude of his troops, assembled his hosts without number . . . In Damaskus, his royal city, I besieged him; his plantations I destroyed . . . To the mountains of Hauran I marched, towns without number I carried away . . . At that time I received the tribute of the Tyrians, Sidonians, of Jehu, son of Omri (ibid., pp. 200, 201).

. . . the town, Ga-al-[ad=Gilead?] . . . the land Beth-Omri (Samaria) the distant . . . the broad, I turned in its entire extent into the territory of Assyria, I set my officers, the viceroys over it. Hanno of Gaza, who took to flight before my troops, fled to the land of Egypt . . . The land Beth-Omri (Samaria) the distant . . . the whole of its inhabitants, together with their property I deported to Assyria. Pekah, their king [I] slew. Hosea I appointed [to rule] over them. Ten talents of gold, a thousand of silver (?) together with their . . . I received from them; [to Assyria brought] I them . . . Indeed the towns of the land Beth-Omri itself are spoken of as cut off from it, among these two whose mutilated names may without difficulty be completed into those two which are mentioned in 2 Kings XV. 29 as taken away by Tiglath-Pileser, viz. Gal-ad=Gilead, and [A] bel-Beth-Maacha (ibid., pp. 247, 248).

[I besieged and captured the town of Samaria; 27,280 of their inhabitants] I carried away; 50 chariots I took as my royal share [among them away] . . . in place of (them, the deported) I assigned abodes to the inhabitants of countries taken [by me]. I imposed tribute on them like Assyria. That we are here dealing with an account of the fall of Samaria, is evident from the mention of exactly 50 chariots taken away by the king which is the number furnished by the other inscription with reference to Samaria . . . (ibid., p. 266).

APPENDIX II

CHRONOLOGY ACCORDING TO USSHER

The Creation of Man 4004
The Deluge..2349
Birth of Abram 1996
Birth of Isaac..1896
Birth of Jacob...1836
Birth of Joseph...1745
Birth of Moses 1571
The Exodus...1491
Death of Joshua 1429
Beginning of the period of the Judges...1429
Termination of the period of the Judges..1095
Commencement of Saul's reign..1095
David king in Hebron 1055
David king in Jerusalem 1047
Solomon made king. Death of David..1015
Death of Solomon...975
Ten Tribes revolt—Jeroboam made their king..975
Rehoboam made King over Judah 975
Omri begins his rule over Ten-Tribed Israel..925
Israel's first invasion..771
Israel's second invasion 742
Israel's third invasion 721
Captivity of Judah...587
Birth of Jesus Christ... 4

BIBLIOGRAPHY

A Guide to the Babylonian and Assyrian Antiquities of the British Museum. Pref. by J.H. Breasted. London: 1922.

Atlas of the Bible. Trans. and ed. by Joyce Reid and H.M. Rowley. Edinburgh: Thos. Nelson and Sons, Ltd., 1956.

The Anglo-Saxon Chronicle. Trans. by James Ingram. London: J.M. Dent and Sons, Ltd.

Annals of Clonmacnoise from the Creation to A.D. 1408. Trans. by C. Mageoghagan. Dublin: Murphy University Press, 1896.

Bain, Robert. The Clans and Tartans of Scotland. London: William Collins Sons & Co., Ltd., 1959.

Baron, Salo Wittmayer. A Social and Religious History of the Jews. 2nd ed., vol. I. New York: Columbia University Press, 1952.

Beddoe. The Races of Britain. London: Trubner and Co., 1885.

Venerable Bede's Ecclesiastical History of England, and The Anglo-Saxon Chronicle. Edited by J.A. Giles, 5th ed. London: George Bell & Sons, 1887.

The Behistun Rock Inscription. Trans. by L.W. King, and R.C. Thompson (The inscriptions of Darius the Great at Behistun, British Museum, 1907), and Sir Henry Rawlinson (Journal of the Royal Asiatic Society, 1847).

The Holy Bible. Various translations and versions.

Bosanquet, J.W. Synchronous History, vol. III. 1874.

Bruce, Robert the. Declaration of Arbroath, or Scottish Declaration of Independence. Edinburgh: Gordon Wilson, 1951.

The Cambridge Companion to the Bible. London: Cambridge University Press, 1892.

Camden, Wm. Britannia. vol. I. 1806.

Chaillu, Paul B. Du. The Viking Age. London: John Murray, 1889.

Chamber's Encyclopedia. vol. XII. London: George Newnes Ltd., 1950.

Childe, V. Gordon. The Aryans. London: Kegan Paul, Trench, Trubner & Co., Ltd., 1926.

The Chronicles of the Kings of Briton. Attr. to Tysilic. Trans. by Peter Roberts. London: E. Eilliamson, 1811.

Church Histories of England. Trans. by Joseph Stevenson. vol. II. London: Seeley's, 1854.

Clarke, Adam. Clarke's Commentary. A New Edition. New York: Abingdon: Cokesbury Press.

Colliers Encyclopedia. vol. 17. P.F. Collier and Son, Corporation, 1959.

Coon, C.S. The Races of Europe. New York: The MacMillan Co., 1954.

Costa, Isaak Da. Israel and the Gentiles. Trans. by M.J. Kennedy. London: James Nisbet & Co., 1850.

The Critical Lexicon Concordance to the English and Greek Testament. Bullinger and Ethelburt. 8th ed. London: Lamp Press, 1957.

Daily Express. April 25, 1961.

Deniker, J. The Races of Man. London: Walter Scott Ltd., 1900.

Dickson. Racial History of Man.

Dinan, W. Monumenta Historica Celtica. vol. I. London: David Nutt, 1911.

Diodorus of Sicily. In 10 volumes, English trans. by C.H. Oldfather. London: William Heinemann Ltd., 1960.

Edersheim, Alfred. The Life and Times of Jesus the Messiah. London: Longmans, Green and Son, 1901.

Encyclopaedia Biblica. Ed. By T.K. Cheyne and others. London: Adam and Charles Black, 1914.

Encyclopedia Americana. 1960 ed. vol. XIII. New York: Rand McNally & Co., 1960.

Encyclopedia Americana. 1957 ed. vol. XXIV. New York: Rand McNally & Co., 1957.

Encyclopedia Britannica. 11th ed. New York: Encyclopedia Britannica, Inc., 1910.

Encyclopedia Britannica. 1958 ed. New York: Encyclopedia Britannica, Inc., 1910.

Encyclopedia Britannica. 14th ed. New York: Encyclopedia Britannica, Inc., 1919.

Evans, I.O. The Observer's Book of Flags. London: Frederick Warne & Co., 1959.

Fleure, H.J. The Peoples of Europe. London: Humphrey Milford, 1922.

Frazer, J.G. The Golden Bough. London: MacMillan and Co. Ltd., 1954.

Fuller. Pisgah Sight of Palestine.

Funck-Brentano, Fr. The Earliest Times. Trans. by E.F. Buckley. London: William Heinemann, Ltd., 1927.

Graetz, Heinrich. History of the Jews. Philadelphia: The Jewish Publication Society of America, 1946.

Grant, Madison. The Passing of the Great Race. 4th Rev. ed. New York: Charles Scribner's Sons, 1923.

Graves, Robert. The White Goddess. London: Faber and Faber, Ltd., 1961.

Guest, Edwin. Origines Celticae. London: MacMillan and Co., 1883.

A Guide to the Babylonian and Assyrian Antiquities of the British Museum. (Printed by order of the Trustees, 1922).

Gunther. Racial Elements of European History.

Haddon, A.C. Races of Man and Their Distribution. Cambridge University Press, 1894.

Haigh, Daniel H. The Conquest of Britain by the Saxons. London: John Russell Smith, 1961.

Halley, Henry H. Bible Handbook. Chicago: Henry H. Halley, 1955.

Hastings, James. Dictionary of the Bible. New York: Charles Scribner's Sons, 1945.

Hastings, James. The Expository Times. Edinburgh: T.&T. Clark, 1898.

Hecateus of Abdera, Fragmenta Historicorum Graecorum. vol. II, English trans. from Muller's comments.

Herodotus. Trans. by Henry Cary. London: George Bell and Sons, 1908.

Hislop, Alexander. The Two Babylons. New York: Loizeaux Brothers, 1948.

The History of Herodotus. Trans. by Prof. George Rawlinson, and others. London: John Murray, 1859.

Holmes, T. Rice. Caesar's Conquest of Gaul. London: MacMillan and Co. Ltd., 1899.

Homer. Odyssey. Trans. by A. T. Murray. London: William Heinemann, 1928.

Huntingdom, Elsworth. The Pulse of Asia.

Hurlbut, Jesse Lyman. A Bible Atlas. New York: Rand McNally and Co.,

Huxley, Julian S., and A.C. Haddon, Sc. D. We Europeans. London: Jonathan Cape, 1935.

Imperial Bible Dictionary. London: Blackie and Son, 1887.

Ingersoll, Robert G. Some Mistakes of Moses. New York: C. P. Farrell, 1892.

International Standard Bible Encyclopaedia. London: Henry Camp.

Jessel, E. E. The Unknown History of the Jews. London: Watts and Co., 1909.

Jewish Chronicle. May 2, 1897.

Jewish Encyclopedia. 1916 ed. London: Funk and Wagnalls Co., 1916.

Jewish Encyclopedia. 1925 ed. London: Funk and Wagnalls Co., 1925.

Jewish Quarterly Review. vol. I.

Johnston, Harry et al. The Living Races of Mankind. 2 vol. London: Hutchinson and Co.

Josephus. The Complete Works of Flavius Josephus. Trans. by William Whitson. New York: John C. Winston Co., 1900.

Kalisch. Phil. Doc., M.A., M.M. Historical and Critical Commentary on the Old Testament. London: Longman, Brown, Green, Longmans, and Roberts, 1858.

Keane. Man Past and Present. Cambridge: University Press, 1899.

Keating, D.D., Geoffrey. The History of Ireland From the Earliest Period to the English Invasion. Trans. by John O'Mahon. New York: 1866

Keith, Sir Arthur. Are We Cousin to the German? (from The Graphic) Dec. 4, 1915.

Keller, Verner. The Bible As History. Trans. by William Neil, M.A. London: Hodder & Stoughton, 1957.

Kephart, Calvin. Races of Mankind. London: Peter Owen Ltd., 1960.

Kinns, Samuel. Graven in the Rock. London: Cassell & Co., Ltd., 1891.

Kraeling, Emil G. Rand McNally Bible Atlas. New York: Rand McNally & Co., 1956.

Langer, William L. An Encyclopedia of World History. Boston: Houghton Mifflin Co.

Latham, Dr. Robert Gordon. Ethnology of Europe. 1852.

Leabhar Gabhal, or the Book of the Conquests of Ireland. Recension of M. O'Cleirigh. Trans. by Macalister and MacNaill. Dublin.

Leeuw, Jan Lohuezen de. The Scythian Period. Leiden: E.J. Brill.

Luckenbill. The Ancient Records of Assyria and Babylonia. Chicago: University Press, 1926.

Lysons. Our British Ancestors. Oxford and London: John Henry and James Parker, 1865.

Mallet, M. Northern Antiquities. Trans. by Bishop Percy. London: Henry G. Bohn, 1847.

Meyers, Philip Van Ness. The Eastern Nations and Greece. Revised ed. New York: Ginn & Co., 1904.

Miller, Dorothy Ruth. A Handbook of Ancient History in Bible Light. New York: Flemming H. Revell Co., 1937.

Milton, History of England.

Minns, Ellis H. Scythians and Greeks. Cambridge University Press, 1913.

Moore, Thomas. The History of Ireland. Paris, 1837.

Muller. Fragmenta Historicorum Graecorum.

Murray, James A.H. A New English Dictionary on Historical Principles.

Noble Families Among the Sephardic Jews. Trans. by B. Brewster. Oxford University Press, 1936.

Norton. Bible Students' Handbook of Assyriology. Kegan Paul, Trench, Trubner and Co., Ltd., 1913.

Owen, Robert. The Kymry. Carmarthen: W. Spurrell & Son, 1891.

Petrie, Sir Flinders. Egypt and Israel.

Pickering, Charles. The Races of Man. London: H. G. Bohn, 1850.

Pinches, Theophilus G. The Old Testament in the Light of the Historical Records and Legends of Assyria and Babylonia. 3rd ed., 1908.

Ploetz, Carl. Epitome of History. London: Blackie and Son, 1884.

Plutarch's Moralia. 15 vols. English trans. by F.C. Baffitt, London: Harvard University Press, 1957.

Proceedings of the Royal Asiatic Society. Comments by Sir Henry Rawlinson. May 12, 1849.

Procopius. History of the Wars. Cambridge University Press.

Rice, Tamara Talbot. The Scythians. London: Thames and Hudson.

Ripley, William Z. The Races of Europe. London: Kegan Paul, Trench, Trubner & Co., Ltd., 1899.

Rostovtseff. The Iranians and Greeks in South Russia. Oxford: 1922.

Sayce, Prof. A.H. Assyria. London: The Religious Tract Society, 1926.

Schrader, Eberhard. The Cuneiform Inscriptions and the Old Testament. London: Williams and Norgate, 1885.

Sergei, G. The Mediterranean Race. London: David Douglas, 1901.

Skene, Wm. F. Celtic Scotland. Edinburgh. David Douglas, 1886.

Smith, Joseph. The Book of Mormon. Salt Lake City: 1920.

Smith, William. A Smaller Classical Dictionary. London: J.M. Dent & Sons, Ltd., 1910.

Spier, Arthur. The Comprehensive Hebrew Calendar. New York: Berhman House, Inc, 1952.

Squire, Charles. Celtic Myth and Legend. London: The Gresham Pub. Co., Ltd.

Stimpson, George. A Book About the Bible. New York: Harper and Brothers Publishers, 1945.

Strong, James. The Exhaustive Concordance of the Bible. New York: Abingdon-Cokesbury Press, 1890.

Taylor, (M.A.) Isaac. The Origin of the Aryans. London: Walter Scott, 1892.

The Scottish Clans and Their Tartans. 39th ed. London: G.W. Bacon Ltd., 1958.

The Scottish Tartans. Edinburgh: W. & A.K. Johnston Ltd.

Torrey, R.A. The Treasury of Scripture Knowledge. 27th ed. London: Samuel Bagster & Sons, Ltd.

Turner, Sharon. The History of the Anglo-Saxons. London: Longman, Brown, Green, and Longmans, 1852.

Walsingam, Thomas. Hypodeigma.

Whatmore, Arthur William. Insulae Britanniacae. London: Elliot Stock, 1913.

Webster's New Collegiate Dictionary, 2nd ed. Springfield, Mass.: G. & C. Merriam Co., 1953.

Webster's Biographical Dictionary, 1st ed. Springfield, Mass.: G. & C. Merriam Co., 1953.

Woolley, Sir Leonard. History Unearthed. London: Ernest Benn Ltd., 1958.

Wylie, J.A. History of the Scottish Nation. London: Hamilton, Adams & Co., 1886.